Edward Duffield Neill

The English colonization of America

During the Seventeenth Century

Edward Duffield Neill

The English colonization of America
During the Seventeenth Century

ISBN/EAN: 9783337152635

Printed in Europe, USA, Canada, Australia, Japan

Cover: Foto ©ninafisch / pixelio.de

More available books at **www.hansebooks.com**

ENGLISH COLONIZATION
OF AMERICA

" Nec falsa dicere, nec vera reticere."

THE ENGLISH COLONIZATION OF AMERICA

During the Seventeenth Century

By EDWARD D. NEILL

CONSUL OF UNITED STATES OF AMERICA AT DUBLIN

STRAHAN & CO., PUBLISHERS
56 LUDGATE HILL, LONDON
1871

EDINBURGH: PRINTED BY THOMAS AND ARCHIBALD CONSTABLE,
PRINTERS TO THE QUEEN, AND TO THE UNIVERSITY.

PREFACE.

THE tracing of the successive steps of the English colonization of North America, during the seventeenth century, is the object of the following chapters.

The writer has carefully searched for facts, in the manuscript transactions, of the great London trading company, under whose auspices the first colonists were despatched, and in other original documents. Those acquainted with the standard historians of America, will find in this volume, statements contradictory of the assertions of Robertson, and other eminent writers. Myths creep into history, as noiselessly as book-worms between the leaves of an old volume, and it is as difficult to dislodge the former, as the latter. A century hence, the sentimentalist will not thank the writer, who calmly states that the touching story of the Scotch maiden, who was the first to hear the slogan and pibroch, and announce the coming of her countrymen to the relief of Lucknow, is a pure and beautiful fiction. As the naturalist, to examine the silk-worm, is obliged to mutilate its delicate and glossy residence, so the historian will not be deterred from tearing away, with the hard steel-pen, the delicate web with which imagination has frequently surrounded the beginnings of a great nation, like Rome.

The accomplished Bancroft speaks of John Rolfe—" a young Englishman, an amiable enthusiast, who had emigrated to the forests of Virginia, daily, hourly, and, as it were, in his very sleep"—hearing a voice, crying in his ears, that he should strive to make Pocahontas, a young Indian maiden, a Christian, and, constrained by the love of Christ, uniting her, to him, by the holy bonds of matrimony. But the prosaic pages of the London Company's transactions, and the old folios of Purchas, show that Rolfe was a married man, some years before this union, and that after his death, there was a white widow and her children, beside the son he had by Pocahontas. The same historian assures us, that the settlers of Maryland were " most of them Roman Catholic gentlemen," while Lord Baltimore, in a letter to the Earl of Strafford, states that the colonists were chiefly poor labouring men, and there is reason to believe that they were mostly Protestants.

The temptation to theorize, and employ rhetorical embellishment, has, as far as possible, been overcome, and naked facts have been submitted to the reader. In the preparation of this volume upon the seed-time of American civilization, the method of the old Roman Vegetius, in his treatise on the "Military Art," has been pursued : " Nihil enim mihi auctoritatis assumo, sed quæ dispersa sunt, velut in ordinem epitomata conscribo."

Dublin, Ireland.
December 1, 1870.

CONTENTS.

CHAPTER I.
EDWARD MARIA WINGFIELD AND ASSOCIATES, . . PAGE 1

CHAPTER II.
LORD DELAWARE, CAPTAIN-GENERAL OF VIRGINIA, . . 25

CHAPTER III.
CAPTAIN SAMUEL ARGALL, DEPUTY-GOVERNOR OF VIRGINIA, . 59

CHAPTER IV.
POCAHONTAS AND HER COMPANIONS, . . 68

CHAPTER V.
NORTH VIRGINIA COLONY, . . . 90

CHAPTER VI.
WILLIAM BREWSTER AND LEYDEN NONCONFORMISTS, . . 95

CHAPTER VII.
PATRICK COPLAND, CHAPLAIN OF EAST INDIA COMPANY, . 104

CHAPTER VIII.
COPLAND'S SERVICES TO VIRGINIA COMPANY, . . 111

CHAPTER IX.
COPLAND'S SERMON AT BOW CHURCH, . . 144

CHAPTER X.

COPLAND'S RESIDENCE AT BERMUDAS; AND THE EDUCATIONAL DEVELOPMENT OF AMERICA, ... 167

CHAPTER XI.

GEORGE, FIRST LORD BALTIMORE, 182

CHAPTER XII.

HENRY FLEET, EXPLORER OF THE POTOMAC RIVER, . 219

CHAPTER XIII.

CECILIUS, SECOND LORD BALTIMORE, AND THE SETTLEMENT OF MARYLAND, ... 238

CHAPTER XIV.

ROBERT EVELYN AND EARLY EXPLORERS OF DELAWARE RIVER, 259

CHAPTER XV.

FATHER ANDREW WHITE, S.J., . . 266

CHAPTER XVI.

DR. THOMAS HARRISON AND THE VIRGINIA PURITANS, . 278

CHAPTER XVII.

FRANCIS HOWGILL AND EARLY QUAKERS, 290

CHAPTER XVIII.

THE PLANTING OF THE CHURCH OF ENGLAND IN THE COLONIES, 314

THE ENGLISH COLONIZATION
OF AMERICA

CHAPTER I.

EDWARD MARIA WINGFIELD AND ASSOCIATES.

A PUPIL of Westminster School one day visited a relative in the Middle Temple, upon whose table were opened books of travel and a map of the world. As distant seas and vast kingdoms but little known were exhibited, the schoolboy resolved, if he ever entered the University, he would pursue geographical studies, and in consequence of the purpose then formed, became Richard Hakluyt, the best authority in England relative to the climate, races, and productions of the four quarters of the globe.

At the time that Sir Francis Drake was fitting out his expedition for America, he was acting as chaplain to the English Embassy in Paris, and so great was his interest in the project, that he wrote he was ready to fly to England " with wings of Pegasus," to devote his reading and observation to the furtherance of the work. And after the gallant navigator sailed up the Pacific coast to the fortieth degree north, " the first to loose the girdle of the world, and encompass her in his fortunate arms,"[1] he was delighted with listening to the tales of returning mariners. The Muscovy, Greenland, and other trading companies did not plan expeditions without seeking his advice. In the minutes of the East India Company, under date of January 29, 1601-2, is the following :—" Mr. Hakluyt, the historiographer of the East India Company, being here before the Committees, and having read unto them out of his notes and books, was requested to set down in writing a note of the principal places in the East Indies, and where trade is to be had, to the end that the same may be used for the better instruction of our factors in the said voyage."[2]

On the 14th of May 1602, Bartholomew Gosnold, a man of integrity, landed from the ship " Concord," with Gabriel Archer and others, on the coast of what is now called Massachusetts, and passed a month in examining the shores now conspicuous with the domes and monuments of Boston, the church spires of peaceful villages, and the tall chimneys of manufacturing towns, and gave to one of its headlands a name still retained, Cape Cod. Embarking for the return voyage on the 18th of June, he cast anchor in English waters on the 23d of July, and astonished the mercantile world not only by the shortness of his passage by the new route, but by his calm and reasonable statements as to the healthfulness of the region visited, and its capabilities for sustaining an English-speaking population.

[1] Purchas's *Pilgrimage*, p. 779.
[2] Cal. of State Papers, East Indies, 1513-1616, p. 120.

Prominent among eager listeners to his statement was Hakluyt, then connected with the cathedral at Bristol, who cordially seconded his desire to found a Nova Britannia on the western continent. Many meetings were held by Gosnold and Hakluyt with the Bristol merchants, and Robert Salterne, who had accompanied the former in the voyage to America, was appointed with Hakluyt to obtain permission from Sir Walter Raleigh to make a settlement under his patent.[1] Raleigh's consent obtained, Salterne in 1603 made a second visit with an expedition that left Bristol, who was followed in 1605 by Captain George Weymouth, who returned with several Indians, who remained for more than two years in England.

These successive voyages, under the auspices of the most distinguished and enterprising men of Bristol, Plymouth, and London, deepened the conviction that British pride and interests demanded that they should separate the French settlements on the St. Lawrence, and the Spanish plantations near the Gulf of Mexico, by an English colony. The stage is always quick to allude to the absorbing questions of the hour, and in 1605 the play of "Eastward Ho," in the coarse language of the period, reproduced the conversations that had taken place on the pavements around the Royal Exchange :—

"*Sea Gull.*—Come, Drawer, pierce your neatest hogshead, and let's have cheer, not fit for your Billingsgate tavern, but for our Virginian Colonel; he will be here instantly.

[1] Gorges.

"*Drawer.*—You shall have all things fit, sir; please you have any more wine?

"*Spend All.*—More wine, slave! whether we drink it or no; spill it and draw more.

"*Sea Gull.*—Come, boys, Virginia longs till we share the rest of her maidenhead.

"*Spend All.*—Why, is she inhabited already with any English?

"*Sea Gull.*—A whole country of English is there, man, bred of those left there in '79; they have married with the Indians, and make 'hem bring forth as beautiful faces as any we have in England; and therefore the Indians are so in love with 'hem that all the treasure they have they lay at their feet.

"*Scapethrift.*—But is there such treasure there, Captain, as I have heard?

"*Sea Gull.*—I tell thee, gold is more plentiful there than copper is with us, and for as much red copper as I can bring I'll have thrice weight in gold. Why, man, all their dripping-pans and chamber-pots are pure gold; and all the chains with which they chain up their streets are massive gold; all the prisoners they take are fettered in gold; and for rubies and diamonds they go forth in holy days and gather 'hem by the sea-shore to hang on their children's coats and stick in their children's caps as commonly as our children wear saffron-gilt brooches and groates with holes in 'hem.

"*Scapethrift.*—And is it a pleasant country withal?

"*Sea Gull.*—As ever the sun shin'd on; temperate, and full of all sorts of excellent viands; wild boar is as common there as our tamest bacon is here; venison as mutton. And then you shall live freely there, without sargeants or courtiers, or lawyers or intelligencers. Then for your means to advancement—there it is simple, and not preposterously mixt. You may be an alderman there, and never be a scavenger; you may be any other officer, and never be a slave. You may come to preferment enough, and never be a pander; to riches and fortune enough, and have never the more villany nor the less wit. Besides, there we shall have no more law than conscience, and not too much of either; serve God enough, eat and drink enough, and 'enough is as good as a feast.'"

The statesmen of the day were not indifferent to the enterprise, for, since the war with Spain had ceased, the streets of London had been filled with men who had been soldiers in Ireland and in the Netherlands, averse to return to the quiet peasant life from which they had been pressed into military service, and yet unfitted to obtain a living by honest industry. Too indolent to handle the spade, they were forced to beg or to steal, and became a terror to the peaceable citizen on the side-walk, or the traveller on the highway.

Military officers also favoured the scheme, in the hope that the development of a new commonwealth would furnish an occasion for them to draw once more the swords that hung upon the wainscoted walls of their houses, and began to rust in the scabbards. Merchants were willing to make pecuniary advances, believing that their money would be returned with interest; and clergymen were eloquent in urging their parishioners to aid in an effort which might lead to the conversion of the savages. Gosnold occupied a whole year in obtaining associates to engage in founding a commonwealth in America, and then a second year in obtaining colonists, and procuring ships and supplies.[1] In answer to a petition to King James, on the 6th of April 1606, a patent was sealed for Sir Thomas Gates, an officer in the employ of the Netherlands; Sir George Somers, well acquainted with navigation; Richard Hakluyt, who had become Prebendary of Westminster; Edward Maria Wingfield; Bartholomew Gosnold, and others, "to reduce a colony of sundry people into that part of America commonly called Virginia," between the 34th and 45th degrees of north latitude.

The patentees contemplated two plantations. Gates, Somers, Hakluyt, and others, chiefly of London, under the charter, were designated the First Colony, and authorized to settle between the 34th and 41st degrees of north latitude, while Hannam, Gilbert, Parker, Popham, and associates of Plymouth, were called the Second Colony, and permitted to plant between the 38th and 45th degrees of the same latitude.

Early in the winter there were gathered a hundred men, no better than those that surrounded David at the cave of Adullam, as the nucleus of the colony.

In view of their departure, the following orders, the result of much thought and observation, were adopted by the Council of the Company on the 10th of December 1606.

[1] Purchas, iv. 1705.

"First, whereas the good ship called the 'Sarah Constant,'[1] and the ship called the 'Good Speed,' with a pinnace called the 'Discovery,' are now ready victualled, rigged, and furnished for the said voyage, we think it fit, and so do ordain and appoint that Capt. Christopher Newport shall have the sole charge to appoint such captains, soldiers, and mariners, as shall either command or be shipped to pass in the said ships or pinnace, and shall also have the charge and oversight of all such munitions, victuals, and other provisions, as are or shall be shipped at the public charge of the adventurers in them, or any of them. And further, that the said Captain Newport shall have the sole charge and command of all the captains, soldiers, and mariners, and other persons that shall go in any of the said ships and pinnaces in the said voyage, from the day of the date hereof, until such time as they shall fortune to land upon the said coast of Virginia; and if the said Captain Newport shall happen to die at sea, then the masters of the said ships and pinnace shall carry them to the coast of Virginia aforesaid.

"And whereas we have caused to be delivered unto the said Captain Newport, Captain Bartholomew Gosnold, and Captain John Ratcliffe several instruments close sealed with the Counsel's seal aforesaid, containing the names of such persons as we have appointed to be of his Majestie's counsel in the said country of Virginia,

---

[1] These orders were copied from a volume of MS. Records of the Virginia Colony, in the Library of Congress of U.S. of America. The ship here called the "Sarah Constant," Purchas calls the "Susan Constant." The former may be a clerical error.

we do ordain and direct that the said Captain Christopher Newport, Captain Bartholomew Gosnold, and Captain John Ratcliffe, or the survivor or survivors of them, shall, within four-and-twenty hours next after the said ships shall arrive upon the coast of Virginia, and not before, open and unseal the said instrument, and declare and publish unto all the company the names therein set down, and that the persons by us therein named are and shall be known and taken to be his Majestie's counsel of his first colony in Virginia aforesaid.

"And further, that the said counsel so by us nominated shall, upon the publishing of the said instrument, proceed to the election and nomination of a president of the said counsel, and the said president, in all matters of controversy and question that shall arise during the continuance of his authority, where there shall fall out to be an equality of voices, shall have two voices, and shall have full power and authority, with the advice of the rest of the said counsel, or the greatest part of them, to govern, rule, and command all the captains and soldiers, and all others his Majestie's subjects of his colony, according to the true meaning of the orders and directions set down in the articles signed by his Majestie and of these presents. . . . And finally, that after the arrival of the said ship upon the coast of Virginia, and the counsellor's names published, the said Captain Newport shall, with such number of men as shall be assigned him by the president and counsel of the said colony, spend and bestow two months in discovery of such ports and rivers as can be found in that country, and shall give order for the present lading and furnishing of the two ships above named, and all such principal commodities and merchandize as can there be had and found, in such sort as he may return with the said ships full laden with good merchandizes, bringing with him full relation of all that hath passed in said voyage by the end of May next, if God permit."

In addition to the orders, the following advisory paper, full of valuable suggestions, probably drawn up by Hakluyt, was given to the officers of the expedition:—

"Instructions given by way of advice by us whom it hath pleased the King's Majesty to appoint of the Counsel, for the intended voyage to Virginia, to be observed by those captains and company which are sent at this present to plant there.

"As we doubt not but you will have especial care to observe the ordinances set down by the King's Majesty and delivered unto you under the privy seal, so for your better directions, upon your first landing, we have thought good to recommend unto your care these instructions and articles following.

"When it shall please God to send you on the coast of Virginia, you shall do your best endeavour to find out a safe port in the entrance of some navigable river, making choice of such a one as runneth furthest into the land, and if you happen to discover divers portable rivers, and amongst them any one that hath two main branches, if the difference be not great, make choice of that which bendeth most toward the north-west, for that way you shall soonest find the other sea.

"When you have made choice of the river on which you mean to settle, be not hasty in landing your victuals and munitions, but first let Captain Newport discover how far that river may be found navigable, that you make election of the strongest, most wholesome, and fertile place, for if you make many removes, besides the loss of time, you shall greatly spoil your victuals and your casks, and with great pain transport it in small boats.

"But if you choose your place so far up as a bark of fifty tons will float, then you may lay all your provisions ashore with ease, and the better receive the trade of all the countries about you in the land, and such as you may perchance find a hundred miles from the river's mouth, and further up the better, for if you set down near the entrance, except it be in some island that is strong by nature, an enemy that may approach you on even ground may easily pull you out, and if he be driven to seek you a hundred miles, and then land in boats, you shall, from both sides of the river, where it is narrowest, so beat them with your muskets as they shall never be able to prevail against you.

"And to the end that you be not surprised, as the French were by Melindus, and the Spaniard in the same place by the French, you shall do well to make this double provision,—first, erect a little store at the mouth of the river, that may lodge some ten men, with whom you shall leave a light boat, that when any fleet shall be in sight, they may come with speed to give you warning. Secondly, you must in no case suffer any of the native people of the country to inhabit between you and the sea-coast, for you cannot carry yourselves so towards them but they will grow discontented with your habitation, and be ready to guide and assist any nation that shall come to invade you, and if you neglect this, you neglect your safety.

"When you have discovered as far up the river as you mean to plant yourselves, and landed your victuals and munitions, to the end that every man may know his charge, you shall do well to divide your six score men into three parts; whereof one party of them you may appoint to fortify and build, of which your first work must be your storehouse for victual, the other you may employ in preparing your ground and sowing your corn and roots, the other ten of these forty you must leave as sentinels at the haven's mouth. The other forty you may employ for two months in discovery of the river above you, and on the country about you, which charge Captain Newport and Captain Gosnold may undertake of these forty discoverers.

"When they do espy any high lands or hills, Captain Gosnold may take twenty of the company to cross over the land, and carrying a half-dozen pick-axes to try if they can find any minerals. The other twenty may go on by river, and pitch up boughs upon the banks' side, by which the other boats shall follow them by the same turnings. You may also take a wherry, such as is used here in the Thames, by which you may send back to the president for supply of munition or any other want, that you may not be driven to return for every small defect.

"You must observe, if you can, whether the river on which you plant doth spring out of mountains, or out of lakes; if it be out of any lake, the passage to the other sea will be the more easy, and is like enough, that out of the same lake you shall find some springs which run the contrary way toward the East India Sea, for the great and famous rivers of Volga, Taxis, and Dwina, have three heads near joined, and yet the one falleth into the Caspian Sea, the other into the Euxine Sea, and the third into the Polonian Sea.

"In all your passages you must have great care not to offend the naturals, if you can eschew it, and employ some few of your company to trade with them for corn, and all other lasting victuals, and this you must do before they perceive you mean to plant among them; for, not being sure how your own seed corn will prosper the first year, to avoid the danger of famine, use and endeavour to store yourselves of the country corn.

"Your discoverers that pass over land with hired guides must look well to them that they slip not from them, and for more assurance let them take a compass with them, and write down how far they go upon every point of the compass, for that country having no way nor path, if that your guides run from you in the great woods or desert, you shall hardly ever find a passage back.

"And how weary soever your soldiers be, let them never trust the country people with the carriage of their weapons, for if they run from you with your shot, which they only fear, they will easily kill all with their arrows.

And whensoever any of yours shoots before them, be sure that they be chose out of your best marksmen, for if they see your learners miss what they aim at, they will think the weapon not so terrible, and thereby will be bold to assault you.

"Above all things, do not advertise the killing of any of your men, that the country people may know it; if they perceive that they are but common men, and that with the loss of many of theirs they may diminish any part of yours, they will make many adventures upon you. If the country be populous, you shall do well also not to let them see or know of your sick men (if you have any), which may also encourage them to many enterprises. You must take special care that you choose a seat for habitation that shall not be over-burthened with woods, near your town, for all the men you have shall not be able to cleanse twenty acres a year; besides that, it may serve for a covert for your enemies round about.

"Neither must you plant in a low or moist place, because it will prove unhealthful. You shall judge of the good air by the people, for some part of that coast where the lands are low have their people blear-eyed and with swollen bellies and legs, but if the naturals be strong and clean made, it is a true sign of a wholesome soil.

"You must take order to draw up the pinnace that is left with you under the fort, and take her sails and anchors ashore, all but a small kedge to ride by, lest some ill-disposed person slip away with her.

"You must take care that your mariners that go for wages do not mar your trade, for those that mind not to inhabit for a little gain will debase the estimation of exchange, and hinder the trade for ever after; and therefore you shall not admit or suffer any person whatsoever, other than such as shall be appointed by the President and Counsel there, to buy any merchandizes, or other things whatsoever.

"It were necessary that all your carpenters, and all other such-like workmen about building, do first build your store-house, and those other rooms of public and necessary use, before any house be set up for any private person; and though the workmen may belong to any private persons, yet let them all work together—first for the Company, then for private men.

"And seeing order is at the same price with confusion, it shall be advisably done to set your houses even, and by a line; that your street may have a good breadth, and be carried square about your market-place, and every street's end opening into it; that from thence, with a few field-pieces, you may command every street throughout, which market-place you may also fortify, if you think needful.

"You shall do well to send a perfect relation by Capt. Newport[1] of all that is done, what length you are seated, how far into the land, what commodities you find, what

---

[1] A Relation was prepared by Newport, but not published by Purchas, who had examined it. The MS. is in the Lambeth Library, and the Relation was lately, and for the first time, printed by the American Antiquarian Society. It is a fair and accurate description of the first Virginia exploration.

soil, woods, and their several kinds, and so of all other things else, to advertise particularly; and to suffer no man to return but by passport from the President and Counsel, nor to write any letter of any thing that may discourage others.

"Lastly and chiefly, the way to prosper and achieve good success is to make yourselves all of one mind, for the good of your country and your own, and to serve and fear God, the Giver of all goodness; for every plantation which our Heavenly Father hath not planted shall be rooted out."

Newport was an experienced mariner, and about a year before had returned from the West Indies with a present to King James, who was fond of the rare and curious, of a wild boar and two young crocodiles.

As the hour for the sailing of the expedition arrived, many prayers ascended for its welfare. Scholars, divines, statesmen, merchants, labourers, all classes and conditions of men heartily adopted the sentiment of Drayton's spirited ode—

> "You brave, heroic minds,
>   Worthy your country's name,
>   That honour still pursue,
>   Whilst loit'ring hinds
>   Lurk here at home, with shame;
>   Go, and subdue!
>
> "Britons! you stay too long,
>   Quickly abroad bestow you;
>   And with a merry gale
>   Swell your stretch'd sail,
>   With vows as strong
>   As the winds that blow you.

"Your course securely steer,
  West and by south forth keep,
    Rocks, lee shores, nor shoals,
    When Eolus scowls,
  You need not fear,
  So absolute the deep.

"And cheerfully at sea,
  Success you still entice,
    To get the pearl and gold,
    And ours to hold
  Virginia,
  Earth's only paradise.

"In kenning the shore,
  Thanks to God first given,
    O you, the happiest men,
    Be frolic then,
  Let cannons roar,
  Fighting the wide heaven.

"And in regions far,
  Such heroes bring ye forth,
    As those from whence we came;
    And plant our name
  Under that star
  Not known to our north.

"And as there plenty grows
  Of laurel, everywhere
    Apollo's sacred tree,
    You it may see
  A poet's brows
  To crown, that may sing there.

"Thy voyages attend,
  Industrious Hackluit,
    Whose reading shall inflame
    Men, to seek fame
  And much commend
  To after-times thy wit."

On the 19th of December the vessels started from the Thames, but, owing to the weather, did not sail from the Downs until the 1st of January 1606-7.

Newport, in command of the fleet, accompanied the "Susan Constant," a ship of one hundred tons, with seventy-one passengers. The zealous promoter of the project, Capt. Bartholomew Gosnold, and fifty-two colonists, were in the "God Speed," a small vessel of fifty tons; and Capt. John Ratcliffe, with twenty others, sailed in the "Discovery," a pinnace of only twenty tons burthen.

Among those who embarked was a quick-witted, unscrupulous, and self-reliant man—John Smith—who, in six weeks after they were out of sight of the coast of England, was suspected of a design to lead a mutiny.

On the 26th of April 1607, the expedition entered the broad and beautiful Chesapeake Bay, and that night the sealed orders were opened, and the following persons were designated as members of the Colonial Council:—Edward Maria Wingfield, Bartholomew Gosnold, John Smith, Christopher Newport, John Ratcliffe, John Martin, and John Kendall. The Council, in accordance with their instructions, soon elected Wingfield, a man of honourable birth, and a strict disciplinarian, as their President.[1]

On the 29th, a cross was planted at Cape Henry, and the country claimed in the name of King James; and the next day the ships anchored off Point Comfort,

---

[1] He was the grandson of Sir Robert Wingfield of Huntingdonshire, and the son of Thomas Maria Wingfield, who was thus christened, in compliment to Queen Mary, by Cardinal Pole.—*Camden Society Pub.*, No. 43. In 1588, Ferdinando Gorges and Edward Wingfield were prisoners of war at Lisle.

now Fortress Monroe. The 1st of May they began cautiously to ascend the James River; and on the 13th landed on a peninsula, in front of which there was good anchorage. All of the Councillors were duly sworn, except Smith, whose conduct during the voyage was disreputable.

In accordance with the orders prepared at London, Captain Newport, in a shallop, with five gentlemen and nineteen others, explored the river above the site of Jamestown.

At one of the Indian villages, not far from where is now the city of Richmond, they saw a lad ten years of age, with yellow hair and light skin, probably the offspring of one of the colonists, left at Roanoke by White, and an Indian concubine.[1] On the 24th of May, at the foot of the falls of the James River, Newport planted a cross on which were inscribed his own name and that of King James. On the 26th, a day before the return of the explorers, two hundred savages attacked Jamestown, and Wingfield bravely resisted them, being foremost in danger, and an arrow of the enemy passing through his beard.

After they had been nearly a month on shore, on the 10th of June, John Smith was permitted to take the oath of councillor. On Sunday, the 21st, the com-

---

[1] Strachey says, "His Majesty hath been acquainted that the men, women, and children of the first plantation at Roanoke, were, by commandment of Powhatan, he persuaded thereto by his priests, miserably slaughtered, without any offence given by the first planted, who twenty and odd years had peaceably lived intermixed with those savages, and were out of his territory."—*Hakluyt Society Pub.*, vol. vi. p. 85.

munion was administered by the devoted Chaplain of the colony, Robert Hunt, and in the evening Newport gave a farewell supper on board of his vessel, and the next day, lifting anchor, sailed and reached England in less than five weeks by the new and more direct route, with the report that neither silver nor gold had been discovered.

On the 18th of August 1607, a gentleman in London wrote to a friend "that Captain Newport has arrived without gold or silver, and that the adventurers, cumbered by the presence of the natives, had fortified themselves at a place called Jamestown, no graceful name, and doubts not the Spaniards will call it Villiaco. A Dutchman, writing in Latin, calls the town Jacobolis, but George Percy names it James Fort, which we like the best of all, because it comes near Chelmsford."

The low situation of the settlement, with the swamps in the rear, soon produced sickness, and during the summer nearly every day a new grave was dug. On the 22d of August, the man who had projected the expedition, and expended money in its behalf, "that worthy and religious gentleman," Bartholomew Gosnold,[1] was buried, and the saddened survivors manifested their respect by firing volleys of musketry over his remains.

The colonists, disheartened by the loss of their associates, and the discomforts of immigrant life, chafed under

---

[1] Anthony, a brother, and Anthony, also a relative, perhaps a son, accompanied Captain Gosnold to Virginia.—*London Co. MSS.*

the prudent measures and military exactness of Wingfield. In September, the members of the Council demanded a larger daily allowance of food, but he refused, because with strict economy their supplies would last but thirteen and a half weeks. As a precautionary measure, he also withheld the ration from any that had upon any day obtained fresh fish or wild game. The two gallons of sack and aqua vitæ reserved for the sick and sacramental purposes were even coveted by members of the Council. The President says they "longed for to sup up that little remnant, for they had now emptied all their own bottles."

As Wingfield would not yield to the clamour of his associates, Ratcliffe, Smith, and Martin, they deposed him, and formed a triumvirate. On the 11th of September he was arraigned before them, and Ratcliffe accused him of refusing him a chicken, a penny whittle, and a spoonful of beer, and of giving him damaged corn. Martin charged him with calling him an indolent fellow, and Smith alleged that he called him a liar. After this procedure, contrary to all the forms of law, he was imprisoned on board of the pinnace.

The colonists soon discovered that it was easier to live by angling, hunting, and roaming with the Indians, than by tilling the earth. The first winter they pursued their own pleasure, and cared little for the interests of the Company they had contracted to serve.

On the 10th of December, Captain Smith ascended the Chickahominy to trade with the Indians, and was treated with great respect and kindness by Powhatan,[1] although two colonists, Emery and Robinson, who went with him, were killed by some hostile savages.

Upon his return to Jamestown, Gabriel Archer, who had become a member of the Council, on the 8th of January 1607-8, placed Smith under arrest for allowing his companions to be killed, but that evening Captain Newport again arrived from England, and ordered the release both of Wingfield and Smith.

After recovering from the fatigue of the sea-voyage, Newport explored the Pamunky River, and was "lovingly entertained" by Powhatan. Returning to Jamestown on the 9th of March, he loaded his vessel with cedar, walnut boards, sassafrass, and iron ore. On the 10th of April 1608, with Archer and Wingfield as passengers, he left Virginia, and on the 20th of May arrived in England.

Wingfield, in reply to the complaints made against him, prepared a full statement of his administration in Virginia for the perusal of the London Company. In it he remarks :[2] "To the President's and Council's objec-

[1] Smith speaks of this kindness in his *Relation* of 1608, but sixteen years after leaving Virginia he published another narrative in which he contradicts his first statement. Honest Fuller, the historian, whose schoolmaster was Arthur Smith, a relative of the Captain's, in his *Worthies of England*, gives the following opinion of the Captain's last work :—

"From the Turks in Europe he passed to the Pagans in America, where such his perils, preservations, dangers, deliverances, they seem to *most men above belief, to some beyond truth*. Yet we have two witnesses to attest them, the prose and the pictures, *both in his own book*, and it soundeth much to the diminution of his deeds, that he *alone* is the herald to publish and proclaim them."

[2] Wingfield's discourse had been perused by Purchas, but he was warped in favour of the sentiments of the plausible Smith. It was copied from the

tions I say that I do know courtesy and civility became a Governor. No penny whittle was asked me, but a knife, whereof I had none to spare. The Indians had long before stolen my knife.

"Of chickens I never did eat but one, and that in my sickness. Mr. Ratcliffe had before that time tasted of four or five. I had by my own housewifery bred about thirty-seven, and the most part of them of my own poultry, [of] all which at my coming away I did not see three living. I never denied him or any other beer when I had it. The corn was of the same which we all lived upon.

"Mr. Smyth, in the time of our hunger, had spread a rumour in the colony that I did feast myself and my servants out of the common store, with intent, as I gathered, to have stirred the discontented company against me. I told him privately in Mr. Gosnold's tent that indeed I had caused half a pint of peas to be sodden with a piece of pork of my own provision for a poor old man which, in a sickness whereof he died, he much desired; and said if out of his malice he had given out otherwise, that he did tell a lie.

"It was proved to his face that he begged in Ireland, like a rogue, without a licence.

"Mr. Archer's quarrel to me was because he had not the choice of the place for our plantation, because I misliked his laying out of our town in the pinnace, because I would not swear him of the council for Virginia, which

manuscript in Lambeth Library, and printed for the first time with Newport's *Relation*, in vol. iv. of the American Antiquarian Society's Collections.

neither would I do nor he deserve; Mr. Smyth's quarrel, because his name was mentioned in the intended and confessed mutiny by Galthropp; Thomas Wootton, the surgeon, because I would not subscribe to a warrant to the Treasurer of Virginia to deliver him money to furnish him with drugs and other necessaries, and because I disallowed his living in the pinnace, having many of our men lying sick and wounded in our town, to whose dressings by that means he slacked his attendance.

"Of the same men also Captain Gosnold gave me warning, misliking much their dispositions, and assured me they would lay hold of me if they could."

Newport, in accordance with his written instructions, also made a report of his explorations. The manuscripts of Wingfield and Newport were both known to Purchas, yet were not published in his collection of voyages, probably because Sir Thomas Smith, who had furnished him with money to aid in printing his *Pilgrimage*, did not approve of their statements.

In the autumn of the year 1608 he completed his third voyage to Jamestown, bringing seventy passengers, among others, Francis West, brother of Lord Delaware, Daniel Tucker, and Raleigh Crashaw. He carried back on the return voyage iron ore, which was smelted and sold to the East India Company.[1]

The first description of the colony was printed in 1608, with the title, "A True Relation of such occurrences and accidents of noate as hath hapned in Virginia

---

[1] Strachey in *Hakluyt Society Pub.*, vol. vi.

since the first planting of that collony which is now resident in the south part thereof, till the last returne from thence."

Some of the copies appeared with the name of Thomas Watson as the author, but most of the edition had on the title-page, " Written by Captaine Smith, Coronell of the said collony, to a worshipful friend of his in England." The work was a small quarto in black letter, and contradicts the statements of Smith in his work on Virginia written at a later period.

CHAPTER II.

LORD DELAWARE, CAPTAIN-GENERAL OF VIRGINIA.

THE winter of 1608-9 was most discouraging to the active members of the London Company. The news of the dissensions with John Smith, now returned, had reached the public ear, former enthusiasm had subsided, and there was a growing conviction that it was a waste of money and of lives to send another expedition to America. "The malicious and looser sort," says a writer of the period, "with the licentious vain stage poets, have whet their tongues with scornful taunts against the action itself, insomuch as there is no common speech, nor public name of anything this day, except it be the name of God, which is more wildly depraved, traduced, and derided by such unhallowed lips, than the name of Virginia."[1]

To preserve the settlement from entire destruction, the Directors of the Company felt that there must be an entire re-organization, and that some one should be placed in charge of affairs there, above the temptations of avarice, actuated by a lofty patriotism, and anxious to civilize the aborigines.

[1] Dedicatory Epistle in *New Life of Virginia*. London, 1612.

Thomas West, Lord Delaware, was therefore selected, and by the free election of the Treasurer and Council of Virginia, with the full consent of the members of the Company, was constituted, during his natural life, Captain-General and Governor of all the English colonies to be planted in Virginia.[1] The appointment was hailed with satisfaction by the public, and the Company began to issue publications setting forth the advantages of emigration, and to prepare a new supply of colonists.

On March 24th, 1607-8, Crakanthorpe delivered a discourse on the divine right of kings at Paul's Cross, and therein alluded to the contemplated voyage in these words :—

"Let the honourable expedition now intended for Virginia be a witness, enterprised, I say not, auspiciis, but by the most wise and religious direction and protection of our chiefest pilot [the King], seconded by so many honourable and worthy personages in this state and kingdom, that it may justly give encouragement with alacrity and cheerfulness for some to undertake, for others to favour so noble and so religious an attempt.

"I may not stay, in this straitness of time, to mention, much less set forth unto you, the great and manifold benefits which may redound to this our so populous a nation by planting an English colony in a territory as large and spacious almost as is England, and in a soil so rich, fertile, and fruitful as that; besides, the sufficiency it naturally yields for itself, may, with best convenience, supply some of the greatest wants and necessities of

[1] *Howe's Chronicle* (London, 1615), p. 942.

these kingdoms. But this happiness which I mention is a happy and glorious work indeed of planting among those poor, and savage, and to be pitied Virginians, not only humanity instead of brutish incivility, but religion also. . . . This being the honourable and religious intendment of this enterprise, what glory! what honour to our sovereign! What comfort to those subjects who shall be means of furthering of so happy a work, not only to see a New Britain in another world, but to have also those as yet heathen barbarians and brutish people, together with our English, to learn the speech and language of Canaan!"

Hakluyt, in view of the enterprise on foot, wrote to the Company April 15, 1609, from his lodging in the college at Westminster, relative to the treatment of the Indians, a subject then, as now, difficult to manage. He remarked that, "for all their fair and cunning speeches, they are not overmuch to be trusted, for they be the greatest traitors in the world. They be also as inconstant as the weathercock, and most ready to take all occasions of advantages to do mischief. They are great liars and dissemblers, for which faults oftentimes they had their deserved payments.

"To handle them gently while gentle courses may be found to serve, it will be without comparison the best; but if gentle polishing will not serve, the one shall not want hammerers and rough masons enough, I mean our old soldiers trained up in the Netherlands, to square and prepare them to our preachers' hands.

"To conclude, I trust by your Honours' Worships'

wise instructions to the noble Governor, the worthy Lieutenant and Admiral, and other chief managers of the business, all things shall be so prudently carried, that the painful preachers shall be reverenced and cherished, the valiant and forward soldiers respected, the diligent rewarded, the coward emboldened, the weak and sick relieved, the mutinous suppressed, the reputation of the Christians among the savages preserved, our most holy faith exalted, all paganism and idolatry little by little utterly extinguished."

During the year 1609 publications urging persons to emigrate appeared. One was entitled *Nova Britannia; offering most excellent fruits by planting in Virginia*, and another a *Good Speed to Virginia*, the dedicatory epistle to which was signed by R. G. from his house at the north end of St. Sythe's Lane, the writer of which regretted that "he was neither in person nor purse to be a partaker in the business."

Tobias Matthew, Archbishop of York, wrote to the Earl of Somerset in the month of June: "Of Virginia there are so many tractates, divine, human, historical, political, or call them as you please, as no further intelligence I dare desire." He had probably read the sermon of William Symonds, preacher of St. Saviour's in Southwark, delivered on April 25, 1609, at Whitechapel before the "most noble and worthy advancers of the standard of Christ among the Gentiles, the adventurers for the plantations of Virginia," which was an earnest appeal to fill up the thinned ranks of the first settlers at Jamestown.

Under one of the heads of his discourse is a statement

of the severance of the husbandman from the soil, and description of the condition of the labouring man of that period, as graphic as any in the English language. His words were—

"Look seriously into the land, and see whether there be not just cause, if not a necessity, to seek abroad. The people, blessed be God, do swarm in the land, as young bees in a hive in June, insomuch that there is very hardly room for one man to live by another. The mightier, like old strong bees, thrust the weaker, as younger, out of their hives. Lords of manors convert townships, in which were one or two hundred communicants, to a shepherd and his dog. The true labouring husbandman that sustaineth the prince by the plow, who was wont to feed many poor, to set many people on work, and pay twice as much subsidy and fifteens to the King, for his proportion of earth, as his landlord did for ten times as much; that was wont to furnish the church with saints, the masters with able persons to fight, is now in many places turned labourer, and can hardly 'scape the statutes of rogues and vagrants.

"The gentleman hath got most of the tillage in his hand; he hath rotten sheep to sell at Michaelmas; his summer-fed oxen at Easter; asking no better price for his hay than his beasts, to keep that till spring that they got at grass. By this means he can keep his corn till the people starve, always provided that the poor husbandmen which are left and the clothier must buy their seed and wool at such a rate, that shall wear them out in a few years.

"And were it not that the honest and Christian merchant doth often help, who putteth all his estate upon the providence of God, which they call venturing to bring corn into the land, for which he hath many a bitter curse of the cursed cornmongers, we should find an extreme famine in the midst of our greatest plenty. The rich shopkeeper hath the good, honest, poor labourer at such advantage, that he can grind his face when he pleaseth.

"The poor metal man worketh his bones out, and sweateth himself in the fire, yet for all his labour, having charge of wife and children, he can hardly keep himself from the alms-box. Always provided that his masters, when he worketh, will give never a penny toward his living, but they can tell, of their own knowledge, that if the poor man were a good husband he might live well, for he receiveth much money in the year, very near fourpence for every sixpenny worth of work.

"The thoughtful poor woman, that hath her small children standing at her knee and hanging on her breast, she worketh with her needle and laboureth with her fingers, her candle goeth not out by night, she is often deluding the bitterness of her life with sweet songs, that she singeth to a heavy heart.

"Sometimes she singeth, 'Have mercy on me Lord,' sometimes 'Help, Lord, for good and godly men do perish and decay,' sometimes 'Judge and avenge my cause, O Lord,' and many such like, which, when a man of understanding doth hear, he doth with pity praise

God that hath given such means to mock hunger with and to give patience. I warrant you her songs want no passion; she never saith O Lord! but a salt tear droppeth from her sorrowful head, a deep sigh breatheth as a furnace from her aching heart, that weepeth with the head, for company, with tears of sweetest blood. And when all the week is ended, she can hardly earn salt for her water-gruel to feed on, upon the Sunday.

"Many such sweets are in England which I know not how better to interpret than to say, the strong old bees do beat out the younger to swarm and hive themselves elsewhere. Take the opportunity, good, honest labourers, which bring all the honey to the hive, God may so bless you that a May swarm is worth a king's ransom."

To advance the welfare of the colony, a more specific charter, with enlarged privileges, was, on the 23d of May, granted to the Company, in which it was provided that as soon as the new Governor or Deputy should arrive, the authority of the President and Council then in power should cease.

With a fair wind, on the first day of June 1609, a fleet of nine vessels, with about five hundred men and material for reorganizing the colony, sailed from Plymouth. Lord Delaware remained behind, but it was accompanied by Sir Thomas Gates, an experienced soldier, still in the service of the Netherlands, as the Lieutenant-General, to reside in and govern the colony, and Sir George Somers as Admiral, who had been an old naval commander, and gave up his seat in Parliament to go to America.[1] These two officers sailed in the vessel under the charge of Captain Newport. Other vessels were commanded by men who had before been at Jamestown, and with the expedition was a pinnace, called the "Virginia," that had been built by the Popham colonists at Sagadahoc, in the State of Maine, and in which, in the year 1608, a portion of them returned to England.

The "Blessing," commanded by Captain Archer, and three others of the fleet, arrived early in August at Jamestown; and soon the "Diamond," Captain Ratcliffe, appeared without her mainmast, which was followed in two or three days by the "Swallow" in like condition.

The "Sea Venture," containing Gates, Somers, and Newport, did not, however, appear; and after waiting for some days, in accordance with the instructions of the new charter, the colonists proceeded to form a government, of which Archer gave the following account:—

"Inasmuch as the President [John Smith] to strengthen his authority, accorded with the mariners, and gave not any due respect to many worthy gentlemen that were in our ships, whereupon they generally, with my consent, chose Master West, my Lord Delawar's brother, their Governor *de bené esse*, in the absence of Sir Thomas Gates, or if he be miscarried by sea, then to continue

---

[1] A debate arose in the House of Commons, on February 14, 1609-10, whether his going to Virginia made it necessary to relinquish his seat as Member of Parliament. Sir George Moore remarked, "that Sir George Sommers ought not to be removed, that it was no disgrace, but a grace to be Governor in Virginia."

till we heard newes from our Counsell in England. This choice of him they made not to disturb the old President during his term, but as his authority expired, then to take upon him the government, with such assistants of the Captains, as discreet persons as the colony affords.

"Perhaps you shall have it blazoned as a mutiny, by such as retain old malice; but Master West, Master Piercie, and all the respected gentlemen of worth in Virginia, can and will testify otherwise, upon their oaths. For the King's patent we ratified, but refused to be governed by the President, that is, after his time was expired, and only subjected ourselves to Master West, whom we labour to have next President."

Soon after this temporary election, George Percy, brother to the Earl of Northumberland, one of the original settlers, a brave and honourable man, was called to the Presidency. West, Ratcliffe, and Martin were made Councillors; and early in October, Captain John Smith was sent home to answer sundry misdemeanours, one of which was a design to marry Pocahontas, a young daughter of Powhatan.

The passengers that arrived in the first ships of the Gates and Somers expedition were "unhallowed creatures." Twenty-eight or thirty were sent in the ship "Swallow" to trade for corn with the Indians, and instead of returning, stole away with one of the best ships, and some returned to England, and declared they had been driven back by famine. To uphold their desertion, they told the tragical story of a man pinched with hunger eating his dead wife, which was based upon the fact that a man who hated his wife had killed her and then secretly cut her in pieces. The woman being missed by friends, his house was searched, and portions of the mangled body found; after which the husband alleged that she had died a natural death, and that he had saved it to eat, being compelled through hunger. But a quantity of provisions having also been found, he was tried, then confessed the murder, and was burned for his fiendish act.

While friends in England were mourning over them as lost, the passengers of the "Sea Adventure" were in good health at the Bermudas, where they had been stranded on the 28th of July 1609; and Sir Thomas Gates and Sir George Somers were busy superintending the construction of two vessels.[1] While on the island the white wife of the afterwards somewhat famous John Rolfe gave birth to a child, which, by Chaplain Buck, was christened Bermuda.

On the 10th of May 1610 Gates and Somers, with their party, embarked in their two rudely constructed ships, and in thirteen days, with one hundred and forty men and women, landed at Jamestown. The bell of the frail chapel was rung, and the emaciated settlers who had survived the winter, assembled to listen to the zealous and sorrowful prayer of Chaplain Buck, after which the commission of Sir Thomas Gates as Lieutenant-

---

[1] On a palmetto tree was cut the following inscription:—

"Conditur in hoc loco navis per Ricardum Frobisherum oneris 70, quæ Virginiæ destinator nos omnes hinc transportabat. Anno 1610, May 4."

In 1670 this was hung as a relic over the chair in the Governor's hall at Bermudas.—Hardy's *Bermudas*, printed in 1671.

General of Virginia, was read, and Percy retired from his temporary command.

When the intelligence of the sad condition of affairs reached the ears of Lord Delaware, "neither whose honour nor fortune needed any desperate medicine," he determined to go in person and assume the duties of Captain-General of Virginia. In view of his departure from his pleasant surroundings in his native land, William Crashaw, preacher at the Temple, and father of the poet, delivered a stirring sermon on February 21, 1609-10, from the text Luke xxii. 32: "But I have prayed for thee that thy faith fail not, therefore when thou art converted, strengthen thy brethren."

The discourse was an argument upon the importance of converting the savage, and founding the English Church and commonwealth in America. In considering the discouragements to the plantation, he alluded to the objection, "that it hath so poor and small a beginning, and is therefore subject to the mocks and flouts of many who say that it is but the action of a very few persons, and they send but poor supplies, and a handful of men at a time, and one good ship would beat them all.

"For answer I say, many greater States than this is likely to prove hath as little or less beginning. The Israelites went down into Egypt being but seventy souls, and were there about two hundred years and little more, and most of that time in miserable bondage, yet did they grow to 600,000 men, besides children, and soon after to one of the greatest kingdoms of the earth. Look at the beginning of Rome, how poor, how mean, how despised it was, and yet on that base beginning grew to be mistress of the world.

"Oh! but those that go in person are raked up of our refuse, and are a number of disordered men unfit to bring to pass any good action. So indeed say those that lie and slander. But I answer for the generality of them that go, they be such as offer themselves voluntarily, for none are pressed, none are compelled, and they be like, for aught I see, to those that are left behind, even of all sorts, better or worse.

"But for many that go in person, let these objectors know they be as good as themselves, and, it may be, many degrees better."

In another portion of the discourse he states that colonists must not expect luxury, but be willing to endure hardness like their forefathers, for "had they been such mecocks and milksops as we are, never would they have expelled the Danes, nor overcome the French."

He confessed to his audience that the three great enemies of the enterprise were the devil, Papists, and players. His language in regard to players is very sharp. He says:—

"As for players—pardon me, right honourable and beloved, for so wronging this place and your patience with so base a subject—they play with princes and potentates, magistrates and ministers, nay, with God and religion, and all holy things,—nothing that is good, excellent, or holy can escape them, how then can this action?

"But this may suffice, that they are players; they abuse Virginia, but they are but players; they disgrace it, but they are but players; and they have played with better things, and such for which, if they speedily repent not, vengeance waits for them.

"But let them play on; they make men laugh on earth, but He that sits in heaven laughs them to scorn, because, like the fly, they so long play with the candle, till first it singes their wings, and at last burns them altogether. But why are the players enemies to the plantation? I will tell you the cause. First, for that they are so multiplied here, that one cannot live by another, and they see that we send all trades to Virginia, but will send no players, which, if we would do, those that remain would gain the more at home."

The eloquent conclusion was in these words:—

"And to you, right honourable and beloved, who engage your lives, and are therefore deepliest interested in this business—who make the greatest ventures and bear the greatest burdens—who leave your ease and honour at home, and commend yourselves to the seas and winds for the good of the enterprise—you that desire to advance the gospel of Jesus Christ, though it be with the hazard of your lives, go forward in the name of the God of heaven and earth, the God that keepeth counsel and mercy for thousands; go on, with the blessing of God, God's angels, and God's Church; cast away fear, and let nothing daunt your spirit, remembering who have broken the ice before you, and suffered that which, with God's blessing, you never shall; remembering what you go to do, even to display the banner of Christ Jesus —to fight with the devil and the old dragon, having St.

Michael and his angels on your side—to eternize your own names both here at home and amongst the Virginians, whose apostles you are, and to make yourselves most happy men, whether you live or die; if you live, by effecting so glorious a work, if you die, by dying as martyrs or confessors of God's religion; and remembering, lastly, whom you leave behind; you leave us, your brethren, of whom many would go with you that yet may not; many will follow you in convenient time, and who will now go with you in our hearts and prayers, and who will second you with new and fresh supplies, and who are resolved, by the grace of that God in whose name they have undertaken it, never to relinquish this action, but though all the wealth already put in it were lost, will again and again renew and continue the supplies, until the Lord gives the hoped harvest of our endeavours.

"And thou, most noble Lord,[1] whom God hath stirred up to neglect the pleasures of England, and with Abraham to go from thy country, and forsake thy kindred and thy father's house, to go to a land which God will show thee, give me leave to speak the truth.

"Thy ancestor, many hundred years ago, gained great honour to thy house, but by this action thou augmentest

---

[1] The West family had for centuries been prominent in politics, and zealous in religion. Alice, the wife of a Sir Thomas West, was buried at St. Sepulchre's, London, in 1395, and she bequeathed £18, 10s. for 4400 masses to be sung and said for the soul of Sir Thomas West, her lord and husband, her own soul, and all Christian souls, in the most haste that might be, within fourteen nights after her decease; also £40 to the Canons of Christ Church to read and sing mass for her lord's soul and her own while the world lasts.

it. He took a king prisoner in the field in his own land,[1] but by the godly managing of this business, thou shalt take the devil prisoner in open field and in his own kingdom, nay the Gospel which thou carriest with thee shall bind him in chains, and angels in stronger fetters than irons, and execute upon them the judgment that is written, yea, it shall lead captivity captive, and redeem the souls of men from bondage. And then the honour of thy house is more at the last than the first.

"Go on, therefore, and prosper with this thy honour, which indeed is greater than any eye discerns, even such as the present age shortly will enjoy, and the future admire. Go forward in the strength of the Lord, and make mention of his righteousness only. Look not at the gain, the wealth, the honour, the advancement of thy house that may fall upon thee, but look at those things and better ends that concern the kingdom of God. Remember that thou art a General of Englishmen, nay a General of Christian men, therefore principally look to religion. You go to commend it to the heathen, then practise it yourselves; make the name of Christ honourable, not hateful unto them. Suffer no Papist, let them not nestle there, nay, let the name of the Pope for Popery never be heard in Virginia. Take

---

[1] This was said to have occurred at the Battle of Poitiers. One of his name, about this period, while passing with English cavalry through a narrow defile, found they were ambuscaded by the French, who pressed upon their rear. He and his fellow-officers halted their troop, and the French rushed at them in full gallop. The English calmly opened their ranks, and after they passed through, fell upon them, and with a fierce clanging of swords upon their metal armour, routed and chased them into the Castle of Romorantin.—*Froissart.*

heed of Atheists, the devil's champions, and if thou discover any make them examples. And if I may be so bold to advise, make Atheism, and other blasphemies, capital, and let that be the first law made in Virginia.

"Suffer no Brownists, nor factious separatists, let them keep their conventicles elsewhere, let them go and convert some other heathen, and let us see if they can *constitute such churches really*, the ideas whereof they have fancied in their brains, and when they have given us such an example, we may then have some cause to follow them. Till then we will take our pattern from their betters.

"Especially suffer no sinful, no lewd, no licentious man, none that live not under the obedience of good laws, and let your laws be strict, especially against swearing and other profaneness. And though vain swearing by God's name be the common and crying sin of England, and no mortal but venial sin in Popish doctrine, yet know that it is a sin under which the earth mourns, and your land will flourish if this be reproved.

"Let the Sabbath be wholly and holily observed, public prayers daily held, idleness eschewed, and mutinies carefully prevented. Be well advised in making laws, but being made let them be obeyed, and let none stand for scare-crows, for that is the way to make all at least to be contemned.

"This course taken, and you shall see those who were to blame at home will prove praiseworthy in Virginia. And you will teach us in England to know (who have almost forgot it) what an excellent thing execution of laws is in a commonwealth.

"But if you should aim at nothing but your private ends, and neglect religion and God's service, look for no blessing, nay look for a curse, though not in the whole action, yet on our attempts, and never think we shall have the honour to effect it. Yet think not that our sin shall hinder the purpose of God, for when this sinful generation is consumed, God will stir up our children after us, who shall learn by our example to follow it in a more holy manner, and so bring it to that perfection which we for our sins and profaneness could not do.

"But you, right honourable, have otherwise learned Christ, and we hope also otherwise practised him, and will declare by the managing of the action, the power of the true religion you have learned in England.

"Then shall heaven and earth bless you, and for the heroical adventure of thy person and state in such a godly course, the God of heaven will make thy name to be mentioned throughout all generations, and thousands of people shall honour thy memory,[1] and give thanks to God for thee while the world endureth.

"And thou Virginia! whom though mine eyes see not my heart shall love, how hath God honoured thee! Thou hast thy name from the worthiest Queen that ever the world had; thou hast thy matter from the greatest King on earth; and thou shalt now have thy fame from

[1] One of the United States of America is called Delaware, and there is also a Delaware County in the States of New York, Pennsylvania, Ohio, and Indiana.

one of the most glorious nations under the sun, and under the conduct of a General of as great and ancient nobility as any ever engaged in action of this nature. But this is but a little portion of thy honour, for thy God is coming towards thee, and in the meantime sends to thee, and salutes thee with the best blessing heaven hath, even the blessed Gospel.

"Look up, therefore, and lift up thy hands, for the God of Israel, who is still the God of England, will shortly, I doubt not, bring it to pass that men shall say, Blessed be the Lord of Virginia, and let all Christian people say Amen.

"And this salutation doth my soul give thee, O Virginia! even this poor New Year's gift, who though I be not likely to be thine apostle, yet do own and devote myself to be in England thy faithful factor, and most desirous to do thee any service in the Lord Jesus Christ, our Saviour and thine, whom we beseech for his precious bloodshedding to advance his standard, and that you may cry for yourselves, as we do now even for you, Even so, come Lord Jesus."

The sermon was dedicated to Parliament by one with the signature L. D., and appears to have been published without the permission of Crashaw.[1]

On the 1st of April 1610, Lord Delaware sailed in the

---

[1] The following is prefixed to the Discourse:—

"To the Printer.

"My earnest desire to further the plantation in Virginia makes me, perhaps, too bold with Mr. Crashaw thus without his leave to publish the same.

"But the great good, I assure myself, it will do shall merit your pains and my pardon. You may give it what title you please, only let this enclosed

ship "Delaware," Robert Tindall, master, from the Cowes, accompanied by the "Blessing" of Plymouth, and the "Hercules." On the 5th of June, he made land to the south of Chesapeake Bay, and that night went ashore at Cape Henry, and the next evening anchored under Point Comfort, when Captain James Davis,[1] in charge of the stockade there, visited the fleet, and "unfolded a strange narrative, mixed both with joy and sorrow." He stated that Sir Thomas Gates and Sir George Somers in two pinnaces had arrived with their company from the Bermudas on the 21st of May. "I was heartily glad," says Lord Delaware in a letter, "to hear the happiness of this news, but it was seasoned with a compound of so many miseries and calamities, as no story ever presented, I believe, the wrath and curse of the Eternal offended Majesty in greater measure."

The pinnace "Virginia" that had been built at Sagadahoc by the Popham colonists, at the time of Delaware's arrival, lay at Point Comfort ready to set sail for Newfoundland as soon as Gates and Somers arrived from Jamestown. Delaware, alluding to the condition in which Gates found Jamestown, remarks, "It appeared rather as the ruins of some ancient fortification than that any people living might now inhabit it; the palisadoes he found torn down, the ports open, the gate from the hinges, the church ruined and unfrequented, empty

Dedication to the Parliament be fairly prefixed in the book for your credit print, to the care whereof I leave you. Your friend, L. D."

The writer was probably Leonard Digges, the father of Sir Dudley Digges. On each page of the book is the running title, "New Yeere's Gift to Virginia."

[1] Davies or Davis had been a member of the Popham colony in the Kenneber River, and the "Virginia" was built there.

houses rent up and burnt, the living not able as they pretended to step into the woods to gather other firewood; and it is true, the Indian as fast killing without as the famine and pestilence within.

"Only the block-house, somewhat regarded, was the safety of the remainder that lived, which now could not have preserved them many days longer from the watching, subtle, and offended Indian, who knew all this their weakness, and forbare too timely to assault the fort, or hazard themselves in a fruitless war on such, whom they were assured in short time would of themselves perish, and being provoked, their desperate condition might draw forth to a valiant defence.

"All these considered, [Sir Thomas Gates] entered into consultation with Sir George Somers and Capt. Newporte, calling unto the same the gentlemen and Counsel of the former Government, interesting both the one and the other to advise with him what was to be done. The provision which both had aboard was examined and delivered, how it being racked to the uttermost, extended not to above sixteen days. The gentlemen of the town who knew better of the country could not give them any hope.

"It soon then appeared most fit, by a general approbation, that to preserve and save all from starving, there could be no readier course thought on than to abandon the country; and accommodating themselves the best that they might in the present pinnaces (as, namely, in the 'Discovery' and the 'Virginia,' and the two brought from and builded at the Bermudas, the one called the 'Deliverance,' of about seventy ton; the other the 'Patience,' of about thirty ton), with all speed convenient to make for the Newfoundland, where, it being then fishing time, they might meet with many English ships, into which, happily, they might disperse most of the company.

"This consultation taking effect, the 7th of June, Sir Thomas Gates having appointed every pinnace his complement and number, and delivered likewise thereunto a proportionable rate of provisions, caused every man to repair aboard; and because he would preserve the town unburned, which some malicious and intemperate people threatened, his one company he caused to be cast ashore, and was himself the last of them, when about noon, giving a farewell with a peal of small shot, he set sail; and that night, with the tide, fell down to an island in the river which our people here call Hog Island, and the next morning the tide brought them to another island, which they have called Mulberry Island, at which time they discovered my long boat."

The "Virginia," which had left several days before, was waiting, as already noticed, at Point Comfort when Delaware arrived there. Immediately he placed a crew on board, and despatched Edward Brewster, captain of his body-guard, with letters to Sir Thomas Gates, whom, on the 8th of June, he met at Mulberry Island. After reading the despatches, Gates bore up helm again, and the same night relanded his men at Jamestown.

On Sunday the 10th, Delaware's ship cast anchor in front of the place, and in the afternoon he went ashore, when, after listening to a sermon by Mr. Buck, the chaplain of Gates, he caused his commission to be read, and then delivered a brief speech, chiding the settlers for their excess and indolence, exhorting them to industry, and hoping that he might not be compelled to draw the sword of justice to cut off delinquents.

There being no house in repair, after his address he returned to the ship, and there on the 12th appointed officers and councillors for the colony.[1]

The first care of the new government was to provide subsistence. During the last winter the Indians and improvident settlers had killed all the hogs, "insomuch as of five or six hundred, there was but one sow left alive," the mares and horses had all been eaten, and for a long time the crow of the morning cock and the cackling of the hen over a new-laid egg had ceased.

Sir George Somers, "the good old gentleman, out of his love and zeal, not motioning, but most cheerfully and resolutely" proposed to go to the Bermudas to obtain some of the wild hogs that were there so numerous. Receiving a commission on the 15th of June, four days later he sailed from Jamestown in the small pinnace, the "Patience," which had been built under his supervision in the island where they had been wrecked the year before.

---

[1] The officers of the Council were Sir Thomas Gates, Knight, Lieutenant-General; Sir George Somers, Knight, Admiral; Captain George Percy, Esq.; Sir Ferdinando Wenman, Knight, Marshal; and William Strachey, Esq., Secretary.

He also nominated Captain John Martin, Master of the Ironworks; Captain George Webb, Serjeant-Major of the Fort; and Daniel Tucker and Robert Wild, Clerks of the Store.

In a communication to the Company dated July 7, 1610, Delaware says :—

"Only let me truly acknowledge they are not an hundred or two of deboisht hands, dropt forth year after year, with penury and leisure, ill provided for before they come, and worse governed when they are here, men of such distempered bodies and infected minds, whom no examples daily before their eyes, either of goodness or punishment, can deter from their habitual impieties, or terrify from a shameful death, that must be carpenters and workers in this so glorious a building.

"But to delude and mock the business no longer, as a necessary quantity of provisions for a year at least must be carefully sent with men, so likewise must there be the same care for men of quality, and painstaking men of arts and practices, chosen out and sent into the business, and such are in due time now promised and set down in the schedule at the end of our own approved discourse, which we have entitled, 'A true and sincere declaration of the purpose and end of our Plantation begun in Virginia.'

"And these two, such men and such provision, are like enough to make good the ends of the employment in all the ways, both for reputation, search, and discovery of the country, and the hope of the South Sea. . . . Whereupon give me leave, I beseech you, further to make inference that, since it hath been well thought on by you to provide for the government, by changing the authority into an absolute command of a noble and well-instructed Lieutenant-General and your industrious

Admiral. . . . Let no imposture nor rumour then, nor any fame of some one, or a few more chanceable actions interposing by the way, or at home, waive any man's fair purpose hitherward, or wrest them to a declining and falling off from the business.

"For let them be assured, as of the truth itself, these promises considered, look what the country can afford, which may by the quantity of our men be safely and conveniently explored, these things shall not be omitted for our part, nor will be by the Lieutenant-General to be commanded; nor our commands received, as in former times, with unwillingness or falseness, either in our people's going forth or in execution, being for each one in his place, whether commander, overseer, or labourer.

"For the causes of idle and restive untowardness being by the authority and unity of our government removed, all hands already set to it, and he that knew not the way to goodness before, but cherished singularity and faction, now can beat out a path to himself of industry, and goodness for others to trade in, such I may well say is the power of exemplar virtue.

"Nor would I have it conceived that we would exclude altogether gentlemen, and such whose breeding never knew what a day's labour meant, for even to such this country I doubt not but will give likewise excellent satisfaction, especially to the better and stayed spirits, for he amongst us that cannot dig, use the square, nor practise the axe and chisel, yet he shall find how to employ the force of knowledge, the exercise of counsel, and the operation and power of his best breeding and quality."

In accordance with the suggestion in Crashaw's sermon, Delaware immediately established a Draconian and intolerant code for the repression of vice and sustentation of true religion, which was enlarged by Deputy-Governors Gates and Dale, and published in 1612,[1] with a preface by William Strachey, Secretary to Lord Delaware.

This early Virginia code prescribed death for blasphemy of the Trinity or the king, and also upon being convicted for the third time of profane swearing. For a want of proper respect to a clergyman, one was publicly whipped, and obliged to ask pardon in church for three successive Sundays. The penalty for not attending church and the Sunday catechetical lesson was, for the first offence, the loss of a week's provisions, for the second, whipping, and for the third, death. If a colonist upon arrival refused to go to the clergyman to give an account of his faith, he was to be daily whipped until he complied.

If a washerwoman stole the linen of an employer she

[1] At first the articles were twenty-one in number; after they were enlarged they were published with this title :—

FOR
THE COLONY IN VIRGINIA,
BRITANNIA.
LAWES DIUINE, MORALL, AND
MARTIALL, &C.
" Alget qui non ardet
Res nostræ subinde non sunt, quales quis optaret,
Sed quales esse possunt."
Printed at London for Walter Barre.
1612.

was publicly whipped. A baker who sold loaves below the standard weight was liable to a loss of his ears.

Although we now shudder at these enactments, they were in accordance with the spirit of the age when it was believed to be doing God a service to coerce men into a certain form of doctrinal belief, and possible to force them to be honest and virtuous citizens.

The daily prayer that accompanied the code was probably prepared by Crashaw. In it is the following petition, which corresponds with a sentiment in the sermon delivered in view of the departure of Delaware, and is the very language used by Crashaw in the preface to Hamor's *Present Estate of Virginia*, published in 1615:—

"And whereas we have, by undertaking the plantation, undergone the reproofs of the base world, insomuch as many of our own brethren laugh us to scorn, O Lord, we pray thee, fortify us against this temptation. Let Sanballat and Tobias, Papists and players,[1] and such other Ammonites and Horonites, the scum and dregs of the earth, let them mock such as help to build up the walls of Jerusalem, and they that be filthy, let them be filthy still."

Sir George Somers, after a stormy passage, reached Bermudas, but in November died from eating too heartily of the wild hog.

Matthew Somers, a young and worthless kinsman, instead of returning to Virginia with a cargo of hogs,

---

[1] In Cook's play of "Tu Quoque," one of the personæ, a penniless fellow, says,—"I dare not walk abroad to see my friends, for fear the sergeants should take acquaintance of me; my refuge is Ireland or Virginia."

persuaded the sailors to steer directly for England, where he remained and pretended to be the heir of Sir George Somers.[1]

In the fall of the year 1610 no tidings having been received of Somers, Sir Thomas Gates was despatched to England to secure a better supply of men, and in December he went to the Netherlands, in whose military service he had remained, to confer with the authorities at the Hague about the overture they had made for uniting in the project of settling Virginia.[2] While Gates was absent the health of Delaware failed, and he was obliged in the spring of the year 1611 to return home. But before the illness of Delaware was known the Company had despatched Sir Thomas Dale with three ships; and in June Gates started on his second voyage to Jamestown with six ships, his wife and daughters, three hundred men, one hundred cows, and a large supply of provisions. The wife of Gates died on the passage, but in August the expedition safely arrived at Point Comfort, and Kecoughtan, now Hampton,[3] was taken possession of as "a delicate and necessary seat for a city."

In the autumn the ship "Star," of 300 tons burthen, sailed from Jamestown with forty fine and large pines

---

[1] London Company MSS.   [2] Winwood.

[3] Strachey says "Pochins was one of Powhatan's sons at Kecoughtan, and was the young weroance there at the same time when Sir Thomas Gates, Lieutenant-General, took possession of it. It is an ample and fair country indeed . . . and is a delicate and necessary seat for a city or chief fortification, being so near,—within three miles by water of the mouth of our bay,—and is well appointed a fit seat for one of our chief commanders, since Point Comfort being out of all dispute to be fortified, to secure our towns above."—*Hak. Pub.*, vol. vi. pp. 60, 61.

suitable for masts. Chamberlain, on December 18, 1611, wrote to Sir Dudley Carleton :—

"Newport, the Admiral of Virginia, is newly come home, and brings word of the arrival there of Sir Thomas Gates and his Company; but his lady died by the way in some part of the West Indies. He hath sent his daughters back again, which, I doubt not, is a piece of prognostication that himself means not to tarry long."

The bloody code enforced by Dale, an officer for years in the service of the Netherlands, and still receiving their pay, did not make men curse less nor pray more.

On the 17th of August 1611, he wrote to the Earl of Salisbury that the three hundred colonists that came with him were "so profane, so riotous, so full of mutiny, that not many are Christians but in name, and their bodies so crazed and diseased that not sixty of them may be employed;" and he implored that the King would send him two thousand able-bodied men to build on sure foundations. The demand, however, was not heeded by the Government, and Delaware and associates, on the 12th of March 1612, received a new charter, giving them the power to establish lotteries. The first public drawing of prizes, to the amount of £5000, took place on the 29th of June 1612, "in a new built house at the west end of St. Paul's, London." Out of the lottery there were drawn out and thrown away sixty thousand blanks, without abating of any one prize; and by the 20th of July the drawings were completed to the full satisfaction of all concerned. Thomas Sharplisse, a London tailor, drew the chief prize—four thousand crowns in fine plate, which was carried to his house in a very stately manner.[1]

The granting of the charter of 1612 by the King, with its special privileges, created some jealousy, and in the Parliament of 1614 led to much discussion. A member named Middleton, in a debate in the House of Commons on April 20, 1614, stated that the Company were willing to yield up their patent, that it had not been their intention to use it otherwise than for the good of all parties; and confessed that there had been some miscarriages. He also declared that the shopkeepers of London, in exchange for their goods, received tobacco instead of coin, which was injurious to the Commonwealth; that many of the divines now smelt of tobacco, and that poor men at night spent fourpence of their day's wages in smoke, and he wished that the patent might "be damned, and an Act of Parliament passed for the government of the colony by a Company."

On the 12th of May the Council of the London Company presented a petition to the House of Commons for aid, which was read, and on the 17th, at seven o'clock, taken up for consideration. The members of the London Company with their attorney, the eminent Richard Martin, entered on that day, followed by the Lords Southampton, Sheffield, and others, who passed within the bar of the House, and stood with heads uncovered.

---

[1] The father of Ogilby the author at this period was in prison for debt, and, borrowing some money of his son, purchased a Virginia lottery ticket, which drew a prize which enabled him to extricate himself from his debtors. —*Aubrey*.

Before Martin commenced his argument the Speaker addressed the Lords, and said it was now the pleasure of the House that they should sit down and be covered.

Martin then arose, made a plea in behalf of the Company and the colony, evincing historical research and broad statesmanship. He told the listeners that the country was theirs by discovery, and the name it had received from the Queen, and should be defended by England as the Spaniards defended the West Indies, the Portuguese the East Indies, and the Hollanders their forts in the Moluccas. The present want of Virginia, he continued, was honest labourers with their wives and children, and he urged that a committee might be appointed to co-operate with the Company in obtaining respectable colonists.

In concluding he reminded the House how Henry the Seventh penuriously turned his face away from Columbus because he could not see the pecuniary profit that would result to England from his projected discoveries, and urged them not to pursue a similar niggardly course toward Virginia, and then, forgetting in the warmth of his oratory that he was only there by a special privilege as the counsel of the Company, he reproved them for neglecting Virginia, and wasting so much time upon matters of less importance.

As soon as Martin concluded there was great feeling manifested in the House. Sir Roger Owen, the member for Shrewsbury, moved that Sir Thomas Smith and other members of the Company withdraw, while the speech of their attorney was under discussion. Sir Edward Montague thought the speech "was the most unfitting that was ever spoken in the House." Mr. Duncombe said he patronized "as a schoolmaster teaching his scholars." Sir G. Moore felt that it was an extraordinary procedure the admission of the counsel of the Company to the floor of the House upon the hearing of a petition, and that the speech was still more strange.

It was finally decided that he should be brought to the bar of the House on the next day, and that after a charge from the Speaker he should make his submission. The next morning he was brought before the House, and offered to kneel. Sir Randall Crew, the Speaker, then said :—

"He had done himself much credit by offering to kneel. The case was this : A petition relative to the Virginia Company had been presented, and an order for the Council to appear; that he as their attorney had presented himself with divers Lords ; that the House at first was disposed to listen to him with all due respect and love ; that the retrospect of the Virginia Plantation was acceptable, for it had been viewed with the eyes of love. But afterwardly he had impertinently digressed, for it was not his place to advise and censure. The House therefore had brought him before them, and, although many were his acquaintances, yet now all looked upon him with the eyes of judges, and not as private friends."

Upon his knees Martin then confessed in substance as follows :—

"All are liable to err, and he particularly so, but he was not in love with error, and as willing as any man to be divorced therefrom; admits that he digressed from the subject, and was like a ship that cutteth the cable and putteth to sea, for he cut his memory and trusted to his invention. Was glad to be an example to others, and submitted to the censure of the House, not with a dejected countenance, for there is comfort in acknowledging an error."[1]

About this time Sir Thomas Smith and others were much engaged with the profitable East India trade, as well as the new London plantations in Ireland at Derry and Coleraine, consequently Virginia for several years languished, a ship seldom arriving at Jamestown. Whitaker, the preacher at Henrico, son of the distinguished Professor of St. John's College, Cambridge, in a tract upon the colony written about this period, said:—

"The continuing and upholding of it hath been most wonderful. I may fitly compare it to the growth of an infant which hath been afflicted from its birth with some grievous weakness, that many times no hope of life hath remained, and yet liveth still. Again, if there were nothing else to encourage us, yet this one thing may stir us up to go on cheerfully with it, that the devil is a capital enemy against it, and continually seeketh to hinder the prosperity and good proceedings of

[1] Richard Martin was a native of Otterton, Devonshire. He was witty, eloquent, convivial, but also an able jurist. He died in 1618, while Recorder of London. The following lines appeared beneath his portrait, engraved in 1620:—

"Legumque lingua, lexque dicendi magis:
Anglorum alumnus, præco Virginiæ, ac parens."

it. Yea, hath heretofore so far prevailed by his instruments, the covetous hearts of many backsliding adventurers at home, also by his servants here, some strong for superiority, others by murmurings, mutinies, and plain treasons, and others by fornication, profaneness, idleness, and such monstrous sins."

Gates, in the spring of 1614, left Virginia never to return, and Sir Thomas Dale, his successor as Deputy-Governor, went to England in 1616, and following the example of Newport, both soon entered the more lucrative service of the East India Company. The administration of the affairs of the colony then devolved upon Captain Samuel Argall, one not fit to be trusted in a position of responsibility. The self-sacrificing Lord Delaware, in view of the languishing state of the Plantation, at length determined to go again and assume command.

In the spring of 1618 he left England in the ship "Neptune," with supplies and two hundred men. Stopping at the isle of St. Michael he was well received by its authorities, but in consequence of something there eaten, supposed by some to have been poisoned, a few days after the ship left, he, and a number of the crew, were taken sick, and on June 7, 1618, he expired.

It was not until the 5th of October that the intelligence reached London of his untimely end. The members of the Virginia Company had no heart for business on that day, and every one felt that he was fairly entitled to the description of one of his ancestors, written three generations before by Lord Morley :—

"Virtue, honesty, liberality, and grace,
  And true religion, this sely grave doth hold.
I do wish, that all our great men would
In good follow this noble Baron's trace,
That from his wise heart did always chase
Envy and malice, and bought of young and old
Love and favour, that passeth silver and gold,
Unto a worthy man, a rich purchase;
These ways he used, and obtained thereby,
Good fame of all men, as well far as nigh,
And now is joyful in that celestial sphere,
Where with saints, he sings incessantly.
Holy honour, praise, and glory,
Give to God, that gave him such might,
To live so nobly, and come to that delight."

CHAPTER III.

CAPTAIN SAMUEL ARGALL, DEPUTY-GOVERNOR OF VIRGINIA.

THE first presiding officer of the London Company was Sir Thomas Smith. During the reign of Queen Elizabeth he was knighted, and in 1604 sent on an embassy to Russia. No one so quick as he engaged in projects calculated to develop the commerce of England, and he was recognised as the ruling spirit of the Muscovia, Greenland, East India, and Virginia Companies, all of which for years held their meetings at his elegant and capacious mansion in Philpot Lane.[1]

It was a measure of policy as well as a source of pleasure for him to patronize those who were writing histories of the brave men who had sailed over distant seas and discovered new lands, one of whom was Purchas, the editor of the *Pilgrimage*, and also of the five folio volumes called the *Pilgrims*.

With all his commercial energy and foresight, and the flattering position he held among the courtiers of King James, he was yet ready to stoop to mean and dishonourable acts to fill his coffers. While acting as the

---

[1] Purchas's *Pilgrimage*, 747.

Governor of the London Company, he used his position for self-aggrandizement; and in 1609, before the expedition of Gates and Somers could arrive, he despatched one of his relatives and favourites—Samuel Argall, described by an old chronicler as "an ingenious, active, and forward young gentleman"—in a fast-sailing vessel, of which Robert Tindall was master, with a cargo of wine and provisions,[1] to be traded on private account.[2] When Argall returned, he was—in 1610—appointed to conduct Lord Delaware to Jamestown; and on the 19th of June followed in another vessel after Sir George Somers, who was bound to the Bermudas for fish and wild hogs.

Losing Somers in a dangerous fog about this time, he followed along the Atlantic coast, and explored that part which Gosnold and Weymouth had not seen. At nine o'clock in the morning of the 27th of July he anchored in a very great bay, into which flowed many rivers, which he named Delaware, in honour of the Captain-General.[3]

When Delaware's health, in 1611, required his return to England, Argall accompanied him; but in September 1612, with the ship "Treasurer," and fifty persons, he was at Jamestown. By the advice of Sir Thomas Gates, in the beginning of November, he went with Sir Thomas Dale to Sir Thomas Smith's Island to see if it was a suitable place for settlement. Three days were passed there, and he reported that there could be a "safe pas-

---

[1] Purchas.   [2] Stith.
[3] Hildreth, and other historians, erroneously state that Delaware died in 1618 at the mouth of the Bay, which on that account bears his name.

sage for boats and barges thither, by a cut out of the bottom of our bay into the Delaware Bay."

During the spring of 1613 he made two trading voyages up the Potomac River; and on the 13th of April proceeded to deliver the captured Pocahontas to the Deputy-Governor at Jamestown. The next month he explored the eastern shore of the Chesapeake, and after this, in the ship "Treasurer," proceeded north toward Sagadahoc, and attacked a French settlement, under the auspices of Madame Guercheville, Lady of Honour to the Queen of France, and killed one Jesuit, and took another back to Virginia. Upon his return to England in 1614 he was called to account for his attack upon the French. To the charges preferred against him and his lieutenant, Turner, he replied that he had captured the French vessel between the 43d and 44th degrees of latitude, within the limits of Virginia, and under his commission bearing the seal of the colony, and that it was a fair and lawful prize. He further declared that the value of the seizure was not more than £200, and at the request of the French was returned. To the charge of inhumanity he replied that no one was detained against his will; and argued that it was proper for him to return to Port Royal and demolish their fortifications.[1]

Returning to Virginia in the "Treasurer," he remained until Dale went back to England in 1616, and the next year succeeded him as Deputy-Governor. The ship that bore him to his new duties anchored in May

[1] British Museum MSS.

15, 1617, off Point Comfort; and on the 9th of June he wrote to the London Company that he had sent Tomakin, the brother-in-law of Pocahontas, to tell Opachankano of this arrival, who, upon receiving the message, railed against England, English people, and particularly his best friend, Sir Thomas Dale.

In the same letter he mentioned that the Rev. Alexander Whitaker, the zealous minister at Henrico, had been drowned, and requested Sir Dudley Digges to obtain from the Archbishop a permit for Mr. Wickham to administer the Sacrament, as there was no other person; and the following March he desired "ordination for Mr. Wickham, and Mr. Macock, a Cambridge scholar; also a person to read to Mr. Wickham, his eyes being weak."[1]

His course in Virginia was so dishonourable, that in August 1618 the London Company forwarded to him the following letter:—

"Sir,—We received your letters by the 'George' directed to the Right Honourable Lords, before the receipt whereof we had finished ours, which we purposed to have sent to you by this conveyance, without expecting the 'George's' coming, but by the unexpected contents of yours we are driven to lay aside our former, and briefly to declare our minds in this, wherein we take no pleasure.

"You know how many ways you have been proceeding chargeable to the Company, not of late only, but formerly when you converted the fruits of their expense to your own benefit without being called to an account.

[1] MSS. Virginia Records.

They have also put honourable reputation upon your person, and presuming of your wisdom and discretion they made you Governor to follow their commission and instructions, which in the person and protestation of an honest gentleman you undertook to do.

"And, therefore, it is very strange to us to see you so change and differ from yourself, which, by your words and deeds being the testimony of your mind, we do sensibly see and feel; and in particular you intimate first unto us that you hold yourself disparaged, in that we sent you our last letters subscribed with so few hands, that we termed you but Deputy-Governor, and that we should think our Cape merchant a fit man to deliver our letters to your hands. You heap up also many unjust accusations against us and the magazine, nourishing thereby, instead of pacifying the malcontented humours of such as seek to bring all to confusion, and to overthrow what is sealed upon wise and equal terms to be props of the Plantation there, and the life of the adventurers here, which both undoubtedly must stand and fall together.

"But we shall easily put by all such your weak imputations when time shall serve to debate the particulars, and when we fear yourself will not be able to answer your own actions, you your own letters dated at Jamestown in March 1617. . . . It is laid unto your charge that you appropriate the Indian trade to yourself, you use our frigate that came from the Somer Islands, and the other with our men, to trade for your own benefit, you proclaim also in the colony that no man shall trade with the Indians, nor buy any furs, but yourself.

"It is also certified that you take the ancient planters of the colony who ought to be free, and likewise those from the common garden, to set them upon your own employments, and that you spend up our store corn to feed your own men, as if the Plantation was only intended to serve your turn.

"We cannot imagine why you should give us warning that Opachankano and the natives have given their country to Mr. Rolfe's child, and that they will reserve it from all others till he comes of years, except, as we suppose, as some do here report it, to be a device of your own to some especial purpose for yourself, but whether yours or theirs, we shall little esteem of any such consequence.

"You say you have disposed of all our kine according to our commission. It seemeth you never look upon our instruments. We gave you no such commission, but the contrary in express words; as that you should preserve and nourish them to the common use. We thought it impossible, when we made you Governor, that ever you should offer us this kind of dealing, not once to mention how many, to whom, nor for what consideration, but to do them all away of your own head, to take satisfaction to yourself, we must let you know we allow of no such sale, nor of the delivery of any one cow by you, further than your instruments do expressly warrant.

"But answerable to this and the rest, you have also dealt with us for the hides, about which it is well known yourself, what trouble we had with the Lord Admiral and the Spanish Ambassador, and how dearly they cost us, and we know how much it would have imported us, to have had them gone by this ship, as well for the reputation of our return, as also for helping to defray the great charge of the voyage, notwithstanding very fairly demanded of you, it hath pleased you to stay them there in your own custody, and to suffer this ship to come home with other men's goods, and not vouchsafing to mention the hides in your general letter, but in this manner: 'That being made Admiral you know how to dispose of unlawful purchase.' And by this we must understand the hides to be yours. As for the debts and wages which you say you have paid for us, we marvel you do not send us a note of the particulars, for to our knowledge we are not in that kind indebted to any man. If there be any such matter, or that you have provided any stuff for the College as you writ, yet you must not imagine that we are insensible of reason as to suffer either of those to be a cloak for you to detain our hides, or to convey away all our cattle and corn. Either you must think highly of yourself or meanly of us, in that being our substitute you will presume to offer us these wrongs, and to suppose you may do what you list in such a public case, without being called to account. We have therefore determined of a course, and we have written to the Lord Governor, which we doubt not but his Lordship will impart unto you."

Unaware that Delaware was dead, they wrote to him to arrest Argall, and send him home in the ship

"William and Thomas" to answer everything whereof he was accused, and to seize his goods as indemnity for the public cattle which he had sold for his own benefit.[1] Chagrined by the Company's letter, when Captain Edward Brewster complained of the unlawful use of Lord Delaware's servants, he arrested him, and on October 15, 1618, had a trial by court-martial, which sentenced Brewster to death. Upon the remonstrance of the clergyman of the colony and respectable citizens, it was commuted to banishment, upon the promise that he would never return to Virginia.

As soon as the Company learned that Delaware had died at sea, they appointed Yeardley in the place of Argall, and the latter was able to escape in a swift sailing pinnace, "Eleanor," sent over by his London friends.

Before he absconded from Virginia, he had sent out the ship "Treasurer," under Captain Elfred, manned with a picked crew, to rove in the Spanish West Indies; and after Yeardley had become Governor, in the year 1619, it returned to Virginia with a certain number of negroes, the first African slaves that arrived in the waters of the Chesapeake. Learning that Argall had been displaced, the Captain of the "Treasurer" sailed for Bermudas. In October of this year, the Governor of this island took from a Miles Kendall fourteen negroes which he said belonged to the ship "Treasurer," but which Kendall alleged he had obtained from a Holland vessel commissioned by the Prince of Orange.

---

[1] In May 1617 the Company had in Virginia 54 servants in their garden, 81 tenants, 80 kine and 80 goats. When he absconded everything was gone but six goats.

To these transactions Rolfe, as quoted by Smith, probably referred when he said, "About the last of August came in a Dutch man-of-war that sold us twenty negars."[1]

In May 1619, Argall became a resident of London, and united with his relative, Sir Thomas Smith, in destroying the London Company, that had detected their dishonourable practices, and for his services against the friends of popular rights was knighted in 1622 by King James.

In April 1624 he was again nominated as Governor of Virginia, and the following minute from the transactions of the London Company tells the result:—

"Sir Francis Wyat being proposed, and some earnestly moving that Sr Samuel Argall might stand in election with him, they were both ballated, and the place fell to Sr Francis Wyat, by having 69 balls, Sir Samuel Argall 8, and the negative box 2."

---

[1] For five years the numbers of negroes in Virginia did not exceed twenty-one. On February 16, 1624, these were reported at:—

Fleur Dieu Hundred,	11
James City,	3
James Island,	1
Plantation opposite,	1
Warasquoyak,	4
Elizabeth City,	1

In 1757 the blacks numbered 58,292, while the white population only amounted to 44,214. In 1860 the negroes were about 560,000, and the whites about 1,300,000.

CHAPTER IV.

POCAHONTAS AND HER COMPANIONS.

IN the first relation of the colony of Virginia, published in 1608, and attributed to Captain Smith, Pocahontas is briefly noticed in these words:

"Powhatan understanding we detained certain saluages sent his daughter, a child of tenne yeares old, which not only for feature, countenance, and proportion much exceedeth any of the rest of his people, but for wit and spirit the only non-pareil of his countrie."

In the same narrative Smith states that he was treated with kindness by Powhatan, who wished him to live in his village, and afterwards he adds, "hee sent me home with 4 men, one that usually carried my Gowne and Knapsacke after me, two other loded with bread, and one to accompanie me."[1]

In 1609 Smith was sent to England to answer several charges, one of which was the design of marrying Pocahontas, and forming an alliance with Powhatan, for the purpose of building up an Anglo-Indian nobility in America. He never again lived in Virginia; but in his *General History,* published more than fifteen years afterwards,

[1] Deane's edition of *True Relation,* p. 38.

he transforms Powhatan to a savage wretch ready to beat out his brains, until "Pocahontas, the king's dearest daughter, got his head into her arms, and laid her owne upon his to saue him from death,"[1] which statement is perpetuated in a sculpture by Capellano, which may be seen over one of the doors of the Capitol at Washington.

William Strachey, secretary of the colony, who arrived with Lord Delaware in 1610, gives a vivid description of Pocahontas. He remarks that "Both men, women, and children have their severall names; at first according to the several humour of their parents, . . and so the great King Powhatan called a young daughter of his, whom he loved well, Pochahuntas, which may signifie little wanton, howbeyt she was rightly called Amonate at more ripe yeares."[2]

In another chapter he states: "Their younger women goe not shadowed amongst their owne companie until they be nigh eleaven or twelve returnes of the leafe old (for soe they accompt and bring about the yeare, calling the fall of the leafe taquitock); nor are they much ashamed thereof, and therefore would the before remembered Pochahuntas, a well featured but wanton young girle, Powhatan's daughter, sometymes resorting to our fort, of the age then of eleven or twelve yeares, get the boyes forth with her into the markett place, and make them wheele, falling on their hands, turning up their heeles upwards, whome she would follow and wheele so herself, naked as she was all the fort over; but being once twelve yeares, they put on a kind of semecinctum

[1] *Smith's History*, folio, 1632, p. 49.   [2] *Hakluyt Soc. Pub.*, vol. vi. p. 65.

lethern apron (as do our artificers or handycrafts men) before their bellies, and are very shame-fac't to be seen bare."[1]

On another page the same writer mentions that "They often reported unto us that Powhatan had then lyving twenty sonnes and ten daughters . . . besides young Pocohunta a daughter of his, using sometyme to our fort in tymes past, nowe married to a private captaine called Kocoum some two yeares since."[2]

During the year 1612, a plan seems to have been arranged among the principal men of Virginia of intermarrying the English with the natives, and of obtaining the recognition of Powhatan and those allied to him as members of a fifth kingdom, with certain privileges. Cunega, the Spanish ambassador at London, on September 22, 1612, writes: "Although some suppose the plantation to decrease, he is credibly informed that there is a determination to marry some of the people that go over to Virginians; forty or fifty are already so married, and English women intermingle and are received kindly by the natives. A zealous minister hath been wounded for reprehending it."[3]

In July of this year the bold and unscrupulous Captain Argall sailed from England, and arrived on the 17th of September at Point Comfort.

Early in the spring of 1613, to employ his own language, "I was told by certaine Indians my friends that the great Powhatan's daughter Pokahuntis was with the

---

[1] *Hakluyt Soc. Pub.*, vol. vi. p. 111.   [2] *Ibid.* p. 54.
[3] *Sainsbury.* Was this clergyman Mr. Buck or Mr. Whitaker?

great King Patowomek whether I presently repaired resolving to possesse myselfe of her by any stratagem that I could use for the ransoming of so many Englishmen as were prisoners with Powhatan as also to get such armes and tooles as hee and other Indians had got by murther and stealing some others of our nation, with some quantity of corne for the colonies reliefe.

"So soone as I came to anchor before the towne I manned my boate, and sent on shore for the King of Pastancy and Ensigne Swift (whom I had left as a pledge of our loue and truce the voyage before) who presently came and brought my pledge with him, whom after I had received, I brake the matters to this King and told him that if he did not betray Pokohuntis into my hands, wee would be no longer brothers nor friends. He alleaged that if hee undertake the businesse, then Powhatan would make warres upon him and his people, but upon my promise that I would joyne with him against him, he repaired presently to his brother the great King of Patowomeck, who being made acquainted with the matter called his counsell together and after some few houres deliberation concluded rather to deliver her into my hands; so presently he betrayed her into my boat, when I carried her aboord my ship. This done an Indian was dispatched to Powhatan to let him know that I had taken his daughter, and if he would send home the Englishman (who he deteained in slaverie with such armes and tooles as the Indians had gotten and stolne and also a great quantity of corne, that then he should have his daughter restored, otherwise not.

This very much grieved this great King, yet without delay he returned the messenger with this answere that he desired me to use his daughter well and bring my ship into his river and then he would give me my demands, which being performed I should deliver his daughter and we should be friends.

"Having received this answer I presently departed, being the 13 of Aprill and repayred with all speed to Sir Thomas Gates to know of him upon what conditions he would conclude the peace, and what he would demand to whom I also delivered my prisoner towards whose ransome within few days the King sent home seven of our men who seemed to be very joyfull for that they were freed from the slavery and feere of cruell murther which they daily before lived in.. They brought also three peeces, one broad axe and a long whip-saw and one canow of corne. I being quit of my prisoner went forward with the frigot which I had left at Point Comfort and furnished her."

John Chamberlain, writing from London on August 1, 1613, to Sir Dudley Carleton, says:

"There is a ship come from Virginia with news of their well-doing, which puts some life into that action that before was almost at the last cast. They have taken the daughter of a King that was their greatest enemy as she was going feasting upon a river to visit certain friends, for whose ransom the father offers whatsoever in his power, and to become their friend, and to bring them where they shall meet with a gold mine. They proposed unto him three conditions, to deliver all the English fugitives, to render all manner of arms or weapons of theirs that are come to his hands, and to give them three hundred quarters of corne. The two first he promised readily, and promiseth the other at the harvest, if his daughter may be well used in the meantime."[1]

Ralph Hamor, Jr., for a time secretary of the colony, and whose father was a member of the Company, and a merchant tailor of London, visited England in 1614, and the next year published *A True Discourse of the Present Estate of Virginia until* 18*th of June* 1614.

It is a narrative of considerable embellishment, and bears evidence of having been composed for the purpose of exciting the king and others to contribute moneys for the use of the colony. He expands the statement of Argall relative to the capture of Pocahontas, and narrates her alliance with John Rolfe, who, with a white wife, came to Virginia in 1610, and whose child was christened at Bermuda by Chaplain Buck,[2] the witnesses being Secretary Strachey and Captain Newport. His statement, which follows, was condensed by Smith, and has been to this day repeated by historians.

"It chanced Powhatan's delight and darling his daughter Pocahuntas (whose fame hath euen bin spred in England by the title of Nonparella of Virginia) in her princely progresse I may so terme it took some pleasure in the absence of Capt. Argal to be among her friends at Pataomecke (as it seemeth by the relation I had) imploied thither as shop keepers to a fare, to exchange

---

[1] *Court and Times of James the First*, i. 262, 263.
[2] Purchas, iv. 1744.

some of her father's corn for theirs, where residing some three months or longer, it fortuned upon occasion either of promise or profit Captaine Argal to arrive there, when Pocahuntas desirous to renue her familiaritie with the English and delighting to see them would gladly visit us as she did: of whom no sooner had Captaine Argal intelligence, but he delt with an old friend and adopted brother of his Iapazeus how and by what meanes he might procure hir captiue, assuring him that now or neuer was the time to pleasure him if he entended indeed that loue which he had made profession of, that in ransome of hir he might redeeme some of our English men armes now in the possession of hir Father promising to vse her curteously, promised his best endeauours and secresie to accomplish his desire; and thus wrought it, making his wife an instrument (which sex haue euer bin most powerfull in beguiling inticements) to effect his plot which hee had thus laid, he agreed that himself, his wife and Pocahuntas would accompanie his brother [Argall] to the water-side, whether come, his wife should faine a great and longing desire to goe aboorde and see the shippe, which being there three or foure times before she had never seene, and should bee earnest with her husband to permit her: he seemed angry with her making as he pretended, so vnnecessary a request as especially being without the company of women, which denial she taking unkindly must faine to weepe (as who knowes not that women can command teares) whereupon her husband seeming to pitty those counterfeit teares gave her leave to goe aboord, so that it would please Pocahuntas to accompany her: now was the greatest labour to win her, guilty perhaps of her father's wrongs, yet by her earnest persuasions she assented; so forthwith aboord they went, the best cheere that could be made was seasonably provided, to supper they went merry on all hands especially Iapazeus and his wife who to express their joy would ere be treading upō Capt. Argal's foot, as who shall say 'tis don, she is your own. Supper ended Pocahuntas was borne in the gunner's roome, but Iapazeus and his wife desired to have some conference with their brother which was only to acquaynt him by what stratagem they had betraied his prisoner as I have already related: after which discourse, to sleep they went, Pocahuntas mistrusting their policy was first up and hastened Iapazeus to be gon. Capt. Argal having secretly well rewarded him with a small copper kettle and some other less valuable toies so highly by him esteemed that doubtless he would have betraied his own father for them, permitted both him and his wife to return but told him that for divers considerations . . . he would reserve Pocahuntas whereat she began to be exceeding pensive and discontented."

Hamor relates that she was taken to Jamestown, and a messenger sent to Powhatan with the terms of ransom, and that three months after he sent word that if his daughter was restored he would give satisfaction. He also stated that in March 1614 Captain Argall's ship and others, carrying Dale and one hundred and fifty men besides Pocahontas, ascended the York river and appeared before Powhatan's town to demand an entire restoration of Englishmen and stolen property. To resume his language :—

"Long before this time a gentleman of approved behaviour and honest carriage Maister John Rolfe had been in loue with Pocahuntas and she with him which thing at the instant that we were in parlee with them, myself made knowne to Sir Thomas Dale by a letter from him[1] whereby he intreated his aduise and furtherance in his loue, if so it seemed fit to him for the good of the plantation, and Pocahuntas acquainted her brethren therewith; which resolution Sir Thomas Dale well approving was the only cause he was so milde amongst them, who otherwise would not have departed the river without other conditions.

"The bruite of this pretended marriage came soone to Powhatan's knowledge, a thing acceptable unto him as appeared by his sudden consent thereunto, who some ten daies after sent an old uncle of hirs named Opachisco to give her as his deputy in the Church[2] and two of her sons to see the marriage solemnized which was accordingly done about the fift of April."

An account is given by Hamor of the council with the Indians at the "Chicohominie, seven miles from Jamestown," and the several articles of the treaty, the

[1] Why Rolfe should not have talked with Dale at Jamestown it is difficult to conceive. The letter referred to is appended to the narrative, and makes about seven printed pages, and is a laboured treatise, giving reasons when a Christian should marry a heathen, and has the musty smell of the dusty study of a London divine, rather than the fragrance of a letter written by a man in love.

[2] All narratives are silent as to where the church was, and the name of the minister who read the marriage-service.

last of which provided that there should be eight chief men under Sir Thomas Dale, each of which was to receive a red coat or livery from the king yearly, a picture of his majesty on copper, with a chain to hang around the neck, these eight to be known as King James's noblemen. Toward the conclusion of the narrative is the following statement :—

"It pleased Sir Thomas Dale (myself being much desirous before my return for England to visit Powhatan and his Court, because I would be able to speak somewhat thereof by mine own knowledge) to imploy myself and on Thomas Salvage (who had lived three years with Powhatan, and speaks the language naturally one whom Powhatan much affecteth, upon a message unto him, which was to deale with him if by any meanes I might procure a daughter of his who (Pocahuntas being already in possession) is generally reputed to be his delight and darling and surely he esteemeth her as his owne soule, for a sure pledge of peace."

After arriving at Powhatan's town, Hamor delivered the following speech :—

"Sir Thomas Dale, your brother, the principal commander of the English men sends you greeting of loue and peace on his part inviolable, and hath in testimonie thereof by me, sent you a worthie present, viz., two large peeces of copper, fiue strings of white and blue beades, fiue wooden combes, ten fish hookes and a pair of knives, (all which I delivered him one thing after another that he might have time to view each particular). He wished me also to certifie you that when you pleased to send men he would give you a great grindstone. My message and gift pleased him. I proceeded thus:—

"The bruite of the exquesite perfection of your youngest daughter being famous through all your territories hath come to the hearing of your brother Sir Thomas Dale who for this purpose hath ordered me hither to intreate you to permit her, with me to return unto him partly for the desire her sister hath to see her, of whom if fame hath not bin prodigall as like enough it hath not, your brother by your favour would gladly make his neerest companion wife and bedfellow and the reason hereof is being now friendly and finally united together and made one people in the bond of loue, he would make a naturall union between us, principally because himselfe hath taken resolution to dwell in your country so long as he liveth, and would therefore not only have the firmest assurance he may of perpetual friendship for you but also hartily bind himself hereunto."

This proposition of Dale was not entertained, for Powhatan had just sold his daughter for a wife, to an Indian, for two bushels of Indian beads. Hamor replied, "I suppose he might restore the beads," and bring the daughter back, not twelve years old, to gratify Sir Thomas Dale, but Powhatan would not listen to the dishonourable proposal, and in a few weeks Hamor sailed for England.[1]

---

[1] Sir Thomas Dale was twice married, and Fanny, the last, was cousin of his first wife. At the time of this proposal his wife was in England. See Greene's *Cal. State Papers* and *Manuscript Transactions of London Company.*

Hamor gives great credit to Rolfe as the first to plant tobacco in Virginia, a fact not mentioned in modern histories.

"I may not forget the gentleman worthie of much commendations, which first took the paines to make triall thereof, his name Mr. John Rolfe, Anno Domini 1612, partly for the loue he hath a long time borne unto it, and partly to raise commodities to the adventurers, in whose behalfe I intercede and vouchsafe to hold my testimony in beleefe that during the time of his aboade there, which draweth neere upon sixe years no man hath laboured to his power there, and worthy incouragement unto England, by his letters than he hath done, witness his marriage with Powhatan's daughter, one of rude education, manners barbarous, and cursed generation, merely for the good and honor of the Plantation."

Appended to Hamor's narrative is the following letter, dated June 18, 1614, and alleged to have been written by the Rev. Alexander Whitaker, and addressed to a cousin, a London clergyman:—

"Sir, the Colony here is much better. Sir Thomas Dale our religious and valiant Geuernour hath now brought that to passe which never before could be effected. For vvarre upon our enemies and kind usage of our freinds, he hath brought them to make for peace of us vvhich is made and they dare not breake.

"But that vvhich is best one Pocahuntas or Matoa the daughter of Powhatan is married to an honest and discreete English Gentleman Maister Rolfe and that after she had openly renounced her country Idolatry, confessed the faith of Jesus Christ, and was baptized, vvhich thing Sir Thomas Dale had laboured a long time to ground in her.

"Yet notwithstanding are the vertuous deeds of this worthy Knight much debased by the letters which some wicked men have written from thence, and especially by one C. L. If you heare any condemne this noble Knight, or doe feare to come further for those slanderous letters you may upon my word reprove them. You know that no malefactors can abide the face of the Judge, but themselves seeming to be reproved doe prosecute with all hatred."

Purchas professes to give the same letter, but the conclusion is different, and adds to the suspicion that the letter is fictitious.

Conclusion in Hamor.	*Conclusion in Purchas.*
"Sir Thomas Dale (with whom I am) is a man of great knowledge in Divinitie and of good conscience. Every Sabbath day wee preach in the forenoone, and chatechize in the afternoone. Every Saturday at night I exercise in Sir Thomas Dale's house. Our church affaires be consulted on by the Minister and foure of the most religious men. Once every month wee have a communion, and once a year a solemn fast. "For me though my promise of three years service to my	"But I much more muse that so few of our English Ministers that were so hot against the Surplis and subscription come hither where neither are spoken of. "Doe they not either wilfully hide their tallents or keepe themselues at home for fear of loosing a few pleasures? But I referre them to the Iudge of all hearts and to the King that shall reward euery one according to the gaine of his talent. "But you, my cosen, hold fast that which you haue, and I

country be expired yet I will abide in my vocation here, until I be lawfully called from hence. And so betaking us all unto the mercies of God in Christ Jesus, I rest for ever."	though my promise of three yeeres seruice to my countrey be expired will abide in my vocation here until I be lawfully called from hence. And so betaking us all unto the mercies of God in Christ Jesus I rest for euer."

Sir Thomas Dale, leaving the affairs of the colony in the hands of Deputy-Governor George Yeardley, early in June 1616 arrived at Plymouth with Pocahontas and a party of Indians, and on the 20th Lord Carew notices the fact in these words :—

"Sir Thomas Dale retourned frome Virginia, he hathe brought divers men and women of thatt countrye to be educated here,[1] and one Rolffe who married a daughter of Pohetan (the barbarous prince) called Pocahuntas hath brought his wife with him into England."[2]

Among those who came with Pocahontas as a counsellor was Tamocomo, who had married her sister. Pur-

---

[1] Before this an Indian lad had been sent to England to be educated. From the *Planter's Plea*, published in London, 1630, is extracted the following :—

"Amongst such as have beene brought over into England from Virginia was one Nanamack, a youth sent over by the Lo : Delaware when he was Governor there, who coming over and living here a yeare or two in houses where hee heard not much of religion but sins, had many times examples of drinking, swearing and like evills, ran as he was, a mere Pagan, but after into a godly family was strangely altered, grew to understand the principles of religion, learned to reade, delighted in the Scriptures, prayers and other Christian duties, mournfully bewailed the state of country, especially his brethren, and gave such testimonies of his love to the truth, that he was thought fit to be baptized, but being prevented by death left behind such testimonies of his desire of God's favor, that it moved such godly Christians as knew him to conceive well of his condition."—P. 53.

[2] *Camden Soc. Pub.*, No. 76, p. 36. Purchas, iv. 1874.

chas says:—"With this savage I have often conversed at my good friends Master Doctor Gulstone where he was a frequent guest and where I have seen him sing and dance his diabolical measures."

After the first weeks of her residence in England she does not appear to be spoken of as the wife of Rolfe by the letter-writers. Rev. Peter Fontaine asserts that "when they heard that Rolfe had married Pocahontas, it was deliberated in Council, whether he had not committed high treason by so doing, that is marrying an Indian princess."[1]

Christmas, his Mask, by Ben Jonson, was played at Court on 6th of January 1616-17, and Pocahontas and Tamocomo were both present. On the 18th of this month Chamberlain writes to Sir Dudley Carleton:[2]—

"On Twelfth night there was a masque when the new made Earl [Buckingham] and the Earl of Montgomery danced with the Queen. . . . The Virginian woman Pocahuntas with her father counsellor have been with the King and graciously used, and both she and her assistant were pleased at the masque. She is upon her return though sore against her will, if the wind would about to send her away."

In the year 1616 the distinguished artist Simon De Passe engraved a portrait, small quarto size, with the following legend:—

"Matoaka als Rebecka Filia Potentiss Princ: Powhatani Imp. Virginiæ."

---

[1] Meade, i. 82.

[2] Nichols's *Progresses, etc., of K. James*, vol. iii. p. 243.

DEATH OF POCAHONTAS.

And beneath :—

"Matoaks, a̅l̅s Rebecka, daughter to the mighty Prince Powhatan, Emperour of Attanoughkornouck a̅l̅s Virginia, converted and baptized in the Christian faith, and wife to the wor͚ M͚r Joh Rolff. Æt. 21. A° 1616."[1]

Chamberlain, in a letter to Carleton, Ambassador at the Hague, dated March 29, 1617, writes :—" The Virginian woman whose picture I sent you, died this last week at Gravesend, as she was returning homeward."[2] Her boy named Thomas, probably after Dale, was left in England, and the father of the child, John Rolfe, having been appointed secretary, was intimately associated with the unscrupulous Argall, now made Governor of Virginia, and arrived, May 15th, at Point Comfort. The Company, on August 23, 1618, wrote to the latter :—

"We cannot imagine why you should give us warning that Opechankano and the natives have given the country to Mr. Rolfe's child, and that they reserve it from all others till he comes of years except as we suppose as some do here report it to be a device of your own, to some special purpose for yourself."

The extravagant statements of John Smith in the *General History*, first published in 1624, called forth

---

[1] *Notes and Queries*, London, second series, vol. vii. p. 403.

[2] In the parish register of Gravesend is this entry :—

"1616 May 2j Rebecca Wrothe
 wyff of Thomas Wroth gent
 a Virginia lady borne, here was buried
 in ye chauncell."

Notes and Queries, vol. v. p. 123, 3d series.

criticism, and he was charged with having written too much and done too little. In the preface to his *Travels and Adventures,* published in 1629, he states that "they have acted my fatal tragedies upon the stage, and racked my relations at their pleasure."

Jonson noticed his heroine, Pocahontas, in the *Staple of News,* first played in 1625. The following dialogue there occurs between Picklock and Pennyboy Canter:

> *Picklock.* " A tavern's as unfit too for a princess.
> *P. Cant.* " No, I have known a Princess and a
>   great one,
>   Come forth of a tavern.
> *Picklock.* " Not go in Sir, though.
> *P. Cant.* " She must go in, if she came forth :
>   the blessed
>   Pokahontas, as the historian calls her,[1]
>   And great king's daughter of Virginia,
>   Hath been in womb of tavern."

The minutes of the Company do not give a very high opinion of Rolfe's honesty.

"April 30, 1621, Sir John Dauers signified that it was the request of my lady Lawarre unto this Courte, that in consideration of her goods remayning in the hands of Mr. Rolfe in Virginia, she might receaue satisfaction for the same out of his tobacco now sent home.

"But forasmuch as it is supposed the said tobacco is

---

[1] Smith, in his dedication of the *General History* to the Duchess of Richmond, says :

"In the utmost of many extremities that blessed Pokahontas, the great King's daughter of Virginia, oft saved my life."

none of the said Rolf's but belonged to Mr. Peirce, it was thought fitt that Mr. Henry Rolfe should acquaint my lady Lawarre of his brother's offer (as he informes) to make her La'p good and faithfull account of all such goods as remayne in his hands, upon her La'ps direction to that effect."

Three months later there is an entry as follows: ·

"July 10, 1621. It was signified that the Ladie Lawarr desyred the court would please to graunt her a comission dyrected to Sir Fraunces Wyatt, Mr. George Sandys and others to examine and certifie what goods and money of her late husband's, deceased, came to the hands of Mr. Rolfe . . . . . and to require the attendinge to his promise that she may be satisfied."

During the year 1622 Rolfe died, leaving a wife and children, besides the child he had by Pocahontas. The following statement appears in the books of the Company under date of October 7, 1622:—

"Mr. Henry Rolfe in his petition desiringe the estate his Brother John Rolfe deceased, left in Virginia might be enquired out and conuerted to the best use for the maintenance of his Relict wife and Children and for his indempnity hauing brought up the Child his said Brother had by Powhatan's daughter w'ch child is yet liuinge and in his custodie.

"It was ordered that the Governor and Counsell of Virginia should cause enquiries be made what lands and goods the said John Rolfe died seized of, and in case it be found the said Rolfe made no will, then to take such order for the petitioner's indempnity, and for the mayntenance of the said children and his relict wife[1] as they shall find his estate will beare (his debt unto the Companie and others beinge first satisfied) and to return unto the Companie here an Account of their proceedings."

The Indian girls that accompanied Pocahontas to England, appear from the minutes to have been a care and expense to the Company. Under date of May 11, 1620, is the following entry:—

"The Court takinge notice from S[r] William Throgmorton that one of the maydes which Sir Thomas Dale brought from Virginia, a native of the countrie, who sometimes dwelt a servant with a mercer in Cheapside, is now veric weake of a consumption at Mr. Gough's in the Black Friers[1] who hath greate care, and taketh great paines to comforte her both in soule and bodie, wheruppon for her recoverie the compainy are agreed to be att the charge of XX[s] a weeke for two moneths (if it please god she bee not before the expiration thereof restored or dye in the mean season,) for the adminstring of Physick and cordialls for her health, and that the first paym't begin this day seavennight because Mr. Threr for this yeare reported his accompts set up.

[1] If the mother of his infant, Bermuda Rolfe, was dead, then this relict wife was the third Mrs. Rolfe.

[1] Rev. William Gouge, D.D., is evidently the person meant. He was educated at Cambridge, an eminent Puritan, cousin of Rev. Alexander Whitaker, called by Bancroft the Apostle of Virginia, and was noted for active benevolence, as well as for scholarship and pulpit oratory. In 1643 he was a member of the celebrated Westminster Assembly of Divines, and frequently occupied the moderator's chair. After a pastorate of forty-five years at Blackfriars, London, he died December 12, 1653, aged seventy-nine. When offered more profitable positions he always declined, saying that "his highest ambition was to go from Blackfriars to Heaven."

"Sir W. Throgmorton out of his private purse for the same purpose hath promise to give XL^s all w'ch monney is ordered to be paid to Mr. Gough through the good assurance that the Company hath of his careful managinge."

The minutes also refer to two other "Virginia maydes."

At a Quarter Court, on the 15th of November 1620, "There were appoynted to take care of the two Virginia maydes remaynninge in the custodie of Mr Webb the husband, viz. Mr Casewell, Mr Roberts, Mr Canninge and Mr Webb who are likewise desyred to place them in good servises where they may learne some trade to live by hereafter for w'ch respect ye Company hath promised to bestowe somethinge with them."

At a Preparative Court held in the afternoon of the 11th of June 1621, "Mr Webb moved that some course might be taken that the two Indian maydes might be disposed of to free the Company of the weeklie charge that now they are att for the keeping of them.

"Whereuppon some havinge moved that they might be sent to ye Somer Ilands att the charge of this Company itt was thought fitt rather to referr itt to the next Court to determyne thereof."

At a great and General Quarter Court held the 13th of June, "Itt beinge referred to this Courte to dyrect some course for the dispose of two Indian maydes havinge byne a longe time verie chargeable to ye Company itt is now ordered that they shall be furnished and sent to the Summer Ilands whyther they were willinge to goe with our servants . . . towards their preferm't in marriage with such as shall accept of them with that meanes —with especiall dyrection to the Gouv'nor and Counsell there for the carefull bestowinge of them."

Six months after this resolution, upon a proposition to bring over some Indian lads to be educated, Sir Edwin Sandys well remarked:—

"Now to send for them into England and to have them educated here, he found upon experience of those brought by Sir Tho. Dale, might be far from the Christian work intended."

A few weeks after the Company's resolution, the Indian girls arrived at the Somers Islands to be married, " that after they were conuerted and had children, they might be sent to their Countrey and kindred to ciuilize them." The following year, Smith says, " the mariage of one of the Virginia maides was consummated with a husband fit for her, attended with more then one hundred guests, and all the dainties for their dinner could be prouided." [1]

Thomas Rolfe, the child of Pocahontas, after being educated, returned to Virginia, and his application to the Virginia authorities in 1641, to go to the Indian country to visit Cleopatra, his mother's sister, is on record.[2] The brilliant but eccentric John Randolph of Roanoke, it is said, prided himself upon his descent from the child of Pocahontas. Campbell, in his *History of*

---

[1] *General History*, etc., London, 1632, pp. 197, 198.
[2] *Manuscript Va. Records* in Library of Congress.

Virginia, states that the first Randolph that came to the James River was an esteemed and industrious mechanic, and that one of his sons, Richard, grandfather of John Randolph, married Jane Bolling, the great-granddaughter of Pocahontas.[1]

[1] Campbell's *History of Virginia*, 1860, pp. 424, 631.

CHAPTER V.

NORTH VIRGINIA COLONY.

THE second colony for Virginia, under the Charter, were empowered to plant between the thirty-eighth and forty-fifth degrees of north latitude, and in 1607 colonists were sent to settle there, some of whom had been taken from prisons[1] by the "huge, heavy, ugly," and stern Chief-Justice Popham. The expedition left England in the ship "Gift," Captain George Popham, and the "Mary and John," Captain Gilbert. On the 6th of August they land at St. George's Island, and discover a cross which they supposed was set up by Captain Weymouth; on Sunday the 9th they listen to a sermon from their chaplain at the cross, and give thanks to God for their safe arrival; on the 12th they proceed toward the river Sagadehoka;[2] and on the 18th having chosen a suitable site for a plantation, the next day a sermon was preached, patent and orders read, after which they commenced to build a fort, Captain George Popham being President, and Raleigh Gilbert Admiral. The following February Popham died, and the settlers being

[1] Aubrey.
[2] This river was also called Sodquin, and now known as the Kennebec.

disheartened, they set sail for England when spring came, in a pinnace called the "Virginia," which they had built, and in a ship which had arrived with supplies.

Prominent among the patrons of the North colony was Sir Ferdinando Gorges, then in command of Plymouth Castle, and through his influence it is probable that Captain John Smith[1] was made Admiral for New England, and in 1614 made one voyage to North Virginia.

On the 8th of March 1615,[2] a ship of 200 tons, of which Edward Brawnde was Master, left Dartmouth, and on 20th of April arrived at Sodquin, or Kennebec, on the Atlantic coast, and on the 24th harboured at Manahegin, nine or ten leagues distant. He left that neighbourhood on the 21st of July, "being bound about Cape Code for the discovery of "Sertayne perell w'ch is told by the saueges to be there. Mr. Brawnde arrived there the 28th of August."[3]

Brawnde's letter "to his worthye good frend Captayne John Smith, Admerall of New England," with its edges burned, and defaced by time, still exists among the Cot-

[1] Among the Cottonian MSS. is a letter, the edges of which are burned, which may have been sent to Gorges and written in 1606 in view of the voyage to the south parts of Virginia. A copy is given with some of the defects supplied :—

"I ham geviu to understand [that] ther ys a voyage prepared for the South partiss yff yt be so that you thiuke good of yt, and that it maye be to enye good porpos I praye to haue youre fordorans in yt. And yt be that youe dealle in the said vyage I ame att your worship commandementt otharewyse nott, nor with outt youre consentt. I wolde [like to make] one vyage 1st in to the North partes. I wolde knowe youre plesure herein and that knowne I wylle make my [plans] as you will asyne me. Your worship shall have me in Plemouthe this the   . God preserve youe. From Brystowe, the laste of November. —Your obeydent   [JOHN] SMYTHE."

[2] Not certain that the year is correctly stated.
[3] Cottonian MSS.

tonian manuscripts, the concluding portion of which we copy without altering the old sea Captain's spelling :—

"To all whome this doth concerne this is to be sertifyed ther ar great voyages to be made in New Englande upon fish take the times of the yeere, and likewise upon ferrs, so far [as it] be not spoyled by the meanes of towe manye factors ... I dow ingage myselfe to load a shippe of 200, between the first of Marche and the midds of June, for in Marche, Aprel and Maye is the best time of making of drye fish, a shippe that will carye 400,000 new freeland fyshe, will not carye aboue 7 or 8 score from New England, the countrye is good and a healthye clemett for ought that I can se or understand, the saueges ar a gentell natural peepel and frequentt the Engleshe vere much, the countrye is worthye of prayes and if I weare of abillitye and able venture I would venture that waye as soone as any way in any cuntrye, that yeldeth such comodetyes as that doth, though my meanes be not able to venture yet my life and labour is willing.

> The M^r is Edward Brawnde.
> His chiff matt John Bennett.
> The second matt Briane Tocker.
> The owner of o^r shippe Willim Treedel.
> The merchantt John Edwards.
> The Bosone John hille.
> The gunner and pilatt Willim Gayneye.
> his matt James ffarre.
> The bossone's matt John downe.
> The quarter misters is
> Nicholas Collins,
> Thomas Weber,

John Barrens,
Hennerye Batteshill.
The steward John Brimelcome.
The cooks Nicholas Head,
    John Hutton.
Some of the comen men's names are:
    John Wiles,
    Philipp Wiles,
    Thomas Roberts,
    John Hept,
    Thomas Tobbe.

I hope I need nott writt enye more of my men's names. So I end, commending all wishers and good adventurers in this voyage to the protection of the Almighty."

It had been customary for the vessels of the South and North colony to use in common the fishing-banks of the North Atlantic coast, but on December 1, 1619, after Sir Edwin Sandys had stated, at a meeting of the Virginia Company, that John Delbridge, a prominent merchant and Member of Parliament, was intending to settle a colony in Virginia, and wished a license to fish at Cape Cod, Sir Ferdinando Gorges, who was present, and a member of the other Company, opposed the proposition, on the ground that it properly belonged to the North colony to give permission for fishing at that point. After some discussion, the question in dispute was referred to the general council, composed of members of both branches of the corporation.

After examining the charter, they decided that it was lawful for either of the colonies to fish within the limits of the other.

Sir Ferdinando Gorges and associates having determined to "replant" in North Virginia early in 1620, petitioned the king for a separate charter,[1] prohibiting the South colony from fishing within their waters, and, after urgent entreaty, obtained a patent. At the request of the London Company a remonstrance was presented in November to the King, by Sir Thomas Roe, who replied, " that if anything were passed in New England patent prejudicial to them of the Southern colony, it was surreptitiously done, and without his knowledge."

On the 15th of the same month, the Earl of Southampton, at a meeting of the Company, said that he had that afternoon stated their objections to the New England patent to the Privy Council, and that it had been ordered for the present that it should be "sequestered."[2]

The controversy continued for about two years, and at length the differences between the two Companies was brought before the House of Commons, who did not acknowledge the Gorges patent.

[1] On July 23, 1620, the warrant was obtained from the King, and on 3d of November seal was affixed.

[2] London Company MSS. Transactions.

CHAPTER VI.

WILLIAM BREWSTER AND LEYDEN NONCONFORMISTS.

WILLIAM BREWSTER was named after his father, the postmaster at Scrooby in Nottinghamshire. For a time he was a student at Cambridge, and then in the employ of Davison, the Secretary of State under Queen Elizabeth. Returning to Scrooby he acted as his father's deputy until his death in 1590, and Samuel Bevercotes was made postmaster. When Davison heard that William Brewster had not obtained the position, he remonstrated with Stanhope, Master of the Posts, and soon the desired appointment was made, and Brewster, until the year 1607, followed in the footsteps of his father.[1]

With others in his neighbourhood he was dissatisfied with the forms of worship in the Church of England, and prepared to leave his native land.

Rapin states that in the first expedition to Virginia there were some Puritans, and that more would have followed, but Archbishop Bancroft obtained an order forbidding their departure. Among the names of adventurers in the Virginia charter of 1609 are those of

[1] *Cal. of State Papers.*

William Brewster and his son Edward,[1] and about this time he removed to Leyden with his family. A man of education and intelligence, he followed printing and bookselling as a means of support, and by the propriety of his conduct obtained the full confidence of his fellow-nonconformists in that city.

The habits of the Dutch were not congenial to the English exiles there, and therefore in the year 1617 the members of the Independent Church at Leyden determined to go to America, and "live as a distinct body under the general government of Virginia, and by their friends to sue to His Majesty that he would be pleased to grant them freedom of religion."[2] Carver and Cushman, two of their number, visited London, and found the Virginia Company willing to grant them a patent with ample privileges. To remove the objections of the King and Bishops as far as possible, the following seven Articles, signed by John Robinson, the pastor, and William Brewster, were submitted:—

ARTICLES.

"1. To the confession of faith published in the name of the Church of England, and to every article thereof, we do, with the Reformed Churches where we live, and also elsewhere, assent wholly.

---

[1] Bradford says his family was large. At the time of the first Virginia expedition he was about forty-five years of age. Among the first settlers to Virginia was William Brewster, gentleman, who died August 10, 1608, who may have been the son of the Elder, and one of the Puritans to whom Rapin alludes. Edward was captain of Lord Delaware's guard.

[2] *Bradford in Mass. Hist. Coll.*, 4 S., vol. iii.

"2. As we do acknowledge the doctrine of faith there taught, so do we the fruits and effects of the same doctrine to the begetting of saving faith, in thousands in the land (conformists and reformists) as they are called, with whom also as with our brethren we do desire to keep spiritual communion in peace, and will practise in our parts all lawful things.

"3. The King's Majesty we acknowledge for supreme governor in his dominion, for all causes, and over all persons, and that none may decline or appeal from his authority and judgment in any cause whatsoever, but that in all things obedience is due unto him, either active, if the thing commanded be not against God's word, or passive if it be, except pardon can be obtained.

"4. We judge it lawful for his Majesty to appoint bishops, civil overseers or officers in authority under him, in the several provinces, dioceses, congregations, or parishes, to oversee the churches, and govern them civilly according to the laws of the land, unto whom they are in all things to give an account, and by them to be ordered according to godliness.

"5. The authority of the present bishops in the land we do acknowledge, so far forth as the same is indeed derived from his Majesty unto them, and as they proceed in his name, whom we will also therein honour in all things, and him in them.

"6. We believe that no synod, classis, convocation, or assembly of ecclesiastical officers hath any power or authority at all, but as the same by the magistrate given unto them.

"7. Lastly, we desire to give unto all superiors due honour, to preserve the unity of the Spirit, with all the fear of God, to have peace with all men, what in us lieth, and wherein we err, to be instructed by any."

On November 12, 1617, Sir Edwin Sandys wrote to Robinson and Brewster expressing the satisfaction with which the articles had been perused, and commending the judicious conduct of Carver and Cushman, who were about to return to have further conference with the Church at Leyden. About the middle of February 1618, a prominent member of the Virginia Company wrote that the King and bishops had consented to wink at their departure. Afterwards, however, the bishops were more exacting.

Towards the close of August a party of Nonconformists, of Presbyterian rather than Independent sympathies, sailed for Virginia, under the leadership of Francis Blackwell, who had been an elder at Amsterdam.

The ship being overcrowded, and fresh water being exhausted, disease broke out, and only thirty out of one hundred and fifty reached Virginia, the captain as well as Blackwell being among the dead.

The seven articles of the Leyden people were examined by Drakes, an Essex clergyman, who in his pamphlet asks "whether it was not good for them, for the avoiding of scandal, and in the expectance of some prosperous success, by the permission of our noble King and honourable counsel, to remove to Virginia and make a plantation there, in hope to convert infidels to Christianity?"

To this, in 1619, a Nonconformist, named Euring, replied, that his brethren would prefer to be members of a scriptural church in the meanest part of England, than either to continue where many of us as yet live, or to plant ourselves in Virginia. "Yet," he adds, "even for Virginia thus much. When some of ours desired to have planted ourselves there, with his Majesty's leave, upon these three grounds,—first, that they might be means of planting the gospel among the heathen; secondly, that they might live under the King's government; thirdly, that they might make way for and unite with others, what in them lieth, whose consciences are grieved with the state of the Church in England, the bishops did by all means oppose them and their friends therein."

The discord, however, in the Virginia Company caused by the discovery of the dishonesty of Sir Thomas Smith, the Treasurer, was for a time the main hindrance to an arrangement with the Leyden Nonconformists. It had been urged that, for prudential reasons, a patent should be issued in the name of a friend, who was not of the Leyden congregation. In the transactions of the Company, under date of May 26, 1619, is the following entry:—

"One Mr. Wencop, commended to the Company by the Earl of Lincoln,[1] intending to go in person to Virginia, and there to plant himself, and his associates, pre-

---

[1] Frances, a sister of the new Earl of Lincoln, was the wife of John, a son of Sir Ferdinando Gorges; Susan, another sister, was the wife of John Humphrey, the first Deputy-Governor of Massachusetts; Arbella, a third

sented his patent now to the Court, which was referred to the Committee that meeteth upon Friday morning at Mr. Treasurer's house, to consider and, if need be, to correct the same."

Sir Edwin Sandys, a friend of Brewster, was now the Treasurer or Governor, having been elected in the place of Sir Thomas Smith two or three weeks before; and he was ready to promote the wishes of the Leyden people in every way. On the 9th of June, at a meeting of the Company, "by reason it grew late, and the Court ready to break up, as yet Mr. John Whincop's[1] patent, for him and his associates to be read, it was ordered, that the Seal should be annexed unto it, and have referred the trust therefore to the Auditors to examine, that it agree with the original, which, if it doth not, they have promised to bring it into the Court, and cancel it."

Bradford, speaking of Wincop, says, "God so disposed as he never went, nor made use of his patent, which had cost them so much labour and charge."

About the 1st of July 1619, William Brewster appears to have removed his family from Holland. Sir Dudley Carleton, Ambassador of England at the Hague, in a despatch of July 22, 1619, writes that Brewster, "within

sister, was the wife of Isaac Johnson, one of the founders of the town of Salem. The ship "Arbella," which bore John Winthrop and associates to America, was named in compliment to Lady Arbella.

[1] John, Samuel, and Thomas Wincop were three brothers, clergymen, settled in different parts of England. On Easter Sunday 1632, they all preached at St. Mary's, Spittle, London.

May not John, in 1619, have been the chaplain in the Earl of Lincoln's house, whose mother was the pious Countess of Lincoln, whose husband had died but a few months before?

three weeks, removed from thence," and one month later again says, "I have made good inquiry after William Brewster at Leyden, and am well assured that he is not returned thither, neither is it likely he will, having removed from thence both his family and his goods."

During the same year his son, Captain Edward Brewster, who had been banished from Virginia by the arbitrary Argall, arrived in England, and conformed to the requirements of the Church of England.[1]

Several months after the Wincop patent was issued, there was a new movement in regard to the emigration of the Leyden Nonconformists; and in January 1619-20 a grant was given to John Peirce and associates to settle in America, within the bounds of the London Company.

Sir John Wolstenholme proposed that the £500 that had been anonymously presented for the education of Indian children[2] might be expended under the direction of the associates of Peirce, but the Company, on the 16th of February, adopted the report of a committee that had considered the proposition, but deemed it inexpedient to assent thereto, *first*, because the proposed colony would be a long time, after their arrival, in settling down in the new country; and *second*, because they were entire strangers to the language and habits of the savage.

At the time that Peirce was making arrangements to

---

[1] Secretary Naunton in August 1619 wrote:—"Brewster frightened back into the Low Countries, his son has conformed, and comes to church." As his father at Leyden, he became a publisher and bookseller in London. In 1637 his shop, with the sign of the Bible, was at Fleet Street bridge. Subsequently he was Treasurer of the Stationers' Company.

[2] For the history of this gift see chapter viii.

leave the Leyden people, the Directors of the New Netherlands Company petitioned their States General in these words,[1] "It happens there is residing at Leyden a certain English preacher versed in the Dutch language, who is well inclined to proceed thither [Manhattan] and live, assuring the petitioners that he has the means of inducing over four hundred families to accompany him, both out of this country and England."

Thomas Weston, a London merchant in the interest of Peirce, now visited Leyden, and urged them not to form an alliance with the Dutch, nor to place too much dependence on the Virginia Company. About the same period several Lords had obtained a large grant from the King of the north part of Virginia, to be wholly separated therefrom and called New England, to which country Weston was disposed to have the colony proceed, on account of its profitable fisheries.

After months of heart-burnings among themselves, and doubts as to the fairness of the London shipping merchants, the Leyden people at length sailed, in the "May Flower," and on the 11th of November 1620 reached Cape Cod,[2] and, after various explorations, on 11th of December (o.s.) landed at Plymouth Rock.

Before they landed there were whisperings among the discontented "that when they came ashore they could use their own liberties, for none had power to command them, the patent they had being for Virginia, and not

[1] N. Y. Col. Documents.
[2] In the compact drawn up in the cabin of the "May Flower" in November, it is stated that the voyage was "to plant the first colony in the *northern* part of Virginia."

for New England, which belonged to another government with which the Virginia Company had nothing to do."

The "May Flower" returned to England in May 1621, and on the 1st of June John Peirce, cloth-worker of London, and his associates, received a patent from the Company for New England. On the 16th of July, at a meeting of the Virginia Company, "It was moved, seeing that Mr. John Peirce had taken a patent of Sir Ferdinando Gorges, and thereupon seated his company within the limits of the Northern Plantations, as by some was supposed, whereby he seemed to relinquish the benefit of the patent he took of this Company, that therefore the said patent might be called in, unless it might appear he would plant within the limits of the Southern Colony."

It would appear from this minute as if there had been some understanding with Gorges on the part of Peirce, to settle the Leyden people in the north colony, and that Captain Jones[1] of the "May Flower," an unscrupulous person, purposely guided his vessel toward Cape Cod.

[1] Captain Thomas Jones was sent by the London Company in November 1621, on a trading voyage to the Hudson and Delaware rivers, in a ship called the "Discovery." The next year he was accused of robbing the New England Indians of their furs. In July 1625 he arrived at Jamestown with a Spanish frigate, which he said he had captured in the West Indies, but his conduct was suspicious, and his story not credited. In a few weeks he died in Virginia.—*London Company* MSS.

CHAPTER VII.

PATRICK COPLAND, CHAPLAIN OF EAST INDIA COMPANY.

FOR years the merchants of London had listened to tales of the wealth "of Ormus and of Ind." As early as 1583, there were hopes entertained of a short and direct route to the renowned and far distant empire of Cathay; and one Apsley, an enterprising man, who dealt in beads, playing-cards, and gewgaws calculated to please the tastes of Orientals, told a friend that he expected to live to see a letter dated at London, on the 1st of May, delivered in China before midsummer, by a short passage over the American Continent, between the forty-third and forty-sixth parallel of north latitude, a thing accomplished nearly three hundred years after the enthusiastic merchant made the prediction.

In the year 1600, the leading men accustomed to assemble at the Royal Exchange, that had been dedicated to commerce by Queen Elizabeth, organized the East India Company with the rich merchant, Thomas Smith, as Governor, and a few years after adopted as a device for their legal seal, three ostrich feathers, with "*Juvat ire per altum*" above, and encircling them, the motto, "*Tibi serviat Ultima Thule.*"

Many of the members sincerely desired that the far-off land should acknowledge Christ, and at the commencement of their trading operations, sent teachers of truth along with the cloths, looking-glasses, glittering toys, and cheap musical instruments. In their deliberations, while they exhibited an anxiety for a fair return for their outlays, in the shape of ivory, gold-dust, and choice pearls, they recognised, nevertheless, that both they and the Chinese, and Japanese, had the same "God o'er head."

An inspection of their minutes shows that they were not despisers of Providence. On one occasion, the Governor of the Company proposed to relieve the poverty of some poor preachers in London, by electing three chaplains, to pray for the safe return of their fleets; and at another period, they gravely deliberated upon the request of the Prince of Sumatra for a white wife. Two years before, John Rolfe brought to England Powhatan's daughter, "of rude education, manners barbarous, and cursed generation, merely for the good and honour" of Virginia, an honourable English gentleman, in view of his child becoming an Asiatic princess, and also out of an alleged desire to propagate the Christian religion in the Pagan world, offered to give away his daughter "accomplished in music, the use of the needle, very beautiful, and of good discourse." Certain members of the Company, alluding to the fact that divines had discountenanced the yoking together of a Christian and barbarian, the anxious parent prepared an answer, showing that his willingness to present a fair daughter to a Sumatran chief was not unscriptural.[1]

As soon as the English had established a trading port at Surat, Patrick Copland, with a faith as pure, and scholarship as elevated, as that of the distinguished Henry Martyn, entered the service of the East India Company as a chaplain.

During the summer of 1614, he returned to England with a talented native youth, whom he had taught chiefly by signs, "to speake, to reade and write the English tongue and hand, both Romane and Secretary, within less than the space of a yeare."[2] Soon after he wrote to the Company that his pupil had increased in the knowledge of the Christian religion, and suggesting that he should be publicly baptized "as the first-fruits of India." Archbishop Abbott having been consulted, the Company acceded to the proposition.

An Indian, either from Hindustan or America, the Bay of Bengala or the Chesapeake, was a great rarity in the streets of London during the reign of James the First; and as he walked, the women with curiosity peeped through cracks of the front doors, and children went before, and followed his steps, their mouths agape with astonishment. Shakespeare, the keen observer of the foibles of his day, alludes in the "Tempest" to this disposition to make much of an Indian :—

---

[1] *Cal. of State Papers. East Indies*, 1513-1616.
[2] *Virginia's God be Thanked.* London, 1622.

"What have we here ? A man or a fish ? Dead or alive ? A strange fish ? Were I in England now, as once I was, and had but this fish painted, not a holiday fool there but would give a piece of silver. Any strange beast there makes a man; when they will not give a doit to relieve a lame beggar, they will lay out ten to see a dead Indian."

For centuries Fenchurch Street has, during Christmas week, been alive with persons busily passing to and fro; but on Sunday, 22d of December 1616, an unusual crowd surged toward the Church of St. Dennis, for it had been announced that, by the rite of baptism, a lad, a native of Bengala, was to be initiated into the Church of Christ. The Privy Council, the Lord Mayor and Aldermen, the members of the East India and the sister Company of Virginia, with difficulty, waded through the "sea of upturned faces" overflowing the approaches to the edifice, and the congregation within the walls was densely packed. The rite was administered by Dr. John Wood, and Petrus Papa, or Peter Pope, the name given in baptism, was chosen by King James, that odd compound of cant, coarseness, and sottishness, who often seemed unable to distinguish between the odour of beer and sanctity, "the spirit of wine and the Spirit Divine," and yet affected to be a special "defender of the faith."

In the "Royal James" that sailed from the Gravesend Feb. 4th, 1616-17, o.s., Copland and Peter Pope departed for India. On the 19th of September 1618, Sir Thomas Dale, late Deputy-Governor of Virginia, arrived in the "Clove," and assumed command as Admiral of the East India fleet. In view of an approaching conflict with the Dutch, on Saturday the 2d of December a sermon was preached in the "Royal James" in the presence of Dale and other captains. On the 9th of August 1619 Dale died at Messulapatam,[1] and about this period Copland received a letter from Adrian Hulsebus, chaplain of the Dutch post on the isle of Java, asking him to co-operate in measures to restore good feeling between the Dutch and English. While the "Royal James" lay off Bantam on the 19th of August, Copland replied to Hulsebus :—

"The thing you touch in your letter is but too true, that the hatred and dissension among Christians, if it continue, will be the cause of much innocent blood-shedding among friends, and of estranging the hearts of the heathen from the worship of the true God.

"And therefore that enmity amongst friends may cease, and that such as are yet without may be allured to submit themselves to the sceptre of Jesus Christ, it standeth upon us, who are preachers of the gospel of peace, to be instruments of peace, which for my own part, how willing I am to be, is not unknown to such as know myself, and among whom I daily converse. . . . All standeth not on one side, there must be a yielding of both sides, if ever there be a sound peace."

On the 26th of April 1620, the fleet sailed for Japan,

---

[1] Camden says that Sir Thomas Gates, the associate of Dale in Virginia, also died in the East India service, July 20, 1620. His children were, Thomas, killed by a cannon ball at Rochelle, Anthony, Mary, and Elizabeth.

and on the 2d of June the "Unicorn," a ship of 800 tons, was lost during a typhoon near Macao, and Copland has vividly described the storm:—

"In this tempest we lost also our pinnace, with twenty-four or thirty men, which we had sent before us to Firando, an island adjoining to Japan, to give notice of our coming, of which we never heard news. We cut off our long-boat, and let her go; we sunk our shallop, with two men in her, who were swallowed up by the waves. Such was this storm, as if Jonah had been flying into Tarshish. The air was beclouded, the heavens were obscured, and made an Egyptian night of five or six days perpetual horror. The experience of our seamen was amazed; the skill of our mariners was confounded; our 'Royal James' most violently and dangerously leaked, and those which pumped to keep others from drowning were half-drowned themselves."[1]

The studies of Pope were continued under the supervision of his first teacher, and the scholar proved to be as quickwitted as the young Chinese and Japanese who are, in the nineteenth century, found in the schools of Great Britain and the United States, or engaged in trade at San Francisco and other centres of commercial transactions. Latin epistles addressed by him early in the year 1620 to the Governor of the East India Company, and to Martin Pring, then in command of the "Royal James," have been preserved, which indicate not only the docility of the youth, but also how "apt to teach" was Copland.

[1] *Virginia's God be Thanked*, page 6.

On the 14th of December 1620, the "Royal James" left Firando, and after stopping at Java for a cargo of pepper, during the next February begun the homeward voyage.

The Isle of St. Helena was reached on the 21st of June 1621, and on the 16th of September the "Royal James" anchored in the Thames, and Copland debarked to labour for the good of the infant plantations in America.

CHAPTER VIII.

COPLAND'S SERVICES TO VIRGINIA COMPANY.

THE Virginia Company were the first to take steps relative to the establishment of schools in the English colonies of America. In a letter written to the authorities of the infant settlement at Jamestown, on November 18, 1618, they use these words: "Whereas, by a special grant and license from his Majesty, a general contribution over this realm hath been made for the building and planting of a college, for the training up of the children of those infidels in true religion, moral virtue, and civility, and for other godliness, we do therefore, according to a former grant and order, hereby ratify and confirm and ordain that a convenient place be chosen and set out for the planting of a university at the said Henrico in time to come, and that in the meantime preparation be there made for the building of the said college for the children of the infidels, according to such instructions as we shall deliver. And we will and ordain that ten thousand acres, partly of the land they impaled, and partly of the land within the territory of the said Henrico, be allotted and set out for the endowing of the said university and college with convenient possessions."[1]

[1] MSS. Virginia Records.

A week after the date of this communication, a ripe scholar in England, the Rev. Thomas Lorkin, subsequently distinguished as secretary of the English embassy in France, writes to an acquaintance : "A good friend of mine proposed to me within three or four days a condition of going over to Virginia, where the Virginia Company means to erect a college, and undertakes to procure me good assurance of £200 a-year, and if I shall find any ground of dislike, liberty to return at pleasure."[1]

The offer, after due consideration, appears not to have been accepted, and nothing more was done until the re-organization of the Company in April 1619, and the election of Sir Edwin Sandys as its presiding officer.

By his integrity, patriotism, scholarship, and great administrative talent, he infused new life into the expiring Society, and associated with him Nicholas Ferrar, the honourable merchant of London, Sir John Danvers, the step-father, and Edward Lord Cherbury, the brother of the sweet poet, George Herbert, also the Earl of Southampton, who in early life extended a helping hand to a poor boy that is said to have held horses for gentlemen at the doors of play-houses, and became Shakespeare, the portrayer of all the varied emotions of the soul, whose reputation as a dramatist has increased in lustre as the centuries have advanced.

The new managers of the Company proceeded to reconstruct Virginia with the most liberal views. By their permission the first representative and legislative

[1] *Court and Times of James the First*, vol. ii. p. 109.

body in America was convened at Jamestown, on July 30, 1619, in the church, the most convenient place they could find, the minister of which was Rev. Richard Buck.

During the sessions of this body, which continued until the 4th of August, a petition was presented relative to the erection of a university and college. From this period until the dissolution of the Virginia Company the design of a university and college was never forgotten.

The collections taken up by order of the King, for a college, in 1619, amounted to £2043, 2s. 11½d., and at a meeting of the Company on May 26, Sir Edwin Sandys, as treasurer, propounded to the court "a thing worthy to be taken into consideration for the glory of God and honour of the Company, forasmuch as the King, in his most gracious favour, hath granted his letters to the several bishops of his kingdom for the collecting of moneys to erect and build a college in Virginia for the training and bringing up of infidels' children to the true knowledge of God and understanding of righteousness. He conceived it the fittest that as yet they should not build the college, but rather forbear awhile, and begin first with the advances they have to provide and settle an annual revenue, and out of that to begin the erection of said college. And for the performance hereof also moved that a certain piece of land be laid out at Henrico, being the place formerly resolved on, which should be called the college land, and for the planting of the same send presently fifty good persons, to be located thereon, and to occupy the same."

On June 14, 1619, it was moved by Mr. Treasurer " that the court would take into consideration to appoint a committee of their gentlemen and other of his Majesty's counsel for Virginia concerning the college, being a weighty business, and so great that an account of their proceedings therein must be given to the State. Upon which the court, upon deliberate consideration, have recommended the rare trust unto the right worthy Sir Dudley Diggs, Sir John Danvers, Sir Nath. Rich, Sir Jo. Wolstenholme, Mr. Deputy Ferrar, Mr. Dr. Anthony, and Mr. Dr. Gulson, to meet at such time as Mr. Treasurer shall order hereto."[1]

On June the 24th the committee by the last court appointed for the college having met, as they were desired, delivered over their proceedings, which the court allowed, being this that followeth :—

" A note of what kind of men and most fit to be sent to Virginia in the next intended voyage of transporting one hundred men.

" A minister to be entertained at the yearly allowance of forty pounds, and to have fifty acres of land for him and his for ever; to be allowed his transportation and his man's at the Company's charge, and ten pounds to furnish himself withall.

" A captain thought fit, to be considered of, to take charge of such people as are to be planted on the college land.

" All the people at this first sending, except some

---

[1] This and following extracts are from the MS. Transactions of the London Company. The varied orthography of proper names has not been altered.

soon to be sent as well for planting the college and public land, to be single men, unmarried.

"A warrant to be made and directed to Sir Thomas Smith for the payment of the collection money to Sir Edwin Sandys, treasurer, and that Dr. Gulstone[1] shall be entreated to present unto my Lord Primate of Canterbury such letters to be signed for the speedy paying of the moneys from every diocese which yet remain unpaid.

"The several sorts of tradesmen and others for the college land: smiths, carpenters, bricklayers, turners, potters, husbandmen, brickmakers.

"And whereas, according to the standing order, seven were chosen by the court to be of the committee for the college, the said order allowing no more, and, inasmuch as Mr. John Wroth came in error to be left out, he is therefore now desired to be an assistant with them, and to give them meeting at such time and place as is agreed of."

At a meeting of the Company held in London at Mr. Ferrar's house, on July 21, 1619, the Earls of Southampton and Warwick, Sir Thomas Gates, and others being present, the following anonymous letter was read:—

+
I. H. S.

"SIR EDWIN SANDYS, *Treasurer of Virginia:*

"Good luck in the name of the Lord, who is daily magnified by the experiment of your zeal and piety in

[1] Gulston was a distinguished physician and founder of the Gulstonian Lectureship.

giving beginning to the foundation of the college in Virginia, sacred work due to heaven and so longed for on earth.

"Now know we assuredly that the Lord will do you good and bless you in all your proceedings, even as He blessed the house of Obed Edom and all that pertaineth unto him because of the ark of God. Now that you seek the kingdom of God, all things shall be ministered unto you. This I well see already, and perceive that by your godly determination the Lord hath given you favour in the sight of all His people, and I know some whose hearts are much enlarged because of the house of the Lord our God to procure you wealth, which greater designs I have presumed to outrun with this oblation, which I humbly beseech you may be accepted as the pledge of my devotion, and as an earnest of the power which I have vowed unto the Almighty God of Jacob concerning this thing, which till I may in part perform I desire to remain unknown and unsought after.

"The things are these: a communion cup with the ewer and vase; a trencher plate for the bread; a carpet of crimson velvet; a linen damask cloth."

On Wednesday, November 17, 1619, at a great and general quarterly meeting of the Virginia Company, the treasurer referred to the instructions sent out by the new governor of the colony, Sir George Yeardley, by which were to be selected ten thousand acres of land for the university to be planted at Henrico, of which one thousand was reserved for the college for the conversion of infidels.

On December 1, "It was propounded that in consideration of some public gifts given by sundry persons to Virginia, divers presents of church plate and other ornaments, two hundred pounds already given toward building a church, and five hundred pounds promised by another toward the educating of infidels' children, that, for the honour of God, and memorial of such good benefactors, a tablet might hang in the court with their names and gifts inserted, and the ministers of Virginia and the Sommer Islands may have intelligence thereof, that for their pious works they may recommend them to God in their prayers; which generally was thought very fit and expedient."

On February 2, 1619-20 :—" A letter from an unknown person was read, directed to the treasurer, promising five hundred pounds for the educating and bringing up infidels' children in Christianity, which Mr. Treasurer, not willing to meddle therewith alone, desired the court to appoint a select committee for the managing and employing of it to the best purpose. They made choice of: Lord Pagett, Sir Tho. Wroth, Mr. J. Wroth, Mr. Deputie, Mr. Tho. Gibbs, Dr. Winstone, Mr. Bamfourde, and Mr. Keightley.

The Copy of the Letter.

" SIR,—Your charitable endeavour for Virginia hath made you a father, me a favourer of those good works which, although heretofore hath come near to their birth, yet for want of strength could never be delivered (envy and division dashing these younglings even in the womb), until your helpful hand, with other favourable personages, gave them both birth and being, for the better cherishing of which good and pious work, seeing many casting gifts into the treasury, I am encouraged to tender my poor mite; and although I cannot with the princes of Issaker bring gold and silver covering, yet offer you what I can, some goats' hair, necessary stuff for the Lord's tabernacle, protesting here in my sincerity, without Papistical merit or Pharisaical applause, wishing from my heart as much unity in your honourable undertaking as there is sincerity in my designs, to the furtherance of which good work, the converting of infidels to the faith of Christ, I promised by my good friends £500 for the maintenance of a convenient number of young Indians taken at the age of seven years, or younger, and instructed in the reading and understanding the principles of Christian religion unto the age of twelve years, and then, as occasion serveth, to be trained and brought up in some lawful trade with all humanity and gentleness until the age of one and twenty years, and then to enjoy like liberties and privileges with our native English in that place.

"And for the better performance thereof you shall receive £50 more, which shall be delivered into the hands of two religious persons with certitude of payment, who shall once every quarter examine and certify to the treasurer here, in England, the due operation of these promises, together with the names of those children just taken, the foster-fathers and overseers, not doubting but you are all assured that gifts devoted to God's service cannot be diverted to private and secular advantages without sacrilege. If your graver judgments can devise a more charitable course for the younger, I beseech you inform my friend, with your security for true performance, and my benevolence shall be always ready to be delivered accordingly.

"The greatest courtesy I expect or crave is to conceal my friend's name, lest importunity might urge him to betray that trust of secrecy, which he hath faithfully promised, who hath moved my heart to this good work. I rest, *ab famo*, DUST AND ASHES.

"SIR EDWIN SANDYS,
"*The faithful Treasurer for Virginia.*"

On the 16th of February the following was passed:—

"Whereas, at the last court a special committee was appointed for the managing of the £500 given by an unknown person for educating the infidels' children, Mr. Treasurer signified that they have met and taken into consideration the proposition of Sir John Wolstenholme, that John Peirce and his associates might have the training and bringing up of some of these children; but the said committee, for divers reasons, think it inconvenient, first, because they intend not to go this two or three months, and then after their arrival will be long in settling themselves; as also that the Indians are not acquainted with them, and so they may stay four or five years before they have account that any good is done.[1]

[1] The associates of John Peirce were William Brewster and the so-called "Pilgrim Fathers," whose landing at Plymouth Rock, Dec. 11, 1620, O.S., is the subject of a poem by Mrs. Hemans. See Chapter VI.

"And for to put it into the hands of private men to bring them up, as was by some proposed, they thought it was not so fit, by reason of the difficulty unto which it is subject.

"But forasmuch as divers hundreds and particular plantations are already there settled, and the Indians well acquainted with them, as namely, Smith's Hundred, Martin's Hundred, Bartlett's Hundred, and the like, that, therefore, they receive and take charge of them, by which course they shall be sure to be well nurtured and have their due so long as these plantations shall hold; and for such of the children as they find capable of learning shall be put in the college and brought up to be Fellows, and such as are not shall be put to trades and be brought up in the fear of God and the Christian religion.

"And being demanded how and by what lawful means they would preserve them, and after keep them, that they run not to join their parents or friends, and their parents or friends steal them not away, which natural affection may inforce in the one and the other, it was answered and well allowed that a treaty and agreement be made with the king of that country concerning them, which if it so fall out at any time, as is expressed, they may by his command be returned.

"Whereupon Sir Thomas Roe promised that Bartlett's Hundred should take two or three, and Mr. Smith to be respondent to the Company, and because every hundred may the better consider thereof they were licensed till Sunday in the afternoon, at which time they sit at Mr. Treasurer's to bring in their answer how many they will have, and bring those that will be respondent for them, and those that others will not take Mr. Treasurer, in behalf of Smith's Hundred, hath promised to take into their charge."

The Treasurer signified, on February 22d, "that the corporation of Smith's Hundred very well accepted of the charge of infidels' children recommended unto them by the court, in regard of their good disposition to do good; but, otherwise, if the court shall please to take it from them they will willingly give £100. And for their resolutions, although they have not yet set them down in writing, by reason of some things yet to be considered of, they will, so soon as may be, prepare the same and present it."

A box standing upon the table with this direction, "*To Sir Edwin Sandis, the faithful Treasurer for Virginia,*" he acquainted them that it was brought unto him by a man of good fashion, who would neither tell him his name nor from whence it came; but, by the subscription being the same as the letter, he considered that it might be the £550 promised them.

It being agreed that the box should be opened, there was a bag of new gold containing the said sum of £550 found therein: Whereupon Doctor Winstone[1] reporting that the committee had requested for the managing thereof, and that it should be wholly in charge of Smith's Hundred, it was desired by some that the resolution should be presented in writing at the next court,

---

[1] A physician who had been educated at Cambridge.

which, in regard of the Ash-Wednesday sermon, was agreed to be upon Thursday afternoon.

At a meeting held at the house of Sir Edwin Sandys, on April 9, 1620, intelligence was given that Mr. Nicholas Ferrar, elder, "being translated from this life[1] unto a better, had by his will bequeathed £300 towards the converting of infidels' children in Virginia, to be paid unto Sir Edwin Sandys and Mr. Jo. Ferrar, at such time as, upon certificate from there, ten of the said infidels' children shall be placed in the college, to be there disposed of by the said Sir Edwin Sandys and Jo. Ferrar, according to the true intent of the said will; and that in the mean [time] till that was performed he hath tied his executors to pay eight per cent. for the same unto three several honest men in Virginia (such as the said Sir Edwin Sandys and John Ferrar shall approve of), of

---

[1] Nicholas Ferrar, Sr., was a rich merchant that had taken an interest in the voyages of Raleigh and Gilbert. After the election, in 1619, of Sir Edwin Sandys to the Governorship of Virginia Company, the meetings were held in the parlours of his capacious house in St. Sythe's Lane. He married Mary Wodenoth; and Arthur Wodenoth, who wrote a brief sketch of the Virginia Company, which was published in 1651, was probably a nephew or brother-in-law.

His son, John Ferrar, was Deputy-Governor of Virginia Company, from 1619, for two years, and after he declined re-election, his brother Nicholas was appointed, and held the office until the Company was dissolved in 1624, and in 1626 the latter was ordained in the Church of England, and retired, with his aged mother, to Little Gidding. William, another son, appears to have gone to Virginia.

John Ferrar had a talented daughter, christened Virginia. She wrote a treatise on silk-worms, and also published in 1651:—

"A Mapp of Virginia discovered to ye Hills, and its latt. from 35 deg. and ½ neer Flora, to 41 deg. bounds of New England.

"Domina Virginia Farrar, Collegit.

"And sold by J. Stephenson, at ye Sunne, below Ludgate, 1651."

John Ferrar died in 1657; his daughter in 1687.

good life and fame, that will undertake each of them to bring up one of the said children in the grounds of Christian religion, that is to say, £8 yearly apiece."

About this period Mr. George Thorpe, a gentleman of sterling character, of his Majesty's privy chamber, and one of his council for Virginia, sailed for the colony, having been appointed by the Company deputy to take charge of the college lands.[1]

At a meeting of the Company on November 15, 1620, as the reading of the minutes of the previous meeting were completed, " a stranger stepped in," and presented a map of Sir Walter Raleigh's, containing a description of Guiana, and with the same four great books, as the gift of one that desired his name might not be known. One of these was a translation of St. Augustine's *City of God;* the others were the works of the distinguished Calvinist and Puritan, Mr. Perkins,[2] " which books the donor desired might be sent to the college in Virginia, there to remain in safety to the use of the collegiate educators, and not suffered at any time to be lent abroad."

For which so worthy a gift my lord of Southampton desired the party that presented them to return deserved thanks from himself and the rest of the Company to him that had so kindly bestowed them.

The next year the interest of the Company in esta-

---

[1] Massacred by Indians, March 22, 1621-22.

[2] William Clayborne, for several years Secretary of Virginia, in 1638, had among his books at Palmer's Isle, near the mouth of the Susquehannah river, one of the large folio volumes of Mr. Perkins.—*Maryland Historical Society MSS.*

blishing schools in America was increased by another unexpected donation.

Mr. Copland, returning home from India in 1621, met some ships on the way to Virginia, and learning the destitution of the New World colony in churches and schools, he longed to do them good. The mode devised for helping them is fully explained in the minutes of the Virginia Company.

At a court held 24th October 1621, Mr. Deputy acquainted the court "that one Mr. Copland, a minister lately returned from the East Indies, out of an earnest desire to give some furtherance unto the plantation in Virginia, had been pleased, as well by his own good example as by persuasion, to stir up many that came with him in the ship called the 'Royal James' to contribute toward some good work to be begun in Virginia, insomuch that he had already procured a matter of some £70 to be employed that way, and had also written from Cape Bona Speranza to divers parties in the East Indies to move them to some charitable contribution thereunto. So, as he hoped, they would see very shortly his letters would produce some good effect among them, especially if they might understand in what manner they intended to employ the same. It was therefore ordered that a committee should be appointed to treat with Mr. Copland about it. And forasmuch as he had so well deserved of the Company by his extraordinary care and pains in this business, it was thought fit and ordered that he should be admitted a free brother of this Company, and at the next quarter court it should be moved that some proportion of land might be bestowed upon him in gratification of his worthy endeavours to advance this extended work; and further, it was thought fit also to add thereunto a number of some other special benefactors unto the plantation whose memorial is preserved. The committee to treat with him are these: Mr. Deputy, Mr. Gibbs, Mr. Nicholas Ferrar, Mr. Bamforde, Mr. Abra. Chamberlyne, Mr. Roberts, Mr. Ayres."

On the last of October 1621, Mr. Deputy signified that, " forasmuch as it was reserved unto the Company to determine whether the said money should be employed towards the building of a church or a school, as aforesaid, your committee appointed have had conference with Mr. Copland about it, and do hold it fit, for many important reasons, to employ the said contribution towards the erection of a public free school in Virginia, towards which an unknown person hath likewise given £30, as may appear by the report of said committee, now presented to be read.

"At a meeting of the committee on Tuesday, the 30th of October 1621, present Mr. Deputy, Mr. Gibbs, Mr. Wroth, Mr. Ayres, Mr. Nicholas Ferrar, Mr. Roberts.

" The said committee meeting this afternoon to treat with Mr. Copland touching the dispose of the money given by some of the East India Company that came with him in the ' Royal James,' to be bestowed upon some good work for the benefit of the plantation in Virginia, the said Mr. Copland did deliver in a note the names of those that had freely and willingly contributed their moneys hereunto, which money Mr. Copland said they desired might be employed towards the building either of a church or school in Virginia, which the Company should think fit. And that although the sum of money was but a small proportion to perform so great a work, yet Mr. Copland said he doubted not but to persuade the East India Company, whom he meant to solicit, to make some addition thereunto; besides, he said that he had very effectually wrote (the copy of which letter he delivered and was read) to divers factories in the East Indies to stir them up to the like contribution towards the performance of this pious work, as they had already done for a church at Wapping, to which, by his report, they have given about £400.

"It being, therefore, now taken into consideration whether a church or a school was most necessary, and might nearest agree to the intentions of the donors, it was considered that forasmuch as each particular plantation, as well as the general, either had or ought to have a church appropriated unto them, there was therefore a greater want of a school than of churches.

"As also for that it was impossible, with so small a proportion, to compass so great a work as the building of a church would require, they therefore conceived it most fit to resolve for the erecting of a public free school, which, being for the education of children and grounding them in the principles of religion, civility of life, and human learning, seemed to carry with it the greatest weight and highest consequence unto the plantations, as that whereof both church and commonwealth take their original foundation and happy estate, this being also so like to prove a work most acceptable unto the planters, through want whereof they have been hitherto constrained to send their children from thence hither to be taught.

"*Secondly.* It was thought fit that the school should be placed in one of the four cities, and they conceived that Charles City, of the four, did afford the most convenient place for that purpose, as well in respect it matcheth with the best in wholesomeness of air, as also for the commodious situation thereof, being not far distant from Henrico and other particular plantations.

"It was also thought fit that, in honour of the East India benefactors, the same should be called the East India School, who shall have precedence before any other to present their children there, to be brought up in the rudiments of learning.

"It was also thought fit that this, as a collegiate or free school, should have dependence upon the college in Virginia, which should be made capable to receive scholars from the school into such scholarships; and fellowships of said college shall be endowed withal for the advancement of scholars as they arise by degree and desert in learning.

"That, for the better maintenance of the schoolmaster and usher intended there to be placed, it was thought fit that it should be moved at the next quarter court that one thousand acres of land should be allotted unto the said school, and that tenants, besides an overseer of them, should be forthwith sent upon this charge, in the condition of apprentices, to manure and cultivate said land; and that, over and above this allowance of land and tenants to the schoolmaster, such as send their children to the school should give some benevolence unto the schoolmaster, for the better increase of his maintenance.

"That it should be specially recommended to the governor to take care that the planters there be stirred up to put their helping hands towards the speedy building of the said school, in respect that their children are likely to receive the greatest benefit thereby in their education; and to let them know that those that exceed others in their bounty and assistance hereunto shall be privileged with the preferment of their children to these said schools before others that shall be found less worthy.

"It is likewise thought fit that a good schoolmaster be provided, forthwith to be sent unto this school.

"It was also informed, by a gentleman of this committee, that he knew one, that desired not to be named, that would bestow £30, to be added to the former sum of £70 to make it an £100, towards the building of the said school."

This report, being read, was well approved of, and thought fit to be referred for confirmation to the next quarter court. On November 19, 1621, the Company again considered the matter.

"Whereas the committee appointed to treat with Mr. Copland about the building of the East India church, or school, in Virginia, towards which a contribution of £70 was freely given by some of the East India Company that came home in the 'Royal James,' did now make report what special reasons moved them to resolve for the bestowing of that money towards the erection of a school rather than a church, which report is at large set down at a court held last October.

"And further, that they had allowed one thousand acres of land and five apprentices, besides an overseer, to manure, besides that benevolence that is hoped will be given by each man that sends his children thither to be taught, for the schoolmaster's maintenance in his first beginning; which allowance of land and tenants, being put to the question, was well approved of, and referred for confirmation to the quarter court; provided that in the establishment hereof the Company reserve unto themselves power to make laws and orders for the better government of the said school and the revenues and profits that shall thereunto belong.

"It was further moved that, in respect of Mr. Copland, minister, hath been a chief cause of procuring this former contribution to be given by the aforesaid Company, and had also writ divers letters to many factories in the East Indies to move them to follow this good example, for the better advancement of this pious work, that therefore the Company would please to gratify him with some proportion of land.

"Whereupon the court, taking it into consideration, and being also informed that Mr. Copland was furnishing out persons to be transported this present voyage to plant and inhabit upon said lands as should be granted unto them by the Company, they were the rather induced to bestow upon him an extraordinary gratification of three shares of land, old adventure, which is three hundred acres, upon a first division, without paying rent to the Company, referring the further ratification of the said gift to the quarter court, as also his admittance of being a free brother of this Company."

About this time a young Puritan minister, John Brinsley, a nephew of the so-called English Seneca, the distinguished Bishop Hall, and the private secretary of his uncle at the synod of Dort, who also in after life became the author of many classical and theological treatises, prepared a little book suitable for the projected school in Virginia. As published, it made a small quarto of eighty-four pages, and was a plea for learning and the schoolmaster. He stated that the incivility "amongst manie of the Irish, the Virgineans, and all other barbarous nations," grew "from their exceeding ignorance of our holy God, and of all true and good learning." On another page he adds that it was his unfeigned desire to adapt the book "for all functions and places, and more particularly to every ruder place, as to the ignorant country of Wales, and more especially to that poor Irish nation, with our loving countrymen of Virginia."[1]

[1] In the library of University of Dublin is a copy of this work, prepared especially for the Virginia Company's plantations, with the following title :—

At a court held for Virginia the 19th of December 1621, Mr. Balmfield signified unto the court of a book "compiled by a painful schoolmaster, one Mr. John Brinsley;" whereupon the court gave order that the Company's thanks should be given unto him, and appointed a select committee to peruse the said book, viz., Sir John Danvers, Mr. Deputy, Mr. Gibbs, Mr. Wroth, Mr. Balmfield, Mr. Copland, Mr. Ayres, and Mr. Nicho. Ferrar, who are entreated to meet when Mr. Deputy shall appoint, and after to make report of their opinions touching the same at the next court.

On Wednesday, the 16th January 1621 [1622], the committee appointed to peruse the book which Mr.

A
CONSOLATION
For our Grammar
SCHOOLES or a faithful and most comfortable in-
couragement for laying of a sure foundation
of a good learninge in our Schooles
and for prosperous building thereunto;
More *specially for all those of the inferiour*
sort and all
rude countries and places, namely,
for *Ireland, Wales, Virginia,* with the *Sommer
Ilands*
and for the more speedie attaining of our
English tongue by the same labour, that all
speake one and the same
language :
And withall for the helping of all such as are de-
sirous speedlie to recover that which they had formerlie
got in the Grammar Schooles and to proceed aright
therein for the perpetual benefit of these our
Nations, and of the churches
of Christ.
London : Printed by Richard Field, for Thomas Man,
dwelling in Paternoster Row, at the sign
of the Talbot : 1622

John Brinsley, schoolmaster, presented at the last court, touching the education of the younger sort of scholars, "forasmuch as they had as yet no time to peruse the same, by reason of many businesses that did arise, they desired of the court some longer respite, which was granted unto them. Mr. Copland, being present, was entreated to peruse it in the meantime, and deliver his opinion thereof to the committee, at their meeting about it."[1]

At a quarter court held on January 30, 1621-2, "the

---

[1] Brinsley in an epistle addresses the Virginia Company concerning his book, as follows :—

"The triall whereof I dare (through God's goodnesse) tender to any by yourselues appointed to make full demonstration of it, to their like, as I haue formerly done to the most learned and fit that I could chuse to this purpose, as appeareth in the Examiner's Censure in the closing of this little Treatise. And withal to help that we may haue by the same not only the puritie of our owne language preserued amongst all our own people there, but also that it may be readily learned in the Schooles, together with the Latin and other tongues, and so more propagated to the rudest Welch and Irish.

"Thus have I presumed to tender vnto you (right Honourable and right Worshipfull) whatsoe the Lord hath vouchsafed me, whereof I haue had hope that it might help you in your gouernment and charges for the good of those poore people committed to you, and specially which might further the happy successe of that so much desired plantation . . . which, if after further triall made by you, it shall be as curteously accepted as it is heartily and cheerefully offered according to that which I haue receiued from the Lord, I shall haue not only some cause to blesse His heavenly Maiesty, but also be encouraged still to prosecute these poore trauels, and to study the further good of them all during life, especially for drawing the poor natiues in Virginia, and all other of the rest of the rude and barbarous from Sathan to God, and so rest

"Yours in all humble observance and hearty prayer to God for you,
"JOHN BRINSLEY."

The examiners to whom he alludes were "James Ussher, Doctour and Professor of Divinitie in Universitie of Dublin ; Daniel Featly, Doctour of Divinitie, and Chaplin in house to his Grace of Canterburie," who wrote their commendation March 15, 1620-21.

letter subscribed D. and A., brought to the former court by an unknown messenger, was now again presented to be read, the contents whereof are as follows :—

"'January 28, 1621.

"'Most Worthy Company,—Whereas I sent the Treasurer and yourselves a letter, subscribed "Dust and Ashes," which promised £550, and did, some time afterward, according to my promise, send the said money to Sir Edwin Sandys, to be delivered to the Company. In which letter I did not directly order the bestowing of the said money, but showed my interest for the conversion of infidels' children, as it will appear by that letter, which I desire may be read in open court, wherein I chiefly commend the ordering thereof to the wisdom of the honourable Company. And whereas the gentlemen of Southampton Hundred have undertaken the disposing of the said £550, I have long attended to see the erecting of some schools, or other way whereby some of the children of the Virginians might have been taught and brought up in the Christian religion and good manners, which are not being done according to my intent, but the money detained by a private Hundred all this while, contrary to my mind, though I judge very charitably of that honourable Society. And as already you have received a great and the most painfully gained part of my estate towards the laying of the foundation of the Christian religion, and helping forward of this pious work in that heathen, now Christian, land, so now I require of the whole body of the honourable and worthy Company, whom I entrusted with the disposal of said moneys, to see the same speedily and faithfully converted to the work intended. And I do further propound to your honourable Company, that if you will procure that some of the male children of the Virginians, though but a few, be brought over into England here to be educated and taught, and to wear a habit as the children of Christ's Hospital do, and that you will be pleased to see the £550 converted to this use, then I faithfully promise to add £450 more, to make the sum £1000, which, if God permit, I will cheerfully send you, only I desire to nominate the first tutor or governor who shall take charge to nurse and instruct them. But if you, in your wisdom, like not this motion, then my humble suit unto the whole body of your honourable Company is that my former gift of £550 be wholly employed and bestowed upon a free school to be erected in Southampton Hundred, so it be presently employed, or such other place as I or my friends shall well like, wherein both English and Virginians may be taught together, and that the said school be endowed with such privileges as you, in your wisdom, shall think fit. The master of which school, I humbly crave, may not be allowed to go over except he first bring to the Company sound testimony of his sufficiency in learning and sincerity of life.

"'The Lord give you wise and understanding hearts, that his work therein be not negligently performed.

"'D. AND A.

"'*The Right Honourable and Worthy the*
"'Treasurer, Council and Company of Virginia.'"

The letter being referred to the consideration of this court, forasmuch as it did require an account of this Company how they have expended the said money, viz., the £550 in gold for the bringing up of the infidels' children in true religion and Christianity, Sir Edwin Sandys declared that the said money coming unto him enclosed in a box in the time of his being treasurer, not long after a letter subscribed "Dust and Ashes" had been directed unto him in the quality of treasurer, and delivered in the court and there openly read. He brought the money also to the next court in the box unopened, whereupon the court, after a large and serious deliberation how the said money might be best employed to the use intended, at length resolved that it was fittest to be entertained by the Societies of Southampton Hundred and Martin's Hundred, and easy to undertake for a certain number of infidels' children to be brought up by them and amongst them in Christian religion, and some good trade to live by according to the donor's religious desire.

But Martin's Hundred desired to be excused by reason their plantation was sorely weakened and then in much confusion; wherefore it being pressed that Southampton Hundred should undertake the whole, they also considering, together with the weight, the difficulty also and hazard of the business, were likewise very unwilling to undertake the managing thereof, and offered an addition of £100 more unto the former sum of £550, that it might not be put upon them.

But being earnestly pressed thereunto by the court,

and finding no other means how to set forward that great work, yielded in fine to accept thereof.

Whereupon, soon after, at an assembly of that Society, the adventurers entered into a careful consideration how this great and mighty business might, with the most speed and great advantage, be effected.

Whereupon it was agreed and reported by them to employ the said money, together with an addition out of the Society's purse of a far greater sum, toward the furnishing out of Captain Bluett and his companions, being so very able and sufficient workmen, with all manner of provisions for the setting up of an ironwork in Virginia, whereof the profits arising were intended and ordered in a rateable proportion to be faithfully employed for the educating of thirty of the infidels' children in Christian religion, and otherwise as the donor had required.

To which end they writ very effectual letters unto Sir George Yeardley, then governor of Virginia, and captain also of Southampton plantation, not only commending the excellence of the work, but also furnishing him at large with advice and direction how to proceed therein, with a most earnest adjuration, and that often iterated in all their succeeding letters, so to employ his best care and industry therein, as a work wherein the eyes of God, angels, and men were fixed. The copy of my letter and direction, through some omission of their officer, was not entered in their book, but a course should be taken to have it recovered.

In answer of this letter they received a letter from Sir

George Yeardley, showing how difficult a thing it was at that time to obtain any of their children with the consent and good liking of their parents, by reason of their tenderness of them, or fear of hard usage by the English, unless it might be by a treaty with Opachankano, the King, which treaty was appointed to be that summer, wherein he would not fail to do his uttermost endeavours.

But Captain Bluett dying shortly after his arrival, it was a great setting back of the ironwork intended; yet since that time there had been orders to restore that business with a fresh supply, so as he hoped will the gentleman that gave this gift should receive good satisfaction by the faithful account which they should be able and at all times would be ready to give, touching the employment of the said money.

Concerning which Sir Edwin Sandys further said that, as he could not but highly commend the gentleman for his worthy and most Christian act, so he had observed so great inconvenience by his modesty and eschewing of show of vain glory by concealing his name, whereby they were deprived of the mutual help and advice which they might have had by conferring with him; and whereby also he might have received more clear satisfaction with what integrity, care, and industry they had managed that business, the success whereof must be submitted to the pleasure of God, as it had been commended to His blessing.

He concluded that if the gentleman would either vouchsafe himself or send any of his friends to confer with the said Society, they would be glad to apply themselves to give him all good satisfaction. But for his own particular judgment he doubted that neither of the two courses particularized in this last letter, now read in court, would attain the effect so much desired. Now, to send for them into England and to have them educated here, he found, upon experience of those brought by Sir Tho. Dale, might be far from the Christian work intended. Again, to begin with building of a free school for them in Virginia, he doubted, considering that none of the buildings they there intended had yet prospered, by reason that as yet, through their doting so much upon tobacco, no fit workman could be had but at intolerable rates, it might rather tend to the exhausting of this sacred treasure in some small fabric, than to accomplish such a foundation as might satisfy men's expectations.

Whereupon, he wished again some meeting between the gentleman or his friends and Southampton Society, that all things being debated at full, and judiciously weighed, some constant course might be resolved on, and pursued for proceeding in and perfecting of this most pious work, for which he prayed the blessing of God to be upon the author thereof; and all the Company said Amen.

In the midst of this narration a stranger stepped in, presenting four books fairly bound, sent from a person refusing to be named, who had bestowed them upon the college in Virginia, being from the same man that gave heretofore four other great books; the names of those he now sent were, viz.—a large Church Bible, the Common Prayer Book, Ursinus's Catechism, and a small Bible richly embroidered.

The court desired the messenger to return the gentleman that gave them, general acknowledgment of much respect and thanks due unto him.

A letter was also presented from one that desired not as yet to be named, with £25 in gold, to be employed by way of addition to the former contribution towards the building of a free school in Virginia, to make the other sum £125, for which the Company desired the messenger to return him their hearty thanks.

Mr. Copland moved that, whereas it was ordered by the last quarter court that an usher should be sent to Virginia, with the first convenience, to instruct the children in the free school there intended to be erected, that forasmuch as there was now a very good scholar whom he well knew, and had good testimony for his sufficiency in learning and good carriage, who offered himself to go for the performance of this service, he therefore thought good to acquaint the court therewith, and to leave it to their better judgment and consideration, whereupon the court appointed a committee, to treat with the said party, viz., Mr. Gibbs, Mr. Wroth, Mr. Wrote, Mr. Copland, Mr. Balmford, Mr. Roberts, who are to join herein with the rest of the committee and to meet about it upon Monday next, in the morning about eight, at Mr. Deputy's, and hereof to make report.

On February 27, 1621-2, the committee's report

touching the allowance granted unto the usher of the free school intended in Virginia being read, Mr. Copland signified that the said usher having lately imparted his mind unto him, seemed unwilling to go as usher or any less title than master of the said school, and also to be assured of that allowance that is intended to be appropriated to the master for his proper maintenance.

But it was answered that they might not swerve from the order of the quarter court, which did appoint the usher to be first established, for the better advancement of which action divers had underwritten to a roll for that purpose drawn, which did already arise to a good sum of money, and was like daily to increase by reason of men's affections to forward so good a work. In which respect many sufficient scholars did now offer themselves to go upon the same condition as had been proposed to this party, yet in favour of him, forsomuch as he was specially recommended by Mr. Copland, whom the company do much respect, the court is pleased to give him some time to consider of it between this and the next court, desiring then to know his direct answer, whether he will accept of the place of usher as has been offered unto him. And if he shall accept thereof, then the court have entreated Mr. Balmford, Mr. Copland, Mr. Caswell, Mr. Mollinge, to confer with him about the method of teaching, and the books he intends to instruct children by.

On the 13th of March the court, taking into their consideration certain propositions presented unto them by Mr. Copland in behalf of Mr. Dike, formerly commended for the usher's place in the free school intended at Charles City, in Virginia, they have agreed in effect unto his several requests, namely, that upon certificates from the governor of Virginia, of his sufficiency and diligence in training up of youth committed to his charge, he shall be confirmed in the place of the master of the said school.

Secondly, that if he can procure an expert writer to go over with him that can withal teach the grounds of arithmetic whereby to instruct the children in matters of account, the Company are contented to give such a one his passage, whose pains they doubt not will well be rewarded by those whose children shall be taught by him.

And for the allowance of one hundred acres of land he desires for his own proper inheritance, it is agreed that after he had served out his time, which is to be five years at least, and longer during his own pleasure, he giving a year's warning upon his remove, whereby another may be provided in his room, the Company are pleased to grant him one hundred acres.

It is also agreed that he shall be furnished with books, first for the school, for which he is to be accountable; and for the children the Company have likewise undertaken to provide good store of books, fitting for their use, for which their parents are to be answerable.

Lastly, it is ordered that the agreement between him and the Company shall, according to his own request, be set down in writing, by way of articles indented.

Upon the same day the following minute was entered on the journal of the Company :—

"Whereas Mr. Deputy acquainted the former court with that news he had received by word of mouth, of the safe arrival of eight of their ships in Virginia, with all their people and provisions sent out this last summer, he now signified that the general letter has come to his hands, imparting as much as had been formerly delivered, which letter for more particular relations did refer to the letters sent by the 'George,' which he hoped they should shortly hear of.

"Upon declaration of the Company's thankfulness unto God for the joyful and welcome news from Virginia, a motion was made that this acknowledgment of their thankfulness might not only be done in a private court, but published by some learned minister in a sermon to that purpose, before a general assembly of the Company, which motion was well approved of and thought fit to be taken into consideration upon return of the 'George,' which was daily expected, when they hoped they should receive more particular advertisement concerning their affairs in Virginia."

Early in April 1622, the following action was taken :—

"Forasmuch as the 'George' was now safe returned from Virginia, confirming the good news they had formerly received of the safe arrival of their ships and people in Virginia, sent this last time, it was now thought fit and resolved according to a motion formerly made to the like effect, that a sermon should be preached to express the Company's thankfulness unto God for this His great and extraordinary blessing.

"To which end the court entreated Mr. Copland, being present, to take the pains to preach the said sermon, being a brother of the Company, and one that was well acquainted with the happy success of their affairs in Virginia this last year.

"Upon which request, Mr. Copland was pleased to undertake it, and therefore two places being proposed where this exercise should be performed, namely, St. Michael's in Cornhill or Bowe Church, it was by erection of hands appointed to be in Bowe Church, on Wednesday next, being the 17th day of this present month of April, about 4 o'clock in the afternoon, for which purpose Mr. Carter is appointed to give notice of the time and place to all the Company."

CHAPTER IX.

COPLAND'S SERMON AT BOW CHURCH.

AFTER the great fire in London, Bow Church was altered and renovated by the celebrated architect, Sir Christopher Wren; but in 1622 it was a venerable time-stained pile, begun in the days of William the Conqueror, and the first in the city built on arches of stone, and hence called St. Marie de arcubus, then St. Mary-le-bow, and at length abbreviated by the busy Londoners into Bow Church. For more than a century the curfew, from its belfry, had been familiar to the citizens, and as it rung at nine o'clock, every apprentice tore himself away from the maiden he loved, or boon companions, and hurried home, fearing, if he was too late, that his unsympathizing master would meet him with a frown.

On Thursday, the 18th of April,[1] about four of the clock in the afternoon, the ringing of Bow Bell signified that there was to be a special service. The wealthy merchants of Lombard Street left the counting-rooms, and handsomely-dressed women, from the fashionable residences on St. Sythe's Lane, slowly moved, in sedans,

[1] The time of delivery was changed from Wednesday to Thursday.

toward this central church, to listen to the Thanksgiving sermon ordered by the Virginia Company, about to be preached by the eloquent and enthusiastic Copland. The text selected was most appropriate, consisting of that portion of the 107th Psalm from the twenty-second verse, describing the actions and feelings of sailors in a violent storm, and their joy at reaching a quiet haven.

He commenced by stating that the occasion of their assembling was to celebrate the goodness of God, and to give public thanks for the arrival of the fleet of nine ships in Virginia, during the last November and December, and the safe landing of eight hundred men, women, and children. In unfolding the text, he spoke of their dangers, deliverance, and consequent duty. In alluding to the dangers of mariners, his sentences were graphic:—

"It is next to famine, imprisonment, and a deadly disease to be a seaman; for as one saith, '*Navigantes neque inter vivos neque inter mortuos*,' sailors are neither amongst the living nor yet amongst the dead, as, having but a few inches of plank between them and death, they hang between both, ready to offer up their souls to every flaw of wind and billow of water wherein they are tossed. The immoveable rocks, and the mutable winds; the overflowing waters and swallowing sands; the tempestuous storms and spoiling pirates, have their lives at their mercy and command. Mariners, living in the sea almost, as fishes, having the waters as their necessariest element, are commonly men void of fear, venturous, and contemners of dangers; yet when God, on a sudden, commandeth a storm, and sitteth himself in the mouth of the tempest, when their ship is foundred with water under them; when life and soul are ready to shake hands and depart this present world, then even these nought-fearing fellows, these high-stomaked men, tremble for fear, like faint-hearted women, that shrink at every stir in a wherry on the River of Thames, in a rough and boisterous tide, or like unto a young soldier, which starteth at the shooting off of a gun."

After he spoke of the dangers of mariners, he continued:—

"But you will say, what needeth all this discourse touching the danger of sea-men: we are met together for another purpose—to giue thanks vnto God? Beloved, I doe confesse, indeed it is so, that the end of our present meeting is for Thankesgiuing. But how can we euer be feelingly thankfull as we should, in word and deed, if wee know not the danger wherein wee are, and the deliuerance vouchsafed vnto us? Will not the true knowledge and deepe consideration of these make vs put so many the more thankes vnto our sacrifice of prayse?

"Wherefore, I beseech you to take to heart—*First*, the danger of your people in their passages both to Virginia and after their landing. *Secondly*, the danger of your whole colony there. *Thirdly*, the danger of yourselues here at home. And lest others that are not of your Honourable Company may thinke this point impertinent to them, let all of us consider the dangers wherein we are, and still are, and the many deliuerances vouchsafed vnto us (for I must intreat you to giue me leave to joyne danger and deliuerance together, for the better stirring of you up to your dvtie. And then I doubt not but all of vs shall have cause to confesse before the Lord his louing-kindnesse and his wonderfull workes before the sonnes of men.

"And, first, to touch the danger of your people both in their passage to Virginia and after their landing there, may I not say, in the words of Job, 'Will yee giue the words of him that is afflicted to the winde?' As if he had said, when affliction itselfe, and the inmost sorrowes of my heart tell my tale, will you regard it? O! that your soules were in my soule's stead, that you felt as much sorrow as I doe. *Loquor in angustia mea, queror in amaritu animæ meæ*, I speake that that I speake from a world of trouble, I make my complaint in the bitternesse of my soule. Surely, if some hundreds of those that miscarried in the infancie, and at the first beginning of your Plantation (which is exceedingly bettered in these two yeeres), were now aliue, I thinke they would speake no otherwise than Job spake: Wil you giue the words of thē that are afflicted to the winde? Will ye not beleeue in what danger we were when some of vs made shipwracke vpon the supposed inchanted Ilands; when others of vs encountred with bloudie enemies in the West Indies; when many of us dyed by the way; and when those that were left aliue, some perished ashore for want of comfortable prouisions and looking vnto, and others were killed with the bowes and arrowes of the savages, vpon our first landing there? I presume I speake to melting hearts of flesh, as tenderly sensible of your brethren's woe, as heartily thankful for your owne good.

"And now, Beloved, since the case is altered, that all difficulties are swallowed vp. And seeing first, there is no danger by the way; neither through encountring of enemy or pyrate; nor meeting with rockes, or sholes (all which to sea-faring men are very dangerous, and from all which your ships and people are farre remoued, by reason of their faire and safe passage through the maine Ocean); nor through the tediousnesse of the passage, the fittest season of the yeare for a speedie passage being now farre better knowne than before, and by that meanes the passage itselfe made almost in so many weekes as formerly it was wont to be made in moneths, which I conceiue to be through the blessing of God, the maine cause of the safe arriual of your last fleete of nine sayle of ships that not one (but one, in whose roome there was another borne) of eight hundred, which were transported out of England and Ireland[1] for your Plantation, should miscarry by the way; whereas, in your former voyages, scarce 80 of a 100 arrived safely in Virginia.

"And, secondly, seeing there is no danger after their landing, either through warres, or famine, or want of

[1] Ireland has always been a hive from which America has derived sturdy hewers of wood to subdue the forests. On April 12, 1621, William Newce, of county Cork, offered to transport two thousand persons to Virginia. Soon after, Daniel Gookin, of county Cork, brother of Sir Vincent Gookin, transported cows and goats from Ireland. Newce and Gookin both settled in Virginia. The former died a few days after his arrival; the latter was living at Newport News at the time of the massacre in spring of 1622, and his descendants are now numerous in United States of America.

conuenient lodging and looking to, through which many miscarried heretofore, for, blessed be God, there hath beene a long time, and still is, a happie league of peace and amitie, soundly concluded and faithfully kept, betweene the English and the Natiues, that the fear of killing each other is now vanished away. Besides, there is now in your Plantation plentie of good and wholesome provisions, for the strength and comfort not onely of the Colony, but also of all such as after their passage doe land ashore. There is also conuenient lodging and carefull attendance prouided for them till they can prouide for themselues, and a faire Inne for recciuing and harbouring them in James Cittie, to the setting up of which both your worshipfull Governour, Sir Francis Wyat, and your worthie Treasurer, Master George Sands,[1] doe write, that they doubt not but there will be raised betweene fifteene hundred and two thousand pounds, to which every man contributeth cheerfully and bountifully, they being all free-hearted and open-handed

[1] In 1621, Christopher Davison, second son of Sir William Davison, and brother of the poets, Walter and Francis, was elected Secretary, and George Sandys, brother of the President of the London Company, was elected treasurer. Before he left England the latter published a translation of five books of Ovid, to which Drayton alluded in a rhyming letter:—

"And worthy George, by industry and use,
Let's see what lines Virginia will produce;
Go on with Ovid, as you have begun
With the first five books ; let y'r numbers run
Glib as the former, so shall it live long,
And do much honour to the English tongue."

While in America, he translated the remaining books, and the whole was published in folio, with illustrations, in 1626, at London. A sixth and pocket edition appeared in 1669. He lived to be an old man, and died at the house of his niece, the widow of Governor Wyatt. In the register of Bexley Abbey is this entry :—" Georgius Sandys, Poetarum Anglorum sui sœculi facile princeps, sepultus fuit Martii 7 stilo Anglic. An. Dom. 1643."

to all publique, good workes. Seeing, I say, that now all former difficulties (which much hindered the progresse of your noble Plantation) are remoued, and, in a manner, ouercome: And that your people in your colony (through God's mercy) were all in good health, euery one busied in their vocations, as bees in their hiues, at the setting saile of your ship, the 'Concord,' from Virginia, in March last, O what miracles are these? O what cause haue you and they to confesse before the Lord his louing-kindnesse, and his wonderfull workes before the sonnes of men!

"But, to passe from the danger and deliuerance of your people, who indangered, yea, lost their liues in setting up your Plantation, consider, I beseech you, *in the second place*, the danger wherein your colony stood at the time of Sir Thomas Gates arriving in Virginia from the Summer Ilands,[1] when it was concluded a few days after his landing, by himself, Sir George Summers, Captaine Newport, and the whole Counsell, by the general approbation of all, to abandon the Colony (because of the want of provisions), and to make for New-found-land, and so for England. And will not the hopefull setling of your Colony there, now under the government of a worthy and worshipfull Commander,[2]

---

[1] Arrived May 21, 1610.

[2] Governor Francis Wyatt was the son of George Wyatt, who died in Ireland. He was nominated to the office by the Earl of Southampton. The MS. Transactions of London Company state:—"His Lordship proposed unto the Company a gentleman recommended unto him for his many good parts, namely, Sir Francis Wyatt, who was well reputed of, both in respect of his parentage, good education, integritie of life, and faire fortunes, being his father's eldest sonne, as also for his sufficiency otherwise, being euery

and a wise and wel-experienced Counsell, stirre you up to confesse before the Lord his louing-kindnesse, and his wonderfull workes before the sonnes of men?

"But if neither the danger of your people, nor the danger of your whole Colony abroad, and the deliuerance vouchsafed to them both be enough to stirre you up to confesse before the Lord His louing-kindnesse; then, I beseech you, *in the third place*, to consider the danger of your own selues here at home, and what masse of money have you buried in that Plantation? How many of you had it not made to wish that you had never put your hand to this plough? Nay, how many of you had it not made to shrinke in your shoulders; and to sinke (as it were) vnder the burden, and to be quite out of hope for euer seeing penny of that you had so largely debursed?

"And now, Beloued, is not the case altered? Are not your hopes great of seeing, nay, of feeling within a few years of double, treble, yea, I may say, of tenfold for one?

"Do not all of you know what that religious and judicious overseer of your College lands there writeth unto you from thence?[1] 'No man,' sayeth he, 'can

---

way, without exception, fitting for this place." In 1626 Wyatt returned to England. In 1639 he was re-appointed Governor, but was soon succeeded by Berkeley. He died in 1644, and was buried at Bexley, in Kent. His mother was Eleanora, daughter of Sir John Finch; his wife Margaret, the child of Samuel Sandys.

Chamberlain, in a letter to Sir Dudley Carleton, dated 19th June 1623, writes:—

"An unruly son of the Lady Finch's, whom she sent to Virginia to be trained, within five or six days after his return, fell into a quarrel with the watch, and was so hurt he died the next morning."

[1] George Thorpe's letter from James City, dated May 17, 1621.

justly say that this country is not capable of all those good things that you in your wisedomes, with great charge, have projected, both for her wealth and honour, and also all other good things that the most opulent parts of Christendome do afford, neither are we hopeless that this country may also yield things of better value than any of those.'

"And surely, by that which I have heard and seene abroad in my travailing to India and Japan, I am confirmed in the truth of that which he doth write; for Japan, lying in the same latitude that Virginia doth—and if there be any ods, Virginia hath them, as lying more southerly than Japan doth—Japan, I say, lying under the same latitude that Virginia doth, aboundeth with all things for profit and pleasure, being one of the mightiest and opulentest Empires in the world, having in it many rich mines of gold and silver.

"And had you not a taste of some marchantable commodities sent vnto you from Virginia some yeeres agoe, whilest that worshipfull and worthy Governour, Sir Thomas Dale, sent home vnto you samples of aboue a dossen seuerall good commodities from thence? Have you not now great hopes of abundance of corne, wine, oyle, lemmons, oranges, pomegranats, and all maner of fruites pleasant to the eye and wholesome for the belly? And of plentie of silke, silke-grasse, cotton, wooll, flax, hemp, &c., for the backe? Are you not already possessed with rich mines of copper and yron, and are not your hopes great of farre richer minerals?

"Have you not read what of late your worthie Treasurer[1] doth write unto you? 'If' (sayth hee) 'we overcome this yeere the Iron-workes, Glasse-workes, Salt-workes; take order for the plentifull setting of corne, restraine the quantitie of tobacco, and mend it in the qualitie, plant vines, mulberry-trees, fig-trees, pomegranats, potatoes, cotton-wooles; and erect a faire Inne in James Citie (to the setting up of which I doubt not but wee shall raise fifteene hundred or two thousand pounds, for every man gives willingly towards this and other public works), you have enough for this yeere.'

"And a little after, in the same letter, 'Maister Pory[2]

---

[1] George Sandys' letter of March 3, 1621-2.

[2] John Pory was a graduate of Cambridge, a protégé of Hakluyt, a great traveller and good writer, but gained the reputation of being a chronic tippler, and literary vagabond and sponger. A letter-writer on August 11, 1612, says:—"It is long since I heard of Master Pory, but now at last understand he lies lieger at Paris, maintained by the Lord Carew."

Sir Dudley Carleton wrote on July 9, 1613, from Venice:—"Master Pory is come to Turin with purpose to see those parts, but wants *primum necessarium*, and hath, therefore, conjured me with these words—*by the kind and constant intelligence which passeth betwixt you and my best friends in England*—to send him fourteen doubloons, wherewith to disengage him, where he lies in pawn, not knowing how to go forward or backward. I have done more in respect of his friends than himself, for I hear he is fallen too much in love with the pot to be much esteemed, and have sent him what he wrote for by Matthew, the post."

A correspondent of Carleton wrote on August 1 of the same year:—"You had not need meet with many such poor moths as Master Pory, who must have both *meat* and *money*, for *drink* he will find out himself, if it be *above* ground, or no deeper than the *cellar*."

In 1619, he was made Secretary of the Colony of Virginia, and after his recall (on account of his intolerable fees), while returning to England, he stopped at the infant Plymouth settlement, and had pleasant intercourse with Governor Bradford and William Brewster, with whom he may have been acquainted in Holland, and received from them some books, which he esteemed as "jewels," he says, in a note to Bradford, dated August 28, 1622, and signed, "Your unfeigned and firm friend." (See Bradford's *New Plymouth*.)

A letter from London, dated July 26, 1623, says:—"Our old acquaintance, deserves good incouragement for his painefull discoveries to the southward, as far as the Choanoack, who, although he hath trod on a little good ground, hath past through great forests of pynes, 15 or 16 myle broad, and above 60 mile long, which will serve well for masts for shipping, and for pitch and tarr, when we shall come to extend our Plantation to those borders.

"'On the other side of the river there is a fruitfull countrie, blessed with aboundance of corne, reaped twise a yeare; aboue which is the copper mines, by all of all places generally affirmed. Hee hath also met with a great deale of silke-grass, which grows there monethly, of which Maister Harriot hath affirmed in print, many yeeres ago, that it will make silke grow-graines, and of which and cotton wooll all the Cambaya and Bengala stuffes are made in the East Indies.'

"Heard you not with your own eares what Mr. John Martin, an Armenian by birth (that hath lived now six or seven yeeres in Virginia, and is but very lately come from thence, who also far preferre Virginia to England, to returne thither againe with this resolution

Mr. Pory, is in poor case, and in prison at the Terceras, whither he was driven by contrary winds, from the north coast of Virginiau, where he had been upon some discovery, and upon his arrival, was arraigned and in danger to be hanged for a pirate."

On his arrival in London, he associated with the disaffected minority of the Virginia Company, who succeeded in arousing the prejudices of the King, so as to deprive them of the government of the Colony.

In 1624, he was one of a commission appointed by order of James to proceed to Virginia, and report upon its condition. At Jamestown he displayed a lack of honour in bribing Edward Sharpless, clerk of the council, to give him a copy of their proceedings, for which the perjured clerk was made by the Virginians to stand in the pillory and lose an ear.

there to live and die), said, in the audience of your whole Court, the 8th of this instant? I have travailed, said he, by land, over eighteen several kingdomes, and yet all of them, in my minde, come farr short of Virginia."[1]

In concluding the second head of the discourse—the deliverances from danger,—he referred to an event which had been much talked of by the members of the Virginia Company.

"I will fear no evill, saith David, neither great nor small; for it is all one with God to deliver from the greater stormes as well as the lesser. Some difference there is, indeed, of *dangers*, and *deliverances* out of them, but it is only such as in books printed on large, and lesse letter and paper, the matter not varying at all. For example, when God brought some of the ships of your former fleetes to Virginia in safty, here God's providence was seen and felt priuately by some; and this was a deliuerance written, as it were, in *quarto*, on a lesser paper and letter. But now, when God brought all of your nine ships, and all your people in them, in safty and health to Virginia; yea, and that ship Tyger[2]

---

[1] Besides Martin, the Armenian, Molasco, a Polonian, was a member of the Virginia Company.

[2] The ships "Warwick" and "Tiger" left the Thames about the middle of September 1621, and carried maids and young women for wives. A MS. letter from the London Company says:—

"By this ship ['Warwick'] and pinnace called the 'Tiger' we also send as many maids and young women as will make up the number of fifty, with those twelve formerly sent in the 'Marmaduke,' which we hope shall be received with the same Christian piety and charity as they were sent from hence. . . . The adventurers for the charges disbursed in setting them forth, which, coming to twelve pounds, they require one hundred and fifty of yours, which had fallen into the hands of the Turkish men-of-war, through tempest and contrary windes, she not being able to beare sayle, and by that meanes driuen out of her course some hundreds of miles; for otherwise, of itselfe, the passage from *England to Virginia* is out of the walke of Turkes, and cleere and safe from all pyrates who commonly lurke neere ilands and head-lands, and not in the maine ocean. When this your Tyger had falne (by reason of this storme, and some indiscretion of her master and people, who, taking the Turkes to have been Flemmings bound for Holland or England, bore up the helme to speak with them; for they needed not, if they had listed, to have come near the Turkes, but have proceeded safely on their voyage,) into the hands of those mercilesse Turkes, who had taken from them most of their victuals, and all of their service-able sayles, tackling, and anchors, and had not so much as left them an houre-glasse or compasse to steere their course, thereby utterly disabling them from going from them and proceeding on their voyage; when I say God had ransomed her out of their hands, as the prophet speaketh, by another sayle which they espyed, and brought her likewise safely to Virginia, with all her people, two English boys only excepted, for which the Turkes gaue them two others, a French youth, and an Irish, was not here the presence of God printed, as it were, in *Folio*, on Royall Crowne paper, and Capitall Letters?"

of the best leaf tobacco for each of them. . . . Their own good deserts, together with your favour and care, will, we hope, marry them all unto honest and sufficient men."

The discourse ended by urging two steps for the welfare of Virginia. First, to send faithful and approved preachers, and not such as "offer themselves hand-over-head."[1] He did not wish them to encourage men like those who had pressed themselves upon the East India Company, one of whom is described in their minutes as a man "of straggling humor, can frame himself to all company, and delighteth in tobacco and wine."[2]

In the second place, he exhorted them to "send over skilfull and painefull tradesmen and husbandmen, to follow their trades and cultivate the ground. Our Countrey aboundeth with people; your Colony wanteth them. You all know that there is nothing more dangerous for the estate of commonwealths than when the people doe increase to a greater number and multitude than may justly parallell with the largenesse of the place and country in which they liue. For even as bloud, though it be the best humour in the body, yet if it abound in greater quantitie then the vessell and state of the body will contayne and beare, doth indanger the body, and oftentimes destroy it; so, although the honour of a king be in the multitude of people, as wise King Solomon speaketh, yet when this multitude of people increaseth to ouer great a number, the commonwealth stands subject to many perilous inconveniences—as famine, pouerty, and sundry other sorts of calamities.

"Thus, hauing falne into this point of exalting God in the congregation of the people, and the assembly of

[1] *Virginia's God be Thanked*, p. 29. [2] Cal. State Papers. East Indies.

the elders, I haue here good occasion offered to mee to blesse God for the *prudence* and *prouidence* of this honourable Lord Maior, and the right worshipfull the Aldermen, his brethren; who, seeing this Cittie to be mightily increased, and fearing lest the ouerflowing multitude of inhabitants should, like too much blood, infect the whole Cittie with plague and pouertie, haue therefore deuised, in their great wisdomes, a remedy for this malady—to wit: the transporting of their ouerflowing multitude into Virginia, which was first put in practise in the Maioraltie of that worthy and famous Lord Maior, Sir George Bowles, who sent ouer a hundred persons, the halfe of this charge being borne by the Citie, the other half by the Honourable Virginia Company, which worthy course was afterwards followed by the right worshipfull Sir William Cockins, in whose Maioraltie were sent ouer a hundred more in the like manner. And now likewise the right Honourable the present Lord Maior and worshipfull the Aldermen, his brethren, intend to continue this course, that they may ease the Citie of a many that are ready to starue, and do starue dayly in our streetes.[1] . . . Right

---

[1] William Cockaine was a distinguished merchant; sheriff in 1609; chief of the new company of merchant adventurers, which gave King James a great banquet on June 22, 1609, at his house, and there knighted. He died in 1626, and the distinguished poet and divine, John Donne, preached his funeral sermon.

In June 1621, the company wrote to the authorities in these words, relative to homeless boys and girls of London :—

"To the Right Honorable Sir William Cockaine, knight lord mayor of the city of London, and the right worthys the aldermen, his brethren, and the worthys the common council of the city :—

". The treasurer, council, and company of Virginia, assembled in their great

Worshipfull, ye are plentifull in other good workes, the maintaining of your hospitals, and other publike workes in this famous Cittie; preach your munificence through all the world, as the faith and obedience of the Romans was published abroad among all. O be rich in welldoing this way likewise, that it may be sayd of you, 'Many have done worthily for the plantation in Virginia, but the honourable Citty of London surmounteth them all.' Your Cittie, as I sayd, aboundeth in people (and long may it doe so), the Plantation in Virginia is capable enough to receive them. O, take course to ease your Cittie, and to prouide well for your people, by sending them ouer thither; that both they of that Colony there and they of your owne Cittie here may

and general court the 17th of November 1613, have taken into consideration the continual great forwardness of this honourable city in advancing the plantation of Virginia, and particularly in furnishing out one hundred children this last year, which, by the goodness of God, have safely arrived (save such as died in the way), and are well pleased, we doubt not, for this benefit, for which, your bountiful assistance, we, in the name of the whole plantation, do yield unto you deserved thanks.

"And forasmuch as we have now resolved to send this next spring very large supplies for the strength and increasing of the colony, styled by the name of the London colony, and find that the sending of these children to be apprenticed hath been very grateful to the people, we pray your lordship and the rest, pursuit of your former so precious actions, to renew the like favours, and furnish us again with one hundred more for the next spring.

"Our desire is that we may have them of 12 years old and upward, with allowance of £3 apiece for their transportation, and 40s. apiece for their apparel, as was formerly granted. They shall be apprenticed; the boys till they come to 21 years of age; the girls till like age, or till they be married, and afterward they shall be placed as tenants upon the public lands, with best conditions, where they shall have houses with stock of corn and cattle to begin with, and afterward the moiety of all increase and profit whatsoever.

"And so we leave this motion to your honourable and grave consideration."

The following letter of Sir Edwin Sandys, to one of the King's secretaries,

liue to bless your prudent and prouident gouernment ouer them. For I haue heard many of the painfullest labourers of your Cittie, euen with teares, bemoane the desolate estate of their poore wiues and children, who, though they rise early, taw and teare their flesh all the day long with hard labour, and goe late to bed, and feede almost all the week long vpon browne bread and cheese, yet are scarce able to put bread in their mouthes at the weeke's end, and cloathes on their backes at the yeare's end; and all because worke is so hard to be come by, and there be so many of the same trade, that they cannot thriue one for another.

"Right Worshipfull, I beseech you, ponder (as I know you doe) the forlorne estate of many of the best members of your Citty, and helpe them, O helpe them, out of their misery: what you bestow vppon them in

Sir Robert Naunton, shows that the children were not always willing to embark:—

"The city of London have appointed one hundred children from the superfluous multitude to be transported to Virginia, there to be bound apprentices upon very beneficial conditions. They have also granted £500 for their passage and outfit. Some of the ill-disposed children, who, under severe masters in Virginia, may be brought to goodness, and of whom the city is specially desirous to be disburdened, declare their unwillingness to go. The city wanting authority to deliver, and the Virginia Company to transport these children against their will, desire higher authority to get over the difficulty." (Cal. State Papers, Colonial Series.)

Another paper will throw some light on the abuses in this business:—
"*Sir Edward Hext, Justice of the Peace of Somersetshire,
to the Privy Council:*

"Upon complaint that Owen Evans, messenger of the Chamber, had a pretended commission to press maidens to be sent to Virginia and the Bermudas, and received money thereby, he issued a warrant for his apprehension. Evans' undue proceedings bred such terror to the poor maidens that forty have fled from one parish to obscure places, and their parents do not know what has become of them."

their transportation to Virginia they will repay it at present with their prayers, and when they are able with their purses; and God, in the meanewhile, will plentifully reward your liberalitie this way, with His blessing vpon your famous Citie, vpon your selues, vpon your posteritie.

"And that I may bend my speech vnto all, seeing so many of the Lord's Worthies haue done worthily in this noble action; yea, and seeing that some of them greatly rejoyce in this, that God hath inabled them to helpe forward this glorious worke, both with their prayers and with their purses, let it be your greife and sorrow to be exempted from the company of so many honourable minded men, and from this noble Plantation, tending so highly to the advancement of the Gospell, and to the honouring of our drad Soueraigne, by inlarging of his kingdomes, and adding a fifth crowne unto his other foure: for 'En dat Virginia quintam' is the motto of the legal seale of Virginia.[1]

"And let mee in a word shut up all, vnto you all, that hath been spoken with that exhortation of the Apostle: My beloved brethren, be yee stedfast, vnmoueable, aboundant always in the worke of the Lord; for as much as you know that your labour is not in vaine in the Lord."

London has at length received its reward for the liberality shown in transportation of the destitute to America. George Peabody, the descendant of an honest immigrant to North Virginia, died toward the

[1] On October 20, 1619, the Company appointed a Committee to meet at Sir Edwin Sandys', "to take a cote for Virginia, and agree upon the Seale." On the 15th of the next month the device was presented for inspection.

The face of the legal seal was an escutcheon, quartered with the arms of

close of the year 1869, having given £500,000 to the poor of that city. After a solemn service in Westminster Abbey, his embalmed body was carried in honour by a British man-of-war, escorted by another bearing the American flag, to his native land, and after landing, the remains of the plain American citizen were followed to their resting-place in the quiet village cemetery by Prince Arthur, the son of Her Majesty, Victoria, Queen of the United Kingdom of Great Britain and Ireland, with some of the highest in rank of the army and navy, the distinguished in science and letters, and most eminent of the public men of the United States of America.[1]

A few weeks after its delivery, the discourse was published with the following title :—

England, France, Scotland, and Ireland ; crested with a maiden Queen, with flowing hair and eastern crown ; supporters, two men in armour.

Spenser, Sir Walter Raleigh's friend, dedicated his *Fairy Queen* to Elizabeth, "Queen of England, France, Ireland, and Virginia." After James of Scotland became King of England, Virginia could be called, in compliment, the fifth kingdom.

[1] "2d April, 1635, embarked on board the 'Planter,' of London; Nicholas Trarine, Master; bound for New England, bringing a certificate from the Minister of St. Alban's, County Herts, and attested by the Justices of the Peace, Francis Peboddy, aged 21 years, husbandman."—*Notes and Queries*, Feb. 12, 1870.

VIRGINIA'S GOD BE THANKED

OR

A SERMON OF

THANKSGIUING

FOR THE HAPPIE

successe of the affayres in

VIRGINIA this last

yeare

Preached by PATRICK COPLAND at
Bow-Church, in *Cheapside*, before the Honorable
VIRGINIA COMPANY, on Thursday, the 18
of *Aprill* 1622. And now published by
the Commandement of the said honorable COMPANY.

Hereunto are adjoyned some Epistles,
written first in Latine (and now Englished) in
the East Indies by *Peter Pope*, an Indian youth,
borne in the Bay of Bengala, who was first taught
and converted by the said P. C. And after baptized by Master *John Wood*, Dr. in Divinitie
*in a famous Assembly, before the Right
Worshipfull, the East India Company*,
at S. *Denis* in Fan-Church Streete
in *London*, December 22,
1616.

LONDON

Printed by J. D. for *William Sheffard* and John Bellamie,
and are to be sold at his shop at the two Greyhounds in Corne-hill, neere the Royall
Exchange. 1622.

Prefixed to the Sermon is the following epistle from Copland, occupying three pages of the original pamphlet, which, as far as possible, is here reproduced.

TO

THE RIGHT

NOBLE AND HO-

NORABLE EARLES, BARONS

And Lords; And to the right worshipfull *Knights, Merchants, and Gentlemen*, Adventurers for the Plantation in VIRGINIA; all happinesse, external, internall, and eternall, in Christ Jesus our blessed SAUIOUR.

AFTER I had discharged the charge laid upon me by your Honourable and Worshipfull Court, and was presently after sollicited by some of your Honourable Societie, to present to the eye, what I had deliuered to the eare. Though at first I was indeed very vnwilling, at their intreatie: yet, being commanded by your Honourable Court to publish what before you had intreated mee to Preach, and weighing well with my selfe, that words spoken, are soone come, soone gone; but that written withall, they make a deeper impression; for, by striking as well the Eye of the Reader, as the Eare of the Hearer, they peirce his heart the better, and saue his soule the sooner. Hereupon that I might testifie how much I honour your lawful commandements, and withall, that I might confirme with my Pen, that grace, which it pleased God to worke by my Voyce, I have now yeelded to all of your Requests, making that common to all, which then was imputed to your Honourable Court, and loue to your Noble Plantation. For seeing many of your Noble and worthy Company have spent a great part of their painefully gained estates vpon this honourable Action, and reioice in nothing more than in this, that God hath giuen them a price in their hand, and a heart to use it for the furthering of this glorious Worke; How could I, at so earnest intreatie refuse to aduenture this mite of mine, among so many worthie adventures of theirs? How could I (I say) refuse to make their publique *Bountie* and your publique Thanksgiuing, yet more publique?

If your Honours will be pleased to take in good part what now I impart; it may proue a spurre vnto me, to vndertake some better piece of seruice for the good of your noble Plantation; at least, if it lie in my poor power to bring it to passe. Thus intreating your Honours fauourable acceptance, I rest

In all humble dutie
to be commanded,

London, this 22 of
May 1622.

P. C.

CHAPTER X.

COPLAND'S RESIDENCE AT BERMUDAS; AND THE EDUCATIONAL DEVELOPMENT OF AMERICA.

THE effect of the Sermon in Bow Church was most happy. Increased interest in the welfare of the colony was manifested by the London people, and the Company resolved to push on the work of education with vigour.

In the month of June there sailed from England Leonard Hudson a carpenter, his wife, and five apprentices, for the purpose of erecting the East India school at Charles city.

The governor and council of Virginia were at the same time informed, that as the Company had failed to secure an usher, upon second consideration it was thought good to give the colony the choice of the schoolmaster or usher, if there was any suitable person for the office. If they could find no one, they were requested to inform them what they would contribute toward the support of a schoolmaster, and they would then again strive to provide "an honest and sufficient man." The letter concludes by saying, "there is very much in this business that we must leave to your care and wisdom, and the help and assistance of good people, of which we doubt not."

On July 3, 1622, the court gave order that a receipt should be sealed for £47, 16s., which the gentleman mariners had given to the East India Company to be employed in laying the foundation of a church in Virginia.

The court thought fit to make Captain Martin Pring (the captain of the 'Royal James') a freeman of the Company, and to give him two shares of land in regard of the large contribution which the gentlemen and mariners of that ship had given towards good works in Virginia, whereof he was an especial furtherer.

The placing and entertainment of Mr. Copland in Virginia being referred by the former court to the consideration of a committee, they having accordingly advised about it, did now make report of what they had done therein, as followeth, viz. :—

1. First, they thought fit that he be made rector of the intended college in Virginia for the conversion of the infidels, and to have the pastoral charge of the college tenants about him.

2. In regard of his rectorship, to have the tenth part of the profits due to the college out of their lands and arising from the labours of their tenants.

3. In regard of his pastoral charge, to have a parsonage there erected, according to the general order for parsonages.

And for that it was now further moved that he might be admitted of the council, then it was referred to the former committee to consider thereof and of some other things propounded for his better accommodation there.

The committee appointed for the college for this present year are the ensuing, viz. :—Sir Edwin Sandys, Sir John Danvers, Mr. Gibbs, Mr. J. Ferrar, Mr. R. Smith, Mr. Wrote, Mr. Barbor.

The report of the committee touching Mr. Copland's placing and entertainment in Virginia was now read, they having thought fit he be made rector of the intended college there for the conversion of the infidels, and to have the pastoral charge of the college there for the conversion of the infidels, and to have the pastoral charge of the college tenants about him; and in regard of his rectorship, to have the tenth part of the profits due to the college out of the lands and arising from the labours of their tenants; and in respect of his pastoral charge, to have a parsonage there erected according to the general order for parsonages which this court hath well approved of; and have likewise admitted him to be one of the council of Virginia.

A few days after the election of Copland as Rector of the College, but before he could make arrangements to leave, a tale of horror spread like wild-fire through the streets of London, the hearing of which made the "hair of the flesh to stand up," and froze the hearts of those who had been devising good things for Virginia.

A ship arrived from America with the horrible tidings, that at the very hour they were engaged in public thanksgiving for the happy league of peace with the

Indians[1] at Bow Church, the Colony was a scene of desolation. The treacherous Indians on Good Friday had risen, and simultaneously attacked the several settlements, and killed nearly three hundred and fifty persons.

Among the mutilated bodies of the slain was that of the refined and educated gentleman, George Thorpe, who had the oversight of the college lands and tenants. After the Company received intelligence of his death, they made a particular request that George Sandys, the brother of Sir Edwin, a poet and translator of the Metamorphosis of Ovid, then Treasurer of the Colony, should take charge of the college interests;[2] and they wrote: "we esteem the college affairs not only a public but a sacred business." After this we know of but one allusion to the college. In 1623, Edward Downes petitioned "that his son Richard Downes, having continued in Virginia these four years, and being bred a scholar, went over in search of preferments in the college there,

---

[1] See page 149.

[2] In the dedication of the completed translation of Ovid to Charles the First, Sandys alludes to his residence as a Colonial Official in Virginia. He writes—"Your gracious acceptance of the first-fruit of my travels, when you were our hope, as now our happiness, hath actuated both will and power to the finishing of this piece: being limn'd by that unperfect light, which was snatcht from the hours of the night and repose; for the day was not mine, but dedicated to the service of your great father and your self; which, had it proved as fortunate, as faithful in me and others more worthy, we had hoped, ere many years had turned about, to have presented you with a rich and well-peopled kingdom, from whence now, with myself, I only bring this composure: 'Inter victrices hederam tibi serpere laurus.' It needeth more than a single denization, being a double stranger, sprung from the stocke of the ancient Romans, but *bred in the New World, of the rudeness whereof it cannot but participate; especially having wars and tumults to bring it to light,* instead of the Muses."

might now be free to live there of himself, and have fifty acres of land."

One year after the dissolution of the Virginia Company, in 1624, another attempt was made to erect the East India free school. Mr. Caroloff and others were sent over for the purpose, but he seems to have become unpopular. The governor and council, under date of June 15, 1625, write :—

"We should be ready with our utmost endeavours to assist the pious work of the East India free school, but we must not dissemble that, besides the unseasonable arrival, we thought the acts of Mr. Caroloff will overbalance all his other sufficiency though exceeding good."

A year before Copland made the collection on board of the "Royal James" for the benefit of Virginia, a company of English Nonconformists that had been residing at Leyden landed on the Atlantic coast, several degrees north of Jamestown, and commenced a settlement called New Plymouth. From that time there were two distinct waves of immigration, the educated and religious preferring the Northern, because King James had made the Southern a penal colony.[1] Early in 1620 the first large instalment of vagabonds and destitute persons arrived in Virginia, and yearly their

---

[1] Wroth published the same year the following lines in his *Abortive of an Idle Hour* :—

> "They say a new plantation is intended,
> Neere or about the Amazonian River,
> But sure that mannish race is now quite ended.
> O that Great Jove, of all good gifts the giver,
> Would move King James, once more, to store that clyme
> With the moll cut-purses of our bad time."

numbers increased, and the desire for schools and churches proportionally decreased.

The social position of the settlers in the northern colony had been far superior. Humphrey, the first Deputy-Governor of Massachusetts, was the son-in-law of the amiable and cultivated Countess of Lincoln, and another of her daughters, Lady Arbella, had married one of the settlers at Salem.

Although the project of Henrico College in Virginia was not carried out, an institution of learning was planted at Cambridge, in New England, called Harvard, after a clergyman, who was one of its earliest benefactors. It soon began to graduate scholars, and upon the restoration of monarchy in England, one of its alumni became a chaplain of Charles the Second. At this period, too, there were thirty or forty graduates of Oxford and Cambridge in the pulpits of Massachusetts and Connecticut, and not more than three or four educated clergymen in Virginia. The year after the accession of Charles the Second a pamphlet was written by a clergyman who had lived in Virginia, and dedicated to the Bishop of London, in which he states that schools there were so few that "there was a very numerous generation of Christian children born in Virginia unserviceable for any employment of Church or State," and also adds that the members of the House of Burgesses were "*usually such as went over servants thither; and though by time and industry they may have obtained competent estates, yet, by reason of their poor and mean condition, were unskilful in judging of a good estate either of Church or Commonwealth, or of the means of procuring it."[1]

Generation after generation the illiterate and unruly continued to be transported to Virginia, until, as the accurate Stith, the first native historian of that commonwealth, admits, it was disgraced in the eyes of the world, corroborating the strong language used by Sir Josiah Child, in his *New Discourse of Trade*, published in 1698 :—

"Virginia and Barbadoes were first peopled by a sort of loose, vagrate people, vicious, and destitute of means at home, being either unfit for labour, or such as could find none to employ themselves about, or had so misbehaved themselves by whoreing, thieving, and debauchery, that none would give them work, which merchants and masters of ships, by their agents or spirits, as they were called, gathered up about the streets of London, and other places, to be employed upon Plantations."[2]

[1] Records show that Edinburgh used to banish the night-walking women to Virginia.

[2] As the descendants of these people increased in wealth they grew ashamed of their fathers, and became manufacturers, not of useful wares, but of spurious pedigrees. A letter written by a native of Virginia, a century ago, alludes to the assumptions of the planters of Virginia and Jamaica in these words :—

"It really seems to me, much as I have heard in Virginia upon the subject of old families, that of all vanity it is the most extravagant. . . . To such an extent is this upstart feeling carried in Jamaica, that the favourite study is heraldry and genealogy. Many who have risen to wealth by cultivating coffee and distilling rum, have immediately turned their backs upon those interesting and useful articles, and employed themselves in manufacturing a pedigree. The ablest members of the College of Heraldry in London have been uniformly unable to send these forth, except with wanting links, bars sinister, and great gaps, rents and fissures, which reminds one of a book with

More than sixty years after the establishment of Harvard University, near Boston, the project of a college for Virginia was revived. In the year 1683 the sum of £20 was paid out of the secret service fund of the King for the transportation of James Blair as chaplain to Virginia. He was a native of Scotland, a country which, a hundred years before, had enacted, in solemn assembly, that there should be a school in every parish, for the instruction of youth in Grammar, the Latin language, and the principles of religion; and at a later period, that the school should be so far supported by the public funds as to render education accessible to even the poorest in the community. Macaulay, in his *History of England*, referring to the school law of Scotland, says the effect of its passage was immediately felt: "Before one generation passed away it began to be evident that the common people of Scotland were superior in intelligence to the common people of any other country in Europe. To whatever land the Scotchman might wander, to whatever calling he might betake himself, in America or India, in trade or in war, by the advantage which he derived from his early training, he was raised above his competitors."

A graduate of the University of Edinburgh in 1673, and gifted with the "*per fervidam vim Scotorum*," he began

---

pages here and there torn from it. Still they pride themselves on this 'open-work' style of genealogy, have these fancy documents recorded, with their arms wholly invented, and at the end of fifty years assume what they suppose to be the air of patricians. While genuine aristocrats hold them in contempt, the middle classes treat with bitter ridicule their spurious reputations."—*Adventures of my Grandfather*. By J. R. Peyton. London, 1867.

to agitate anew the scheme of a college, which had been so dear to Copland. The project met with opposition from the masses, who were too ignorant to appreciate its advantages, and from Sir Edmund Andros; but Blair did not shrink from a good fight, and at last obtained a charter for the College of William and Mary, at Williamsburgh. The preamble to the Statutes of the College gives the following sad account of the illiterate condition of Virginia at the commencement of the eighteenth century :[1]—

"Nowhere was there any greater danger on account of ignorance and want of instruction than in the English colonies of America, in which the first planters had much to do in a country overrun with weeds and briers, and for many years infested with the incursions of the

---

[1] It is a great relief to the true but dark picture of the ignorant condition of the first families in Virginia, to consider the high degree of intelligence that now prevails in America.

The *godless* system of Public Instruction, as its opponents in America term it, has produced the following fruits:—

The report prepared by Prof. Henry B. Smith, D.D., in behalf of the American Branch for the Fifth General Conference of the Evangelical Alliance, held in Amsterdam, furnishes a mass of valuable information, from which we glean the following facts:—

Three-fourths of the entire population are under the dominant influence of the chief Protestant Churches; and the largest development and increase of Christianity in this century has been found in the United States. The Methodists have increased in the number of their communicants from 15,000 to over 2,000,000; the Baptists from 35,000 to nearly 1,700,000; the Presbyterians from 40,000 to 700,000; the Congregationalists from 75,000 to 275,000; the Lutherans number over 300,000 communicants; the Episcopalians over 160,000; and the German Reformed more than 100,000. Each of these churches reaches a population about four times as large as the number of its church members.

The increase of church-membership has relatively outrun the increase of population, and this in spite of the growing influx of foreign and largely papal population. In 1800 the total population was 5,305,935; and the

barbarous Indians, to earn a mean livelihood with hard labour. There were no schools to be found in those days, nor any opportunity for good education.

"Some few, and a very few, indeed, of the richer sort, sent their children to England to be educated, and there, after many dangers from the seas and enemies, and unusual distempers occasioned by the change of country and climate, they were often taken off by small-pox and other diseases. *It was no wonder if this occasioned a great defect of understanding and all sort of literature, and that it was followed with a new generation of men far short of their forefathers, which, if they had the good fortune, though at a very indifferent rate, to read and write, had no further commerce with the muses or learned sciences, but spent their life ignobly with the*

church members numbered 350,000: in 1860 the total population was 31,443,321; church members 5,035,250. Thus the ratio in 1800 was one communicant to about fifteen of the population; in 1832 it was one to ten; and in 1860 one to six.

The church edifices in this country in 1860 numbered 54,000, of the value of $171,390,432; and the number had increased 50 per cent. during the previous ten years. The Methodists had 19,883, averaging $2000 each; the Baptists, 11,211, at $1700 each; the Presbyterians and Congregationalists, 8953, at $5500 each; the Romanists, 3795, etc.

The aggregate receipts of twenty-five missionary and philanthropic associations one year before and one year after the war, were about $2,250,000 in 1860, and over $5,000,000 in 1866. And the total amount given in large sums during the four years ending with 1866, to colleges, seminaries, and schools of high grade cannot have been less than seven or eight millions of dollars: thus illustrating the safety of relying on the voluntary principle, even amid the distresses and sacrifices of war.

The land grants in aid of Education by the United States of America have been—

For Common Schools, ...	Acres—67,983,914
„ Universities, ...	„ 1,082,880
„ Agricultural and Scientific Schools, .	„ 9,510,000

hoe and spade, and other employments of an uncultivated and unpolished country. There remained still, notwithstanding, a small remnant of men of better spirit, who had the benefit of better education themselves in their mother country, or at least had heard of it from others. These men's private conferences among themselves produced at last a scheme of a free school and college."

A nature as benevolent as the junior Nicholas Ferrar's responded to every good wish for the plantations of the Virginia Company. His biographer, alluding to Copland, says: "He was a worthy man, and very zealous for the conversion of the infidel natives in America.[1] He had many conferences with Nicholas Ferrar upon the subject, and the best way and means to effect it, and

---

[1] It is interesting to note how largely the attention of good men was called to the establishment of Christianity in America. Crashaw, in the year 1610, hoped the Church would make "a bridge" between the Old and New World. Sir William Alexander, Secretary of State for Scotland, and proprietor of Nova Scotia, as early as 1614, wrote, in one of his poems—

> " In this last age, Time doth new worlds display,
> That Christ a Church o'er all the earth may have ;
> His righteousness shall barbarous realms away,
> If their first love more civil lands will leave :
> America to Europe may succeed ;
> God may stones raise up to Abram's seed."

From year to year the enthusiasm on this subject increased. Poets and divines vied with each other in portraying a bright future for the New World. John Donne, Dean of St. Paul's, in closing his sermon before the Virginia Company, said :—

"Those among you that are old now, shall pass out of this world with this great comfort, that you contributed to the beginning of the Commonwealth and the Church, although not to see the growth thereof to perfection ; Apollos watered, but Paul planted ; he that begun the work was the greater man. And you that are young men may live to see the enemy as much impeached by that place, and your friends, yea, children, as well accommodated in that place as any other. You shall have made this *island*,

he seriously informed Sir Edwin Sandys and others of the Company that he verily believed Mr. Ferrar was determined to leave the old world and settle in Virginia, and there employ the talents with which God had blessed him, and spend his life in the conversion of the natives, adding, "*If he shall do so, I will never forsake him, but wait upon him in that glorious work.*"

Ferrar did not leave his country, but he did "prove a spur" to Copland to sail for America.

The Virginia Company, on account of its popular which is but as the *suburbs* of the Old World, a bridge—a gallery to the New, to join all to that world that shall never grow old, the kingdom of Heaven."

George Herbert, the holy singer of the Church of England, crystallized this thought a few years later in the words—

> "Religion stands tip-toe in our land,
> Ready to pass to the American strand.
> When height of malice and prodigies, lusts,
> Impudent sinning, witchcraft, and distrusts,
> The marks of future bane, shall fill our cup;
> When Seine shall swallow Tiber, and the Thames,
> By letting in them both, pollutes her streams;
> When Italy of us shall have her will,
> And all her calendar of sins fulfil;
> Whereby one may foretell what sins next year
> Shall both in France and England domineer;
> Then shall religion to America flee,
> They have their time of Gospel, e'en as we."

As he drew near death, the author, placing the manuscript containing these lines in the hands of one by his bedside, said, "I pray, deliver this little book to my dear brother Ferrar." When Nicholas Ferrar applied at Cambridge for permission to publish the poem, the Vice-Chancellor at first refused to allow it to be printed unless the above verses were stricken out; but Mr. Ferrar refusing to comply, a license to print was reluctantly granted. Two or three years later, Dr. Twisse, writing to the learned Mede, said :—

"Now, I beseech you, let me know what your opinion is of our English Plantation in the New World. Heretofore I have wondered in my thoughts at the providence of God concerning that world, not discovered till this old world of ours is almost at an end, and there no footsteps found of the knowledge of the true God, much less of Christ. And then, considering our English Plantations of late, and the opinion of many grave divines concerning the Gospel's fleeing westward, sometimes I had such thoughts—Why may not that be the place of the New Jerusalem?"

sympathies, was looked upon by King James as the nursery of a seditious Parliament. After its charter was revoked, the £300 which had been bequeathed by his father, for the educating of Indian children, was transferred by Nicholas Ferrar to the Bermudas, or Somers Islands Company, an outgrowth of the Virginia Company. Copland then proceeded to Bermudas, as a planter of Christian civilisation, and laboured there for many years. His friend, Nicholas Ferrar, jr., of a retiring and contemplative disposition, forsook the marts of busy London, and receiving ordination in the Church of England, retired with his aged mother, to Little Gidding, where, with nieces and nephews, he passed his days in doing good, and his nights in holy vigils, inclined to adopt the ritualism of Laud, yet sincere, self-denying, zealous in good works, and beloved by the sweet poet, George Herbert, and other intimate friends.

Copland, on an isle of the sea, as suitable for contemplation as Patmos, inclined to the simplest forms of worship consistent with propriety, efficacy, and solemnity, and was convinced that the State should never interfere with any religious worship that did not disturb its peace, nor retard the prosperity of the commonwealth.[1] In the year 1642 the London directors of the Bermuda Company declared that settlers should be left " free in matters which concern the Church as may

[1] Norwood, who came to Bermudas in 1615, as Surveyor and Schoolmaster, in 1642, aged 71 years, wrote to William Prynne, protesting against the new church organization to which Copland and others belonged. The new Church observed a weekly love-feast, and used a catechism prepared by Oxensteirn, called "Milk for Babes." The officers were—*Pastor*, Rev. N. White, formerly of Knightsbridge, near Westminster; *Elders*, Rev. Mr. Golding, a young man, and Rev. P. Copland; *Deacon*, Robert Cesteven, Esq., Councillor.

be, that they be not infringed of the liberty of their conscience;" and about the same period an Independent Church was formed at Bermudas, of which the Rev. N. White was elected pastor, and Copland, described in a pamphlet as "a grave and reverend dispenser of the glorious gospel," was made one of the deacons. In 1645 White was in England, and published a reply to the aspersions which the celebrated William Prynne had cast upon his Church, and contended for liberty of conscience. On the 27th of October 1645, the House of Commons, upon the petition of those in Bermudas, "Ordered that the inhabitants of the Summer Islands, and such others as shall join themselves to them, shall, without any molestation or trouble, have and enjoy the liberty of the conscience in matters of God's worship, as well in those parts of Amiraca where they are now planted, as in all other parts of Amiraca, where hereafter they may plant."

Copland, with his wife and others, soon left Bermudas, and went to a small isle of the Bahamas group, to form a church which should have no connection with the State; and the Puritans on the James River, in Virginia, were invited to seek the same spot, which, in view of the entire freedom of worship, was called Eleuthera. The Virginia Nonconformists declined the proposition, but soon after moved to the vicinity of Annapolis, on the shores of the Chesapeake, and by their influence that Province passed the "Act of Religious Toleration," which gave Maryland a favourable reputation throughout the civilized world.

The isle upon which Copland and his associates landed proved a dreary place, and the friends of religion in Boston, Massachusetts, were obliged to send them supplies, and, in 1651, many of them returned to Bermudas, where Copland, then more than fourscore years of age, must have soon died.

Living in a period of political and ecclesiastical convulsions, indulging neither in political acerbity nor the *odium theologicum*, yet not afraid to differ from popular modes of thought and worship, to correspond with Hugh Peters, once the fiery preacher at Salem, Massachusetts, and at the same time call Nicholas Ferrar his friend, it is not strange that his name was not written in large letters by the trimming historians of the era of the vacillating Charles and determined Cromwell, who seemed to think it a work of merit to hurl words, like barbed arrows, against all who differed from them an iota.

Adjoining San Salvador, the first island of the Western World descried by Columbus, Eleuthera appears on the maps. It is but a small isle of the sea, of no more commercial importance than Nazareth of Galilee, but the principles advocated there have lived and spread, and the United States of America has become an Eleuthera, the land of civil and religious freedom, where each State instructs its youth in morality and such knowledge as will make them industrious, and thus diminishes vice and pauperism, but devolves upon the Church and parents the delicate responsibility of preparing them for the kingdom which is not of this world.

CHAPTER XI.

GEORGE, FIRST LORD BALTIMORE.

GEORGE CALVERT, the first Baron of Baltimore, was one of the most brilliant and talented of those who shared the confidence of the sottish and pedantic James the First of England. His father was a respectable Yorkshire farmer, living at Kipling, in the valley of the Swale. Graduating at Oxford,[1] Calvert became secretary to Robert Cecil, Earl of Salisbury. His talents and diligence attracted attention, and he was frequently intrusted with important public business. In 1604 he was a member of Parliament for Bossiney, in Cornwall,[2] and afterwards visited the Continent. Returning from France, he wrote the following chatty letter, on March 10, 1610-11, to Sir Thomas Edmondes, residing at Paris as English ambassador :—

"But that I could not let pass any servant of your

---

[1] He received the degree of A.B. on February 23, 1596, at the same time as Francis Rouse, afterwards Sir Francis, the versifier of the Psalms of David. In 1605 he received the degree of A.M., with Thomas West, afterwards Lord Delaware, and John Pott, probably Dr. Pott, for a time Governor of Virginia.

[2] He was chosen to fill the seat of George Upton, deceased.

own, without saluting you, I should perhaps have stayed a few days longer, for more matter, desiring together with the advertisement of my safe arrival, to let your lordship understand the state of our court here, our country, and our friends.

"But I am yet but a stranger, and know little, and besides the extraordinary good usage I received from your lordship and your worthy lady, which I preach to all my friends here, with that acknowledgment which it deserveth, hath so debauched me, as my spirits are still with you, and I cannot yet well draw them from the Faubourg of St. Germain to incline anything here. I arrived in England, at Hythe, in Kent, upon Saturday last, late at night, having been six days and one night at sea, with foul weather, and upon Sunday I came hither, where I was not unwelcome or unlooked for, as I perceived. I presently went to the court and delivered my despatch. I found my lord[1] in a disposition calm and sweet, using me with that favourable respect wherewith he is pleased to grace those poor servants he makes account of.

"He read not your letter presently, being at that time in hand, as it seemed, with some other despatch, neither had I any other speech with him of your lordship than that he asked me how you did, when I remembered your service to him. He dismissed me for that night because it was very late, and since I have seen him but once, for the next day he went to Hatfield, and from thence is gone to the king at Royston, and at

[1] **Earl of Salisbury.**

Audley End, where my Lord Chamberlain is at this present, and returns again hither within these three days, as I understand. . . . I had forgotten to put with the news of the clergy a famous conversion of a revolted minister of our Church, Mr. Theophilus Higgins, who your lordship may remember fled from England to Brussels, some three or four years since, and was undertaken by Sir Edward Hoby,[1] who wrote an 'Anti-Higgins,'[2] answered afterwards, as I take it, in part or whole, by my Lady Lovell.

"This Mr. Higgins, upon Sunday last, the day of my arrival, preached at Paul's Cross his penitential sermon, where were present my Lord Treasurer and divers others Lords of the Council, besides an infinite number of all sorts of people. The self-same day was born to Sir Edward Hoby a son and heir, inasmuch as he saith he will bless that day for the birth of two children, a spiritual and temporal, for a *natural* I dare not say, though more proper perhaps for this division, because this word sometimes receives a base interpretation. And yet himself said, as I hear, as soon as the midwife brought

---

[1] Hoby was educated at Oxford. Knighted in 1582. The pamphlet alluded to was entitled, "A Letter to Mr. Theophilus Hygons, late Minister, now at Fugitive, in answer to his First Motive."

[2] Theophilus Higgins, at the age of fourteen, in 1592, went to Oxford, and was there at the same time as Calvert. He was subsequently the popular preacher at St. Dunstans, London, but under Jesuit influence united with the Church of Rome, and lived two years at Douay. In 1609 he published his reasons for the step in a pamphlet, called "First Motive to Adhere to the Roman Church." The sermon, preached upon his return from Douay, to which Calvert alludes, was published with this title, "Sermon at St. Paul's Cross, March 30, 1610, on Eph. ii. 4, 5, 6, 7. In Testimony of his hearty Reunion with the Church of England, and his hearty submission thereto. London, 1611."

him his son to see him, that 'it was a goodly child—God bless him! and wonderfully like his father, whosoever he were.'"

About this time Calvert was made Clerk of the Privy Council, and accompanied King James to Royston. "In his journey," says a chronicler of the day, "Calvert, Clerk of the Council, is settled about him, and is wholly employed in reading and writing."

Winwood, Ambassador at the Hague in 1611, forwarded a copy of the book on *Attributes of the Deity* by Vorstius, the candidate for the chair of Arminius in the University of Leyden, with a note stating that there "was matter enough in it for a wit that hath either spirit or courage."

The excessive conceit of the King made him believe that he was justly styled "Defender of the Faith," and that he was as well versed in theology as Paul or Augustine,[1] and in his vanity he urged the maintenance of the Calvinistic views upon the States of the Low Countries. Winwood, on the 1st of January 1611-12, received a note from his correspondent, John More, in which he remarks,—"According to your lordship's command, it hath been my business to inform myself what construction is made of your late proceedings in the affair of Vorstius, which by general report I understand to have been exceedingly well liked by his Majesty; and Mr. George Calvert, falling of himself upon the subject at his house, whither I went with my wife, on a visit unto him and his, told me that the King had publicly declared

[1] *Villeroi in Raumer*, vol. ii. p. 211.

that in the course of this business Winwood hath done *secundum cor meum.*"

At this time James commenced the tractate against Vorstius, and in a letter to the Earl of Salisbury, Calvert mentions "that he is writing out the discourse which the King began concerning Vorstius."

Calvert was appointed, in 1613, one of the Commissioners to go to Ireland to listen to grievances, and to examine the condition of affairs. Soon after this, it was rumoured that he would be made Ambassador at the Hague, but a friend of Sir Dudley Carleton who was the incumbent, wrote to him: "I have both before and since made all the inquiry I could, and can find no ground of any fresh report. Only I have heard Mr. Calvert named, but when the question is asked him he doth utterly renounce any such intention in himself, and I do rather believe him, for it is not likely he should affect such a journey, being reasonably well settled at home, and having a wife and many children, which are no easy carriage, specially so far."

One of the favourites of the Court, he was in 1617 made a knight,[1] and known as Sir George Calvert. Advancing in the estimation of the pleasure-loving monarch, he was soon made principal Secretary. A letter written on February 20, 1618-19, says: "The King went to Theobald's on Tuesday, but before his

---

[1] Chamberlain wrote to Sir Dudley Carleton: "On 20th September the King knighted Sir Clement Edmondes of Northamptonshire, Sir George Calvert of Yorkshire, and Sir Albert Morton of Kent, three of the Clerks of the Council, the chief reason whereof was that Secretary Lake's son, being but extraordinary, had gotten start of his fellows."—Nichols, vol. iii. p. 437.

going Sir George Calvert was sworn Secretary. I had an inkling of it two or three days before, though the patent was drawn with a blank, and the voice ran generally with Packer. The night before he was sworn the Lord of Buckingham told him the King's resolution, but he disabled himself divers ways, but specially that he thought himself unworthy to sit in that place, so lately possessed by his noble lord and master. The King was well pleased with his answer and modesty, and, sending for him, asked many questions, most about his wife. His answer was, that she was a good woman, and had brought him ten children, and would assure his Majesty that she was not a wife with a witness."

In another letter it is stated that the King, on the 16th of February, "appointed, in the place of Sir Thomas Lake, Sir George Calvert, Secretary, who was Clerk of the Council, whose prudence and fidelity in State matters Robert Cecil, Secretary, was thoroughly acquainted with, of whose assistance also the King made use, yea, and he judged also he would be a great help to Sir Robert Naunton, the other Secretary."[1]

Gondomar, the Spanish ambassador, had discovered the power of money and flattery at the Court. The wife of the King had no respect for her husband, and was ready to accede to the wishes of the Pope, and under the fascinating attentions of the Spaniard, Buckingham, Calvert, and others became pliable, and to gratify Spain they disgraced England by beheading the gallant navigator, Sir Walter Raleigh. The whimsical monarch now incensed

[1] Nichols, vol. iii. p. 529.

the English people by arbitrary grants and rewards to those who fawned. In 1619 he gave to Calvert an annual pension of one thousand pounds, and a grant of the increased custom on silk for twenty-one years.

It at last became vital to the interests of the King to have a stout defender of his prerogative, in opposition to the popular will, upon the floor of the House of Commons, and Calvert, with Sir Thomas Wentworth, offered himself for Yorkshire.

With an energy and rapidity not excelled by an active politician of the nineteenth century, Wentworth daily wrote canvassing letters, urging the claims of himself and Calvert, and was profuse in promises and flattery.

To Sir Thomas Fairfax,[1] the grandfather of the hero of Naseby, he writes:—

"I was at London much entreated, and indeed at last enjoined, to stand with Mr. Secretary Calvert for to be knight of this shire the next Parliament, both by my

---

[1] The Fairfaxes, Wentworths, Calverts, and Washingtons of Yorkshire are all represented in America. One of the descendants of Sir Thomas Fairfax, first Baron of Cameron, is Commander Fairfax of United States Navy, who distinguished himself in quelling the slaveholders' rebellion; and another, the eleventh Baron of Cameron, is John Fairfax, M.D., who lives in Maryland, a few miles from the city of Washington, D.C., U.S.A.

William Wentworth of Yorkshire emigrated to New Hampshire, three of his descendants, John, Benning, and Sir John, were colonial governors, another a member of the Continental Congress, and recently John Wentworth, of the same stock, has represented the city of Chicago, Illinois, in the Congress of the United States of America.

John Washington, the ancestor of the first President of the United States of America, came to Virginia in 1658, and John Parke Custis, a stepson of General George Washington, married Eleanor Calvert, whose father was an illegitimate son of Benedict, Lord Baltimore.

Lord Clifford and himself, which after I had assented unto and despatched my letters, I perceived that some of your friends had motioned the like to Mr. Secretary on your behalf, and were therein engaged, which was the cause I write sooner unto you. Yet hearing, by my cousin Middleton, that he moving you on my behalf for your voices, you were not only pleased to give over that intendment, but freely to promise us your best assistance, I must confess that I cannot forbear any longer to write unto you how much this courtesy deserves of me, and that I cannot choose but to take it most kindly from you, as suitable with the ancient affection which you have always borne me and my house. And presuming of the continuance of your good respects towards me, I must entreat the company of yourself and friends with me at dinner on Christmas-day, being the day of the election, when I shall be most glad of you, and then give you further thanks for your kind respects."

To one friend he writes:—" In my next letters I will let Mr. Secretary know your good respect and kindness toward him, whereof I dare assure you he will not be unmindful."

To another voter he remarks:—" I have got an absolute promise that if I be chosen knight, that you shall have a burgess-ship at Appleby, wherewith I must confess I am not a little pleased, in regard we shall sit there, judge, and laugh together."

To a relative he makes a practical suggestion:—" The course my Lord Darcy and I hold, is to entreat the high constables to desire the petty constables to set down the names of all freeholders within their townships, and which of them have promised to be at York, and bestow their voices with us, or as we may keep the vote as a testimony of their good affections, and know whom we are beholden unto, desiring them further to go along with us to York on Sunday, being Christmas-eve, or else meet us about two o'clock of the day at Tadcaster. I desire you would please to deal effectually with your high constables, and hold the same course, that so we may be able to judge what number we may expect out of your wapentake. I hope you will take the pains to go along with us, together with your friends, to York, so that we may all come in together, and take part of an ill dinner with me the next day, when yourself and friends shall be right heartily welcome."

Sir Arthur Ingram is informed,—"As touching the election we now grow to some heat; Sir John Saville's instruments closely and cunningly suggesting underhand Mr. Secretary's non-residence, his being the king's servant, and out of these reasons by law cannot, and in good discretion ought not, be chosen of the country. Whereas himself is their martyr, having suffered for them, the patron of the clothiers, the fittest to be relied on, and that he intends to be at York on the day of election."

To Sir George Calvert he suggests that the pressure of court influence be applied to carry the election :—
" May it please you, sir, the Parliament writ is delivered to the sheriff, and he by his faithful promise deeply engaged for you. I find the gentlemen of these parts generally ready to do you service. Sir Thomas Fairfax

stirs not, but Sir John Saville by his instruments exceeding busy, intimating to the common sort underhand, that yourself being not resident in the county, cannot by law be chosen, and being his Majesty's Secretary and a stranger, one not safe to be trusted by the country, but all this, according to his manner, so closely and cunningly, as if he had no part therein, neither doth he as yet further declare himself, than only that he will be at York the day of the election, and thus finding he cannot work them from me, labours to supplant you.

"My Lord President hath writ to his freeholders on your behalf, and seeing he will be in town on the election day, it were, I think, very good if he would be pleased to show himself for you in the Castle-yard, and that you writ a few lines unto him, taking notice that you hear of some opposition, and therefore desire his presence. I have heard that when Sir Francis Darcy opposed Sir Thomas Lake in a matter of like nature, *the Lords of the Council writ to Sir Francis to desist.* I know my Lord Chancellor is very sensible of you in this business; *a word to him and such a letter would make an end of all.*"

The Christmas of 1620 in the old city of York was a day long remembered. To the usual hilarities were added the noise and confusion of an exciting election. Amid the drinking of mugs of beer and cups of gooseberry wine, there was angry discussion of the merits of the contestants, emphasized by round and coarse Saxon oaths, until toward night the cheers for Calvert and Wentworth declared the victorious party.

Previous to the assembling of Parliament, public

opinion was decidedly against James. "Consider, for pity's sake," said a French ambassador, "what must be the state and condition of a prince whom the preachers from the pulpit publicly assail, whom the comedians of the metropolis covertly bring upon the stage, whose wife attends these representations in order to enjoy the laugh against her husband, whom the Parliament braves and despises, and who is universally hated by the whole people."[1]

One could not walk the streets of London without seeing in the windows of bookshops ludicrous caricatures and sarcastic pamphlets hitting the king. In the library of Sir Robert Cotton were frequently closeted Pym, Selden, Coke, and other loyal and talented men, to arrange a policy of opposition to a monarch who thought more of the deer in his hunting-parks than of his subjects, and who had in a rage announced that "he would govern according to the good of the commonwealth, but not according to the common will." At the opening of the Parliament he said, "It is the king that makes laws, and ye are to advise him to make such, as will be best for the commonwealth."

No man was so thoroughly opposed to the doctrine of popular rights as Sir George Calvert, and early in the session, as the right-hand man of the King, he urged the House of Commons to accede to the demands for money, and to say less about their liberties and freedom of speech, and his remarks were so offensive that he was much censured by members for his forwardness. Cham-

[1] Raumer, vol. ii. p. 206, 207.

berlain, in a letter to Sir Dudley Carleton on February 10, 1620-21, wrote:—

"The first day of their sitting,[1] Secretary Calvert made a speech for the supply of the King's wants, which was thought untimely, before anything else was treated of. . . . There was some crossing and contestation 'twixt Secretary Calvert and Coke at a committee, about the Spanish ambassador, who is said to have almost as many come to his mass, as to the sermon at St. Andrews, over against him, and there is great complaint of the increase of Popery everywhere."

When Calvert mentioned that the Parliament proposed an address asking that the Prince of Wales might marry a Protestant, the King was so enraged that he sent a letter to the Speaker complaining of the "fiery, popular, and turbulent spirits" in the lower House, and forbidding them to inquire into the mysteries of State, or to concern themselves about the marriage of his son. The arrogant tone of the communication roused Pym and others to protest, and Calvert tried to still the storm of indignation by a mild admission of the impropriety of the closing expressions of the King, and calling them a slip of the pen at the close of a long letter.

Calvert's intimacy at this period with Gondomar, the Spanish, and Tillieres,[2] the French ambassador, called

[1] The third Parliament of King James met January 30, 1620-21, sat until March 27, and adjourned. Re-assembled April 17; adjourned June 4. Re-assembled November 14, and dissolved February 8, 1621-22.

[2] Tillieres became Lord Chamberlain to Henrietta Maria on the eve of her marriage to Charles the First. Shortly after her arrival in England, on Sunday, 19th of June 1625, at high mass at Denmark House, he was made Knight of the French Order of the Holy Ghost. The Queen brought in her

forth much remark. Tillieres, who despised both the English religion and English people, in a despatch to his government on November 25, 1621, said: "The third man in whose hands the public affairs are ostensibly lodged is the Secretary of State, Calvert. He is an honourable, sensible, well-minded man, courteous to strangers, full of respect towards ambassadors, zealously intent for the welfare of England, but by reason of these good qualities entirely without consideration or influence."

On August 8, 1622, the wife of Calvert,[1] called by train from France twenty-nine priests, who exercised so much influence over her that at length Lord Conway, by order of Charles, dismissed all her French attendants.

"The women howled," says an old writer, "and lamented as if they had been going to execution, but all in vain, for the yeomen of the guard thrust them and all their country-folks out of the Queen's lodgings, and locked the doors after them."

The King issued the following order to Buckingham:—

"I command you to send all the French away to-morrow out of town, if you can by fair means, but stick not long in disputing, otherwise force them, driving them away like so many wild beasts until you have shipped them, and so the devil go with them. Let me hear no answer but of the performance of my command."

John Pery, who had been Secretary of the first legislature at Jamestown, Virginia, in a letter dated September 2, 1626, at London, wrote that Tillieres was expected to return to England, and remarked:—

"His Majesty hath sent an express prohibition to Tillieres that he shall not presume to set foot on English shore in that quality [ambassador], because he will not admit of his late sworn servant to be checkmate with him. But the truth is, Tillieres is too much Jesuited for our State to endure, and hath lately done ill offices against us."

[1] She was Anne, daughter of George Mynne. Her children were:—

Cecilius,	the second Lord Baltimore.
Leonard,	Keeper of the Rolls, Connaught, Ireland, then Governor of Maryland from 1634 to 1647, where he died.
George,	came to America with Leonard, and died before 1653.
Francis,	died young.
Henry,	,, ,,
Anna,	baptized April 1, 1607; married Wm. Peasley.
Dorothy.	

Camden a most modest woman, died in childbirth, leaving a large family, and not long after this sorrow, Cecil, the eldest son of Calvert, married Anna,[1] daughter of Thomas Earl Arundel, one of the most influential Roman Catholic noblemen in the realm. For months Calvert was now occupied with Gondomar in preparing the articles for the proposed marriage of Prince Charles with the Infanta of Spain. He devoutly wished for the consummation of this scheme, and it was with great pleasure he read a letter on February 27, 1622-23, by an associate secretary, informing him that the Prince and Duke of Buckingham, disguised as traders, and with the assumed names of Jack and Tom, had quietly sailed for Spain. To prevent improper disclosures, it was arranged that the communications of Buckingham to the King should be first transmitted in cypher to Calvert. Upon the intelligence of the Prince's arrival in Madrid, Calvert wrote from St. Martin's Lane on 3d of April 1623: "Here is amongst all men an universal joy for the good news brought us by Mr. Grymes, and we have made the best expressions of it we can for the present. I hope it shall every day increase, first, for the general good, and next for the great part of honour

Elizabeth.
Grace, married Sir Robert Talbot of Kildare, Ireland.
Helen.
John.
Philip Calvert, Governor of Maryland, was not her child, but an illegitimate son of her husband.

[1] Ann Arundel, county Maryland, bears her name. She died at the age of thirty-four, on July 24, 1649. On her tombstone at Tisbury she is described as "Anna Arundelia, pulcherrima et optima conjux Cecilii Calverti, Baronis de Baltemore, et absolu: domini Terræ Mariæ et Avaloniæ."

your Lordship hath in it, wherein God make you as happy as ever man was!"

Eight months after his wife's death, Calvert was the life of the party at the King's festival at Windsor in honour of St. George. An old letter-writer says, "He was very gay and gallant, all in white, cap-a-pie, even to his white hat and white feather."

From the hour, however, that Buckingham broke off the negotiations at Madrid, Calvert's position became uncertain. He had been fully committed to the scheme, he did not dream of its failure, and late in May 1623 he wrote that "orders are given for all things needful for the reception of the Prince and the Infanta." When the intelligence reached England that the deep-laid plan had failed, he not only suffered from disappointment, but with the populace he was an object of obloquy, because one of the acknowledged leaders of what was called the Spanish party in politics.

Buckingham after his return from Spain was shy of those that had been under the seductive influences of Gondomar, and withdrew his confidence from Calvert. In a letter to the King he says, "I hope to have the happiness to-morrow to kiss your hands, therefore I will not send you the letter you writ to the Pope, which I have got from Secretary Calvert. When he delivered it to me, he made this request, that he hoped your Majesty would as well trust him in a letter you were now to write, as you had heretofore in the former. I did what I could to dissemble it, but when there was no means to do it, I thought best to seem to trust him absolutely, thereby to tie him to secrecy."

The whole of the year 1624 proved embarrassing to Calvert. Early in April one wrote that Secretary Calvert was in ill health, and talked of resigning. A day or two after it was said "he is on ill terms with the King and Prince Charles, and is called to account, among other things, for detaining letters a year ago at the request of the French ambassador." The next month some one thinks the Secretary does not mean to resign, but by feigning it, to induce the King to give him a large share of business. But the letters written to Sir Dudley Carleton by his nephew probably tell the truth, "that he is willing to sell the secretaryship to him for six thousand pounds, that Lord Hollis had offered eight thousand, and Sir John Suckling seven thousand."

During the summer he "drooped and kept out of the way"[1] at Thistleworth, where he was cheered by pleasant letters from his constant friend Wentworth, who was rusticating at his ancestral seat in Yorkshire. In a letter dated August 24, 1624, Wentworth alludes to the retirement in these words:—

"Since you are like those ancient Romans retired from court to the harmless delights of Tusculanie, 'Ereptus specioso ejus damno,' like another Æneas from burning Troy. . . . . Believe it, we may not yet admit you a countryman throughout; your neighbours of Thistleworth may tell you one summer is too little to

[1] Letter to Sir Dudley Carleton from a friend.

purge away the leaven of a courtier, and it is time that must approve,

> 'Fitque color primo turbati fluminis imbre
> Purgaturque mora;'

we must have more trial, more experience, first initiatus, then adultus, lest you might come to spy out our liberty rather than to keep our counsel, to enjoy the contentment and freedom of our life, with peace and quietness."

Before the end of the month Calvert received another as redolent of country life as a bucolic of Virgil:—

"Our harvest is all in, a most fine season to make fish-ponds, our plums are all past and gone, peaches, quinces, and grapes, almost fully ripe, which will, I trow, hold better relish with a Thistleworth palate, and approve me how to have the skill to serve every man in his right end. These only we countrymen muse of, hoping in such harmless retirement for a just defense from the higher powers, and possessing ourselves in contentment, may with Dryope in the poet,

> 'Et siqua est pietas, ab acutæ vulnere falcis
> Et pecoris morsu, fundes defendite nostras.'"

Returning to London in the autumn, Calvert found the Court busy in the arranging of a French match for Prince Charles. In October Parliament, of which he was now a member for Oxford, was adjourned by the King, to which Wentworth pleasantly alludes in a letter written soon after:—

"We conclude that the French treaty must first be consummate before such unruly fellows meet in Parliament, lest they might appear as agile against this, as that other, Spanish match. . . . For is it a small matter, trow you, for poor swains to unwind so dextrously your courtly true love-knots? You think we see nothing; but, believe it, you shall find us legislators no fools, albeit you of the Court (for by this time I am sure you have by a fair retreat from Thistleworth quit your part of a country life for this year) think to blear our eyes with your sweet balls, and leave us in the suds when you have done. Thus much for the common weal. For your own self I am right glad for your ague recovered, hoping it will cleanse away all bad disposed humors."[1]

The relations of Calvert and Buckingham were now more pleasant, but still it was inexpedient that the former should continue in the secretaryship. A nephew of Sir Dudley Carleton, on November 23, 1624, writes to his uncle that "Secretary Conway declares that there was no one whom he should prefer as colleague, but that Calvert was reconciled to Buckingham, who had assured him that he should have the option of refusing any offer made for his place." Six weeks before the death of King James, the transfer of the secretaryship was made. Chamberlain writes to a friend,—" Sir Albert Morton is not yet returned from New Market, though I hear he be sworn, and hath the seals delivered him by Sir George Calvert, who had £3000 of him, and is to have as much more somewhere, besides an Irish barony for himself, or where he list to bestow for his benefit. Young Hungerford is made a baron *en payant*,

[1] Strafford's *Despatches*, vol. i.

for this is the true Golden Age, no penny, no *pater noster*." Two weeks after he sold the secretaryship, in company with Toby Matthew, son of the Archbishop of York, who had become a member of the Church of Rome, he visited Yorkshire, which, said a letter-writer of the day, "confirms the opinion that he is a bird of that feather."

Archbishop Abbot, a cotemporary, referring to the affair of the resignation, says :—

"Secretary Calvert hath never looked merrily since the Prince's coming out of Spain. It was thought he was much interested in the Spanish affair. A course was taken to rid him of all employments and negotiations. This made him discontented, and, as the saying is, 'desperatio facit monachum,' so he apparently turned Papist, which he now professeth, this being the third time he hath been to blame that way. His Majesty to dismiss him suffered him to resign his Secretary's place to Sir Albertus Morton, who paid him £3000 for the same, and the King hath made him Baron of Baltimore in Ireland."

Goodman, formerly Bishop of Gloucester, who had left the Church of England and joined the Church of Rome, gives a milder version. He says:—"The third man who was thought to gain by the Spanish match was Secretary Calvert, and as he was the only secretary employed in the Spanish match, so undoubtedly he did what good offices he could therein for religion's sake, being infinitely addicted to the Roman Catholic faith, having been converted thereunto by Count Gondmar and Count Arundel, whose daughter Secretary Calvert's son had married; and as it was said the Secretary did actually catechise his own children, so as to ground them in his own religion, and in his best room having an altar set up, with chalice, candlesticks, and all other ornaments, he brought all strangers thither, never concealing anything, as if his whole joy and comfort had been to make open profession of his religion."

Toward the end of March 1625, King James died, and on Tuesday his successor, Charles the First, came to White Hall, and the oath of allegiance being offered to Lord Baltimore, as one of the Privy Council, he asked time for deliberation,[1] on account of which hesitation he was relieved of attendance at the Court, and soon departed for Ireland.

Although an active courtier, he had watched with interest the expeditions for trade and discovery in distant climes. For years he was a member of the East India, and also the Virginia Company, and with members of the latter he had many conferences, in consequence of their disputes with the King and Privy Council as to their rights under their patent.

The day that Sir Edwin Sandys was elected Governor of the Virginia Company, April 28, 1619, the members were informed that Secretary Calvert had sent a letter notifying that the King had sent a man suspected of deer-stealing for transportation to Virginia. The following November the King also sent a letter informing them that he wished divers dissolute persons transported,

---

[1] *Court and Times of Charles the First*, vol. i.

and it was agreed by the Company that Sir Edwin Sandys should inform Secretary Calvert that it would be very acceptable to the colonists to receive them as servants.

A few days later, Sandys informed the Company that he had been with Secretary Calvert, and that the King was displeased that the convicts had not been shipped, and that fifty or one hundred must be sent away with all speed. He then told the members "what a pinch he was put into," for "they could not go in less than four ships, for fear they would, being many together, mutiny and carry away the ships." After many plans were discussed, the Company decided that they would maintain the convicts at their own charges, until they could devise means of transportation. When this resolution was made known to Secretary Calvert, he replied that he feared the King would not be satisfied, as he wished no delay.

A ship was at last found. At a meeting on 23d of December, "a commission to John Damyron, Master of the Duty, being read, and allowed for taking the first opportunity of wind and weather to sail for Virginia, with the passengers of the Company, shipped by command of his Majesty, it was now ordered that the seal should be thereunto affixed." Deputy Ferrar then stated that the Knight Marshal had informed Sir Edwin Sandys that upon the next Monday morning fifty of the persons to be transported would be at Bridewell for the Company to make choice of such as they think fit for the present to be sent.

In May 1622, Mr. Bell told the Company that a

messenger one night came to him, and told him that Secretary Calvert wished to see him at his chamber. After he went there, Calvert told him that the King did not wish to infringe their liberty of free election, but that it would be pleasing to him if they would elect for annual officers some of those names written on paper, which they so far complied with as to place two names of the King's choice, to stand with one of the Company's nomination. The nominees selected as candidates for the Governorship of the Company from the King's list were Mr. Clethero and Mr. Hanford; the Company's nominee was the Earl of Southampton. The balloting took place on the 22d of May, and Hanford received seven, and Clethero thirteen, while the Earl of Southampton received one hundred and thirteen ballots, showing clearly how slender was the influence of the King's faction.

The day before the annual election of the next year, 1623, a servant of Secretary Calvert brought a letter from the King requesting them to postpone the election of officers for two weeks, but at length Southampton was re-elected by an overwhelming vote, and continued the presiding officer until the 16th of June 1624, when Chief-Justice Ley decided that the charter of the Company was null and void. On the 15th of July the King appointed Calvert one of the commissioners to look after the affairs of Virginia. The 16th of February 1624-25 he was created Baron of Baltimore,[1] in the

[1] In the reign of King James an order of nobility was created which had not the privileges of English barons, but were only called lords of some place, either in England or Ireland, without owning a foot of land in the locality. Baltimore, after which Calvert was called, is an ancient town in the county

county of Longford, Ireland, and 2304 acres of arable, and 1605 of bog and wood-land, were granted to him in fee-simple, in free and common soccage as of the Castle of Dublin.

While residing in Ireland he determined to visit America. As early as 1620 he purchased an interest in the New Foundland Plantation, which had been established several years before. Whitbourne, in a description of New Foundland, published in 1622, says: —" The Right Hon. Sir George Calvert, secretary to the King's most excellent Majesty, hath undertaken to plant a colony of his Majesty's subjects in the country, and

of Cork, on a promontory not far from Cape Clear. It is said to have been the site of a Druid temple, and that the name is a contraction of Beal-tee-more, the great residence of Beal. The bay in front of the place, in the fifteenth century, was frequented by Spanish rovers, who often fought with O'Driscoll sept, who there resided. Hill, in his history of Bandon, says an old ballad is still sung, of which the concluding verses are :—

" O'Driscoll gazed round on sea and land,
And call'd to his vassals on the strand ;
Ready his commands they did obey,
And launched his galleys into the sea.
He little thought on that fatal day,
That the Algerines would come that way ;
They came on shore and caused great slaughter,
And carried off O'Driscoll's daughter.

Behold her anguish ! Also her fears !
A poor captive carried into Algiers ;
Whilst in the harem, she stood alone,
And the son about her brightly shone,
To her, flattering tales the Pacha told,
And showed her his pearls and his gold ;
But this virtuous maiden, nobly born,
His love and his treasures she did scorn.

By force, she was by him caressed ;
But she plunged a dagger into his breast ;
He loudly screamed, and on Allah cried,
Then fell upon the ground and died !
The sentence was passed, that she should die,
She thought of her home, and heaved a sigh ;
Resigned to her fate, with pious love,
Her stainless spirit found a home above :
Thy pride is gone, and thy glory is o'er,
Ruined and neglected Baltimore."

hath already most worthily sent thither in these last two years a great number."

Sir William Alexander, also secretary to King James, wrote: " Master Secretary Calvert hath planted a Company at Ferriland, who both for buildings and making trial of the ground, have done more than was ever performed by any in so short a time, having on hand a brood of horses, kowes, and other beastials, and by the industry of his people he is beginning to draw back yearly some benefits from thence."

On the 1st of March 1626-7, Lord Baltimore arrived in London to complete his arrangements for the voyage, and on the 7th of April he wrote from his lodgings in the Surry to the Duke of Buckingham's secretary, asking for the speedy despatch of the warrant for his ships the " Ark of Avalon," one hundred and sixty tons burden, and " George of Plymouth," one hundred and forty tons, to be exempted from the general stay, as Sir Arthur Aston was waiting to sail.

Charles the First, from the day of his accession, manifested a desire to be " every inch a King." Restive under the restrictions of Parliament, he resorted to raising moneys under the Privy Seal, and his extortions were so great that an opposition arose styled the party of the Country, and arrayed itself against the party of the King.

To the people's party Wentworth first allied himself, and when the King, under the Privy Seal, demanded a loan of him, he refused it as unconstitutional.

Lord Baltimore, now in London, and with his whole

heart on the side of the King, was distressed at the position of his old friend, and on May 1, 1627, urgently wrote: "I have been here now some two or three months, a spectator upon this great scene of state, where I have no part to play, but you have, for which your friends are sorry. It is your enemies that bring you on the stage, where they have a hope to see you act your own notable harm, and therefore keep yourself off I beseech you, 'et redimas te quam queas minimo.' Furnish not your enemies with matter of triumph, when without detriment either to your honour or conscience, you may give them the foil if you will, and remember the old tale of the rain that fell upon all the world except two that kept themselves in a cellar, and how sorry they were afterward for the Providence."

About the 1st of June Baltimore sailed for New Foundland, not as a religious exile, as some historians declare, but simply to see if he might save the money invested in the plantation. Frankly he told a friend, "I must either go and settle it in better order, or else give it over, and lose all the charges I have been at hitherto for other men to build their fortunes upon. And I had rather be esteemed a fool by some for the hazard of one month's journey, than to prove myself one certainly for six years[1] by past, if the business be now lost for the want of a little pains and care."[2]

Three or four days before he departed for America he made his final appeal to Wentworth to yield to the

[1] He adventured in the plantation in 1620. In March 1623 a new grant was given, which was again altered on 7th April, and the plantation called the Province of Avalon.   [2] Strafford's *Despatches*, vol. i.

King's demand: "I should say much more to you were you here, which is not fit for paper, but never put off the matter of your appearance here for God's sake, but send your money into the collector's without more ado."

"At Michaelmas I hope to be with you, God willing. In the meantime I shall be in great fear that your too much fortitude will draw upon you suddenly a misfortune which your heart may perhaps endure, but the rest of your body will ill suffer. . . . The conquering way sometimes is yielding, and so is it I conceive in this particular of yours, when you shall both conquer your own passions and vex your enemies, who desire nothing more than your resistance."

These earnest words, with the hint of bodily suffering if he did not yield, touched the impulsive Wentworth, and he joined the Court party. When he came to act in opposition to the people's party, Pym, who had been intimate with him, made the prophetic speech, "Though you leave us now, I will never leave you while your head is upon your shoulders."

Parliament was dissolved on the 26th of June, and on the 14th of July the King rewarded Wentworth with a baronetcy, with the intimation of further honours, which speedily followed.

Lord Baltimore departed for New Foundland in a ship of three hundred and twenty tons and forty guns, and arrived at Ferryland on the 23d of July, bringing with him Longvyll and Anthony Smith, two seminary priests.[1] The colonists, however, were Protestants, and

[1] William Robinson of Timwell, Lancashire, also came with him.

the Rev. Erasmus Sturton was the minister. Hayman, the governor of the plantation, was the author of the following dedication and poem :—

" To my reverend kind friend, Erasmus Sturton, Preacher of the Word of God, and Parson of Ferryland, in the Province of Avalon in New Foundland.

> " No man should be more welcome to this place
> Than such as you, Angel of peace and grace.
> As you were sent here by the Lord's command,
> Be you the blest Apostle of this land.
> To infidels do you evangelize,
> Making those that are rude, sober, and wise,
> I pray the Lord, that did you hither send,
> Our cursings, swearing, jouring, mend."

In accordance with his expectation, Lord Baltimore returned to England in the autumn, bringing back the priest Longvyll, and commenced to arrange for the removal of his family to the New World. During the spring of 1628, he again sailed, taking with him a lady to whom he was not legally married, a priest named Hacket and all his children, with the exception of Cecil and two married daughters. The summer was a season of trial; and, in a letter dated the 25th of August, tells his troubles to the Duke of Buckingham :—

" The King once told him that he wrote as fair a hand to look upon afar off, as any man in England, but that when any one came near, they were not able to read a word. He then got a dispensation to use another man's, for which he is thankful, as writing is a great pain to him now. Owes an account of his proceedings in this plantation to the Duke, since it was under his Grace's patronage he went out. He came to build and set and sow, but he has fallen to fighting with Frenchmen."

He then gives an account of a capture of fishing vessels by De la Rade, in command of three ships, with four hundred men, "many of them gentlemen of quality, la fleur de la jeunesse de Normandye."[1]

He sent two ships, the "Victory" and "Benediction," in pursuit—one carrying twenty-four guns, and when they came in sight, the French dropped their six prizes and sailed away, while Baltimore had to support the crews, amounting to sixty-seven men. During the autumn of 1628, his son Leonard went to England to ask for a share in the prizes that had been taken, and for a letter of marque ante-dated, and his brother-in-law, William Peasley, about the same time petitioned the Lords of the Admiralty for the use of the ship "St. Claude," for preservation of the King's rights, and many subjects in New Foundland.

The advent of priests of the Church of Rome led to dissension at Ferryland, and the Protestant clergyman, Sturton, left on 26th of August, and after arriving in England, in the following October, complained of the proselyting efforts of the priests; and that, in opposition to the laws of England, every Sunday, mass and all the ceremonies were observed, and that a child of one William Pool, without the father's consent, had been baptized.

In the spring of the year 1629, the ship "St. Claude," under a letter of marque, with Leonard Calvert as factor, sailed for New Foundland; and on the 19th of August,

[1] Sainsbury's *Cal. of State Papers.*

Lord Baltimore writes to the King, and "gives thanks upon his knees for the loan of a fair ship," confesses that he has met with difficulties no longer to be resisted, "his house has been a hospital all the winter of one hundred persons; fifty were sick at one time,[1] and nine or ten had died." He also requested a grant of land in Virginia, where he desires to remove, with some forty persons.

Waiting for no reply, he sent his children home, and with a lady and servants arrived in October at Jamestown, to the surprise of the Virginians.

Governor Pott[2] and Council inquired his purpose, and

---

[1] Sir David Kirk, on October 2, 1639, after his arrival at Ferryland, wrote to Archbishop Laud :—

"Out of one hundred persons they took over, only one died of sickness. The air of Newfoundland agrees perfectly well with all God's creatures, except Jesuits and schismatics. A great mortality among the former tribe so affrighted my Lord of Baltimore, that he utterly deserted the country."— *Cal. State Papers.*

[2] Dr. John Pott was, on July 16, 1621, recommended to the Virginian Company by Gulston, the distinguished physician of London, as a suitable successor to Dr. Bohun, the first physician-general, who had been killed in March, during a fight between the vessel in which he was a passenger and two Spanish men-of-war.

The minutes of the Company speak of "one Mr. Potts, a Mr. of Arts, well practised in chirurgerie and physique, expert also in the distilling of waters, and that he had many other ingenious devices."

The Company accepted and allowed him £20 for a chest of physic, and £10 for "books of physic," besides a free passage for himself, wife, man and maid servant.—*MSS. London Co. Transactions.*

Soon after he signed the remonstrance against Baltimore he was succeeded in the governorship by the rough John Harvey, who immediately charged him with malfeasance, and ordered him to stay under arrest at Harrope, his plantation, seven miles from Jamestown, near Williamsburg.

Elizabeth, the wife of the doctor, went to England, and complained of the arbitrary conduct of Harvey. Commissioners were appointed to examine the case, and they reported that the condemning of Potts on superficial hearing had been very rigorous, and, on July 25, 1631, he was pardoned by the King, "especially as he was the only physician in the colony."

his reply was, " to plant and dwell." " Very willingly, my Lord," they answered, "if your Lordship will do what we have done, and what your duty is to do." Refusing to obey the statutes of England, he was told that they could not allow him to settle, and that he must depart in the first ship. Leaving his lady and servants, he accordingly sailed for England, and at the same time the Virginia authorities forwarded the following statement to the Lords of the Privy Council :—

" May it please your Lordships to understand, that about the beginning of October last, there arrived in the colony the Lord Baltimore, from his plantation at New Foundland, with an intention, as we are informed, rather to plant himself to the southward of the settlement here, although he hath seemed well affected to this place, and willing to make his residence therein with his whole family.

" We were readily inclined to render to his Lordship all those respects which were due unto the honour of his person, which might testify with how much gladness we desire to receive and to entertain him, as being of that eminence and degree whose presence and affection might give great advancement to the plantation.

" Thereupon, according to the instructions from your Lordships, and the usual course held in this place, we tendered the oaths of supremacy and allegiance to his Lordship and some of his followers, who, making profession of the Romish religion, utterly refused to take the same, a thing which we could not have doubted in him, whose former employments under his late Majesty might have endeared to us a persuasion he would not have made a denial of that, in point whereof, consists the loyalty and fidelity which every true subject oweth unto his Sovereign.

"His Lordship, therefore, offered to take the oath, a copy whereof is included, but, in true discharge of the trust imposed on us by his Majesty, we could not imagine that so much latitude was left for us to decline from the prescribed form so strictly exacted, and so well justified and defended by the pen of our late Sovereign, King James of happy memory; and among the blessings and favours for which we are bound to bless God, and which this colony hath received from his Most Gracious Majesty, there is none whereby it hath been made more happy than in the freedom of our religion which we have enjoyed, and that no Papists have been suffered to settle their abode amongst us, the continuance whereof we now humbly implore from his Most Sacred Majesty, and earnestly beseech your Lordships, that by your meditations and counsels, the same may be established and confirmed unto us."

On the 22d of November the King wrote to Lord Baltimore that since his plantation in New Foundland had not fulfilled expectations, and that he was now in pursuit of a new place, "and weighing that men of his condition and breeding are fitter for other employments than the farming of new plantations, which commonly have rugged and laborious beginnings," he thought fit to advise him to desist from further prosecution of his designs.[1]

---

[1] Sainsbury's *Cal. of State Papers*.

But this discussion did not repress his desire to make another settlement, and in December he petitioned the Privy Council for a grant of land in Virginia, and that the Governor there might be instructed to aid in returning to England the lady he had left there.

Pory, the celebrated scholar and traveller, and at one time secretary of the colony of Virginia, in a letter to Joseph Mead, chaplain of Archbishop Laud, on February 12, 1629-30, writes of Baltimore:—" Though his Lordship is extolling that country to the skies, yet he is preparing a bark to send to fetch his lady and servants from thence again." It seems that soon after this Baltimore must have sailed for Virginia, for in the records of the colony, under date of March 25, 1630, is the following entry:—" Thomas Tindall to be pilloried two hours for giving my Lord Baltimore the lie and threatening to knock him down."[1]

The Duke of Norfolk contemplated at this time a settlement on the south shores of the James River, and the Virginia Assembly, in compliment to him, made a new country, bearing his name, and the same year, 1629, Sir Robert Heath, the Attorney-General, obtained from the King a grant of those parts of America between the degrees of 31 and 36 of north latitude, inclusive, not yet planted or cultivated, to be designated as "the Province of Carolana."[2] In February 1631, Baltimore

---

[1] Hening's *Statutes*, vol. i.

[2] A charter for Carolana was given to Heath on October 20, 1629. On the 10th of next February certain parties apply to settle a colony there, to occupy from 34 to 35 north latitude, with power to erect courts, and payments to be made to Heath as lord-paramount. Two weeks later, at the

secured a tract of land, lying south of James River,[1] and a charter was prepared therefor, and signed, but it caused so much opposition from Francis West, brother of Lord Delaware, who had been Governor of Virginia, William Clayborne, Secretary, and William Tucker, one of the Virginia Council, who were in London, that it was abandoned. He then persuaded the King to give him a grant, embracing the more remote lands north and east of the Potomac River.

In preparing the charter for the proposed province, a blank was left, although Baltimore had thought of calling it Crescentia. The King, when the patent was brought, asked what he should call the country that he was about to cede. Baltimore replied that it would have been pleasant to have called it after the King, but that could not be, as another province was already desig-

---

request of Heath, the Privy Council made Hugh L'Amy Receiver-General of Rates in Carolana. On April 30, 1630, the Privy Council ordered that no aliens should be settled in Carolana without special direction, nor any but Protestants. About this time Baron de Sancé arrived for the settling of a colony of French Protestants in this province.

It was agreed by Heath that the French should bring certificates from their Protestant pastors, to be examined and attested by the minister of the French church in London, when the Attorney-General would issue a permit to sail.

On the 15th of May, George Lord Berkley, Samuel Vassal, a prominent London merchant, and others, proposed to settle from the 34th, 35th, and 36th degrees of latitude, under Heath's charter. In 1633, Edward Kingswell contracted with Vassall to transport himself, wife, and family, a Mr. Wingate, and others, to Carolana. In October they sailed from London in the Mayflower, but were landed in Virginia instead of Carolana. In May 1634 Kingswell returned to England, and sued Vassall for breach of contract. Sir Henry Martin, Judge of Admiralty, after examining the case, in December, decided in his favour.

[1] This may have been the same tract as that which the Duke of Norfolk obtained, who was the brother of his daughter-in-law, the wife of his son Cecilius.

nated as Carolana. Charles then said : " Let us name it after the Queen. What think you of Mariana ?"

Baltimore, a firm believer in the divine right of kings, disapproved, because he said it was the name of the Spanish historian who taught that the will of the people was higher than the law of tyrants.[1] Charles, still disposed to compliment his wife, said, " Let it be Terra Mariæ," and this name was inserted.

A few days later the charter passed the privy seal, but, upon the advice of Attorney-General Noy, the affixing of the great seal was delayed, and meanwhile, on April 13, 1632, the first Baron of Baltimore died at his lodgings at Lincoln's-Inn-Fields, and was buried in the chancel of the Church of St. Dunstan's West, London.

A few months after his death, the charter of Terra Mariæ, or Mary Land, was made out in the name of his son, Cecilius, and contained no provisions for civil or religious liberty.

By it the proprietor and his heirs were created true and absolute lords and proprietaries of the province, with free, full, and absolute power to ordain, make, and enact laws, with the advice, assent, and approbation of the freemen of the province, and with authority to appoint all judges, justices, and constables.

The freemen could only meet in assembly with the proprietor's permission, and it was expressly provided that he might make wholesome laws from time to time, to be kept and observed, on the ground that it might be

[1] Ayscough MSS.

necessary before the freeholders could be convened for the purpose.

The charter of Maryland appears, with one important exception, to be the same as that of Carolana, granted to Sir Robert Heath :—

CHARTER OF CAROLANA, 1629, A.D.	CHARTER OF MARYLAND, 1632, A.D.
"Charles, by the Grace of God," etc. : "To all to whom these presents shall come, Greeting :	"Charles, by the grace of God," etc. : "To all to whom these presents shall come, Greeting :
"Whereas, our trusty and well beloved subject, Sir Robert Heath, our Attorney-General, being excited with a laudable zeal for the propagation of the Christian faith, the enlargement of our Empire and dominion, and the increase of trade and commerce of our Kingdom, has humbly besought leave of us, by his own industry and charge, to transport an ample colony of our subjects," etc., "into a certain country hereafter described in the parts of America between the degrees of 31 and 36 of northern latitude, inclusive, not yet cultivated or planted," etc.	"Whereas, our well beloved and right trusty subject, Cecilius Calvert, Baron of Baltimore,", etc., "being animated with a laudable and pious zeal for extending the Christian religion, and also the territories of our Empire, hath humbly besought leave of us that he may transport, by his own industry and expense, a numerous colony of the English nation to a certain region, hereinafter described, in a country hitherto uncultivated in the parts of America," etc.
"Know ye, therefore, that we favouring the pious and laudable purpose of our said Attorney-General, of our special grace, certain knowledge, and mere motion, have given, granted, and confirmed unto the said General,	"Know ye, therefore, that we, encouraging with our royal favour the pious and noble purpose of the aforesaid Barons of Baltimore, of our special grace, certain knowledge, and mere motion, have given, granted,

his heirs and assigns for ever, all that [the boundaries here inserted.]

"And we do grant and confirm," etc., "all patronages, and advowsons of all churches, which, by increase of Christian religion, shall hereafter happen to be built within the said region, territory, island, and limits aforesaid, with all and singular, and with as ample rights, jurisdictions, privileges, prerogatives, royalties, liberties, immunities, and royal rights, and temporal franchises whatsoever, as well by sea as by land within the said region, islands, and limits aforesaid, to have, use, exercise, and enjoy in as ample manner as any Bishop of Durham in our Kingdom of England.

and confirmed, and by this our present charter for us, our heirs and successors, do give, grant, and confirm unto the aforesaid Cecilius, now Baron of Baltimore, his heirs and assigns" [the boundaries here inserted], "so that the whole tract of land," etc., "may entirely remain excepted for ever to us, our heirs, and successors."

"And we do grant, and likewise confirm," etc., "furthermore the patronages and advowsons of all churches, which, with the increasing worship and religion of Christ, within the said region, islands, islets, and limits aforesaid hereafter shall happen to be built, together with licence and faculty of erecting and founding churches, chapels, and places of worship in convenient and suitable places within the premises, *and of causing the same to be dedicated and consecrated according to the ecclesiastical laws of our Kingdom of England;* with all and singular such, and as ample rights, jurisdictions, privileges, prerogatives, royalties, liberties, immunities, and royal rights, and temporal franchises whatsoever, as well by sea as by land, with the region, islands, islets, and limits aforesaid, to be had, exercised, used, and enjoyed as any Bishop of Durham," etc.

"Know ye that we, upon further grace, certain knowledge, and mere motion, have thought fit to erect the same tract of ground, country, and island into a Province; and out of the fullness of our royal power and prerogative, we do for us, our heirs, and successors, erect and incorporate the same into a Province, and do name it Carolana, or the Province of Carolana, and the said islands, the Carolana islands, and so for ever henceforth will have them called."

"Know ye, that we, of our mere special grace, certain knowledge, and mere motion, have thought fit that the said region and islands be erected into a Province, as out of the plenitude of our royal power and prerogative, we do for us, our heirs, and successors, erect and incorporate the same into a province, and nominate the same Maryland, by which name we will that it shall from henceforth be called."

The clause in the charter of Maryland which is in italics, expressly requiring the churches to be consecrated according to the ecclesiastical law of England,[1] must have been inserted by the Attorney-General to prevent the Church of Rome from obtaining a foothold in the province.

Strange that such a charter should have ever been designated as a charter of religious liberty!

---

[1] Many years after, Sir Edward Northey, Attorney-General of England, gave this decision:—

"As to the said clause in the grant of the province of Maryland, I am of opinion the same doth not give him power to do anything contrary to the ecclesiastical laws of England."—*Chalmers' Opinions.*

CHAPTER XII.

HENRY FLEET, EXPLORER OF THE POTOMAC RIVER.

THE region now known as Maryland, its eastern shore washed by the Atlantic Ocean, its western limits marked by the Potomac River, with the Chesapeake, one of the most expansive bays in the world, flowing far into the centre, dividing the province into two peninsulas, serrated with many rivers, was uncommonly accessible to the mariner, and explored at an early period. After the preliminary reconnoissance previous to the publication of the first map in Virginia, the country began to be visited by Europeans to obtain furs from the Indians. The islands near the mouth of the Pocomoke River, named after Sir Thomas Smith, the Governor of the London Company, were examined as early as 1612 by Captain Argall and Sir Thomas Dale, with the view of establishing a settlement.

Ensign Savage and John Pory, in 1620, pushed toward the head of Chesapeake Bay, and in the days of Governor Wyatt, near one hundred English were very happily settled in this region with the hope of a very good trade in furs.[1]

William Clayborne[2] sent out by the London Company

---
[1] *Purchas*, iv. p. 1784.
[2] He was the second son of Sir Edward Cleburne or Clayborne of Westmoreland, and born about 1583.

to be Surveyor of Virginia, was the first to make a settlement at Kent Island, and to establish trading posts at Accomack, near the mouth of the Pocomoke River and Palmer's Isle at the upper end of the Chesapeake Bay near the Susquehanna River. The isle was probably named after Edward Palmer of Leamington, Gloucester County, England, an uncle of the unfortunate Sir Thomas Overbury. Camden calls him a curious and diligent antiquary; and Fuller in his *Worthies* says:—
"His plenteous estate afforded him opportunity to put forward the ingenuity implanted by nature for the public good, resolving to erect an academy in Virginia. In order whereunto he purchased an island, called Palmer's Island unto this day, but in pursuance thereof was at many thousand pounds expense, some instruments employed therein not discharging the trust reposed in them with corresponding fidelity. He was transplanted to another world,[1] leaving to posterity the monument of his worthy, but unfinished intention."

Henry Fleet was as active in developing the resources of the Potomac River as Clayborne of the Chesapeake Bay. A brief journal kept by him in the year 1631 and now for the first time printed,[2] is valuable as giving the first full description of the country and Indians then living where the lofty dome of the capitol at Washington is now the prominent object.

[1] A patent was granted to Edward Palmer, on July 3, 1622, by the Virginia Company. He died about 1625 at London.
[2] The MS. is in the Lambeth Library. In 1664 it belonged to William Griffith, A.M., who was probably the son of Henry Griffith, one of the owners of the "Warwick."

The manuscript is entitled, "A brief Journal of a Voyage made in the bark 'Warwick' to Virginia and other parts of the continent of America," and the contents are as follows :[1]—

" The 4th of July 1631 we weighed anchor from the Downes, and sailed for New England, when we arrived in the harbour of Pascattowaie the 9th of September, making some stay upon the coast of New England. From thence, on Monday the 19th of September, we sailed directly for Virginia, where we came to anchor in the bay there, the 21st of October, but made little stay. From thence we set sail for the river of Patomack, where we arrived the 26th of October at an Indian town called Yowaccomoco,[2] being at the mouth of the river, where I found that, by reason of my absence, the Indians had not preserved their beaver, but burned it, as the custom is, whereupon I endeavoured by persuasions to alter that custom, and to preserve it for me against the next spring, promising to come there with commodities in exchange by the first of April. Here I was tempted to run up the river to the heads, there to trade with a strange populous nation, called Mowhaks, man-eaters, but after good deliberation, I conceived many inconveniences that might fall out. First, I considered that I was engaged to pay a quantity of Indian corn in New England, the neglect whereof might be prejudicial both to them that should have it, and to me that promised

---

[1] The bad and obsolete spellings of the Journal are not given. Fleet's proper names are however retained.

[2] Afterwards the site of St. Mary, the old capital of the province of Maryland.

payment. And then I observed that winter was very forward, and that if I should proceed and be frozen in, it might be a great hindrance to my proceedings; therefore I did forbear, and making all the convenient haste I could, I took into the barque her lading of Indian corn as I supposed, being persuaded and overruled by John Dunton, whom I entertained as master. But upon the delivery of our lading found not above 800 bushels to our great hindrance.

"The 6th of December we weighed anchor, shaping our course directly for New England, but the wind being contrary, ending with a fearful storm, we were forced into the inhabited river of James Town. There were divers envious people, who would have executed their malice upon us, had it not been for a rumour of a commission they supposed I had, which I took great pains to procure, but (time being precious and my charge great) I came away only with the copy. Divers that seemed to be my friends advised me to visit the Governor. I showed myself willing, yet watched an opportunity that might be convenient for my purpose, being not minded to adventure my fortunes at the disposing of the Governor.

"Then we did a little replenish our provisions. But at this time I was much troubled with the seamen, all of them resolving not to stir until the spring, alleging that it was impossible to gain a passage in winter, and that the loading being corn, was the more dangerous. But the master and his mate, who were engaged for the delivery of the corn, laboured to persuade and encourage them to proceed, showing that it would be for their benefit; so that, with threats and fair persuasions, at last I prevailed.

"On Tuesday the 10th of January, we set sail from Point Comfort and arrived at Pascattoway, in New England,[1] on Tuesday the 7th of February, where we delivered our corn, the quantity being 700 bushels.

"On Tuesday, the 6th of March, we weighed anchor and sailed to the Isle of Shoals, where we furnished ourselves with provisions of victual. Sunday, the 11th of March, we sailed for the Massachusetts Bay, and arrived there on the 19th day. I wanted commodities to trade with the Indians, and here I endeavoured to fit myself if I could. I did obtain some, but it proved of little value, and was the overthrow of my voyage.

"From the Massachusetts was sent with me a small pinnace of the burthen of twenty tons, the which I was to freight with Indian corn for trucking stuff, which proved to me like that I had before from the Bay, and Pascattoway, from whence I had some likewise. Yet this was not the greatest wrong I received by this barque, as shall hereafter be related.

"Upon Monday, the 9th of April 1632, we both weighed anchor, and shaped our course for Virginia, but the sixth day being stormy weather we lost our pinnace. Contrary winds and gusty weather, with the insufficiency of the Master, made our return to Virginia tedious, to the overthrow of the voyage. But it so pleased God

---

[1] There was Pascattoway in New England, as well as on the Potomac river.

that we anchored against the English colony the 13th of May, when, for want of wind, being a flat calm, we came to an anchor at Acomack. Having some English commodities I sold them for tobacco. Wednesday, the 16th of May, we shaped our course for the river of Patomack, with the company of Captain Cleybourne,[1] being in a small vessel. By the relation of him and others of the plantation of Acomack, the Governor of Virginia[2] was much displeased with me, unto whom complaints had been made by divers of the country, and it had been discovered by one of my company that was run away, how that I had but the copy of my commission. Friday, the 17th of May, we might discern a sail making toward us about two o'clock in the afternoon. She came up to us, and we found that it was the pinnace that came out with us, which having had a short passage, had been up the river of Patomack, at Yowocomaco, an Indian town, where she had stayed three weeks, and then I was certified that had usually been in those parts with me, after my last departure came there and went up the river to truck, where he found good store of beaver, and being furnished with commodities such as Virginia affords, did beat about from town to town for beaver, but prevailed not. And in the end, coming where my barque had been, that town having 300 weight of beaver, he then reported that I was dead, they supposing that his vessel to be the same that I was

[1] William Clayborne represented Accomac in the Virginia House of Burgesses. In 1629 he defeated the Indians at Candayack, at the mouth of the Pamunky river, and received a grant of land at that point for his services.
[2] John Harvey.

to come in, desired them to bring me ashore dead or alive, and this report caused some distraction for the present, who supposed that by reason of my long absence, past my appointed time, some mischance had befallen me. And the Indians there disposed of their beaver to Charles Harmon, being 300 weight, who departed but three days before I came there.

"This relation did much trouble me, fearing (having contrary winds) that the Indians might be persuaded to dispose of all their beaver before they could have notice of my being in safety, they themselves having no use at all for it, being not accustomed to take pains to dress it and make coats of it. Monday, the 21st of May, we came to an anchor at the mouth of the river, where, hastening ashore, I sent two Indians, in company with with my brother Edward, to the Emperor,[1] being three days' journey toward the Falls. And so sailing to the other side of the river, I sent two Indians more, giving express order to all of them not to miss an Indian town, and to certify them of my arrival. But it so happened that he [Harmon] had cleared both sides of the river, so far as the Emperor's, where these Indians, when they came, certified him of my being well, and of my brother's being there, so that afterwards he could not get a skin, but he had made a very hand of it, and an unexpected trade for the time, at a small charge, having gotten 1500 weight of beaver, and cleared fourteen towns. There were yet three that were at the disposing of the Emperor, so the barque and myself passing by divers

---

[1] At Piscataway, still the name of a post town.

towns, came to the town of Patomack on Saturday, the 26th of May. There I gave the pinnace her lading of Indian corn, and sent her away the 1st of June, with letters from our Company to their friends in London, and elsewhere in England, which were safely conveyed from New England. The same day, with a north-west wind (Charles Harman staying no longer), we set sail, and the third we arrived at the Emperor's, but before we could come to the town, he was paddled aboard by a petty king in a canoe. When he came he used divers speeches, and alleged many circumstances for the excuse of the beaver which Charles Harman had of his men in that river, and after compliments used, he presented me with one hundred and fourteen beaver skins, which put me into a little comfort after so much ill success. Yet this was nothing, in regard of the great charge at his town, and at a little town by him called the Nacostines,[1] where I had almost 800 weight of beaver. There is but little friendship between the Emperor and the Nacostines, he being fearful to punish them, because they are protected by the Massomacks or Cannyda Indians, who have used to convey all such English truck as cometh into this river to the Massomacks.

"The Nacostines before, here occasioned the killing of twenty men of our English, myself then being taken prisoner and detained five years, which was in the time

---

[1] The Anacostans lived where Washington, the capital of the United States of America, is now built. The Navy Yard is on the Anacostan or eastern branch of the Potomac. A suburban post-office at the end of Navy Yard bridge is called Anacostia, and an island in the main stream, opposite the city, is called Analostan, a corruption of Anacostan.

of Sir Francis Wyatt,[1] he being the Governor of Virginia. The 13th of June I had some conference with an interpreter of Massomack and of divers other Indians that had been lately with them, whose relation was very strange in regard of the abundance of people there, compared to all the other poor number of natives which are in Patomack and places adjacent, where are not above five thousand persons, and also of the infinite store of beaver they use in coats. Divers were the imaginations that I did conceive about this discovery, and understanding that the river was not for shipping, where the people were, nor yet for boats to pass, but for canoes only. I found all my neighbour Indians to be against my design, the Pascattowies having had a great slaughter formerly by them to the number of one thousand persons in my time. They coming in their birchen canoes did seek to withdraw me from having any commerce with the other Indians, and the Nacostines were earnest in the matter, because they knew that our trade might hinder their benefit. Yet I endeavoured to prosecute my trade with them nevertheless, and therefore made choice of two trusty Indians to be sent along with my brother, who could travel well.

"I find the Indians of that populous place are governed by four kings, whose towns are of several names, Tonhoga, Mosticum, Shaunetowa, and Usserahak, reported above thirty thousand persons, and that they have palisades about their towns made with great trees,

[1] He came to Virginia 1621, and returned to England in 1626. Was reappointed in 1639. For notice of him see page 150.

and with scaffolds upon the walls. Unto these four kings I sent four presents in beads, bells, hatchets, knives, and coats, to the value of £8 sterling.

"The 14th of June they set forth, and I entreated them to bring these Indians down to the water to the Falls, where they should find me with the ship. On Monday, the 25th of June, we set sail for the town of Tohoga, when we came to an anchor two leagues short of the Falls,[1] being in the latitude of 41, on the 26th of June. This place without all question is the most pleasant and healthful place in all this country, and most convenient for habitation, the air temperate in summer and not violent in winter. It aboundeth with all manner of fish. The Indians in one night commonly will catch thirty sturgeons in a place where the river is not above twelve fathom broad. And as for deer, buffaloes, bears, turkeys, the woods do swarm with them, and the soil is exceedingly fertile, but above this place the country is rocky and mountainous like Cannida.

"The 27th of June I manned my shallop, and went up with the flood, the tide rising about four feet in height at this place. We had not rowed above three miles, but we might hear the Falls to roar about six miles distant,[2] by which it appears that the river is separated with rocks, but

---

[1] Burnaby, who visited them in 1759, gives this description: "The channel of the river is contracted by hills. It is clogged, moreover, with innumerable rocks, so that the water for a mile or two flows with accelerated velocity. At length, coming to a ledge of rocks, it divides into two spouts, each about eight yards wide, and rushes down a precipice with incredible rapidity."

[2] The Falls are nine miles from Washington.

only in that one place, for beyond is a fair river. The 3d of July, my brother, with the two Indians, came thither, in which journey they were seven days going, and five days coming back to this place. They all did affirm that in one palisado, and that being the last of thirty, there were three hundred houses, and in every house forty skins at least, in bundles and piles. To this king was delivered the four presents, who dispersed them to the rest. The entertainment they had I omit as tedious to relate. There came with them, one-half of the way, one hundred and ten Indians, laden with beaver,.which could not be less than 4000 weight. These Indians were made choice of by the whole nation, to see what we were, what was our intent, and whether friends or foes, and what commodities we had, but they were met with by the way by the Nacostines, who told them we purposed to destroy those that came in our way, in revenge of the Pascattowaies, being hired to do so for 114 skins, which were delivered aforesaid, for a present, as a preparative.

"But see the inventions of devils; the life of my brother, by this tale of the Nacostines, was much endangered. The next morning I went to the Nacostines to know the reason of this business, who answered they did know no otherwise, but that if I would make a firm league with them, and give their king a present, then they would undertake to bring those other Indians down. The refusal of this offer, was the greatest folly that I have ever committed, in mine opinion.

"The 10th of July, about one o'clock, we discerned

an Indian on the other side of the river, who, with a shrill sound, cried, 'Quo! Quo! Quo!' holding up a beaver skin upon a pole. I went ashore to him, who then gave me the beaver skin, with his hatchet, and laid down his head, with a strange kind of behaviour, using some few words, which I learned, but to me it was a foreign language. I cheered him, told him he was a good man, and clapped him on the breast with my hands. Whereupon he started up, and used some complimental speech, leaving his things with me, and ran up the hill.

"Within the space of half an hour, he returned, with five more, one being a woman, and an interpreter, at which I rejoiced, and so I expressed myself to them, showing them courtesies. These were laden with beaver, and came from a town called Usserahak, where were seven thousand Indians. I carried these Indians aboard, and traded with them for their skins. They drew a plot of their country, and told me there came with them sixty canoes, but were interrupted by the Nacostines, who always do wait for them, and were hindered by them. Yet these, it would seem, were resolute, not fearing death, and would adventure to come down. These promised, if I would show them my truck, to get great store of canoes to come down with one thousand Indians that should trade with me. I had but little, not worth above one hundred pounds sterling, and such as was not fit for these Indians to trade with, who delight in hatchets, and knives of large size, broad-cloth, and coats, shirts, and Scottish stockings. The women desire bells, and some kind of beads.

"The 11th of July there came from another place seven lusty men, with a strange attire; they had red fringe, and two of them had beaver coats, which they gave me. Their language was haughty, and they seemed to ask me what I did there, and demanded to see my truck, which, upon view, they scorned. They had two axes, such as Captain Kirk traded in Cannida, which he bought at Whits of Wapping, and there I bought mine, and think I had as good as he. But these Indians, after they came aboard, seemed to be fair conditioned, and one of them, taking a piece of chalk, made a plain demonstration of their country, which was nothing different from the former plot drawn by the other Indians. These called themselves Mostikums, but afterwards I found they were of a people three days' journey from these, and were called Hereckeenes, who, with their own beaver, and what they get of those that do adjoin upon them, do drive a trade in Cannida, at the plantation, which is fifteen days' journey from this place. These people delight not in toys, but in useful commodities.

"There was one William Elderton very desirous to go with them, but being cannibals I advised him rather to go with the others, whither I had sent a present, telling him they had no good intentions, yet upon his earnest entreaty, though unwillingly, I licensed him to proceed, and sent a present with him to their king, one of them affirming that they were a people of one of the four aforenamed nations. But I advised my man to carry no truck along, lest it might be a means to endanger his life. Nevertheless, as I was afterwards informed, he carried a coat, and other things, to the value of ten shillings more, and on the 14th of July departed.

"The 15th of July the Indians were returned with the interpreter, according to promise, and, being come, looked about for William our interpreter, to whom I made relation whither he was gone, and they seemed to lament for him, as if he were lost, saying, that the men with whom he went would eat him, that these people were not their friends, but that they were Herecheenes. At the departure of these Indians, they told me that two hundred Indians were come to the place from whence they came with store of English truck to trade for beaver, and told us they had a purpose to come down and visit us, and take a view of our commodities, and they inquired after divers kinds of commodities, of which I had some very good, part of which I gave them, and sent them away, desiring them to follow after the other Indians, and to get away my man. All this time did my truck spend not so much upon beaver as upon victuals, having nothing but what we bought of the Indians, of whom we had fish, beans, and boiled corn. The seamen, nevertheless, hoped to sell away all their clothes for beaver.

"The 18th of July I went to the Pascattowaies, and there excused myself for trading with those that were their enemies, and from thence I hired sixteen Indians, and brought them to the ship, and made one of them my merchant, and delivered to them, equally divided, the best part of my truck, which they carried up for me, to trade with their countrymen; and I gave charge to the factor to find out my man, and to bring him along with them when they came back.

"The 7th of August these Indians returned, and the Tohogaes[1] sent me eighty skins with the truck again, who showed these Indians great packs of beaver, saying there were nine hundred of them coming down by winter, after they had received assurance of our love by the Usserahaks, although the Nacostines had much laboured the contrary. And yet they were all at a stand for a time, by reason of two rumours that had been raised,—the one, that I had no good truck, neither for quantity, nor for quality; the other, that one of our men was slain by the Hirechenes, three days' journey beyond them, and that they had beguiled us with the name of Mosticums, one of their confederate nations. Nevertheless, they being desirous to have some trial of us, had sent us these skins, minding to have an answer whether we would be so satisfied of this deceit or no, and that they would come all four nations and trade with us upon their guard.

"I liked this motion very well, but was unwilling to protract time, because I had but little victuals, and small store of trucking stuff, and therefore I sailed down to Pascattowie, and so to a town on this side of it called Moyumpse. Here came three cannibals of Usserahak, Tohoga, and Mosticum; these used many complimenting speeches and rude orations, showing that they desired us to stay fifteen days, and they would come with

[1] Tiogas?

a great number of people that should trade with us as formerly they had spoken. I gave them all courteous entertainment, and so sent them back again.

"At this time I had certain news of a small pinnace with eight men, that made inquiry in all places for me, with whom was Charles Harman. The Indians would willingly have put them by from me, or I could have shifted them in the night, or taken them, as I pleased; but, knowing my designs to be fair and honest, I feared nothing that might happen by this means. And now, after much toil and some misery, I was desirous of variety of company.

"The 28th of August, in the morning, I discerned the barque, and having the shallop which I built amongst the Indians, I manned her with ten men and all manner of munition, with a full resolution to [discover] what they were, and what were their intentions. Being come near them, I judged what they were and went aboard, where I found Captain John Uty,[1] one of the Council of Virginia. In which barque I stayed with them by the space of two hours, and then invited them aboard my ship, where, being entered into my cabin, after a civil pause, this salutation was used:—

"'Captain Fleet, I am sorry to bring ill news, and to trouble you in these courses, being so good; but as I am an instrument, so I pray you to excuse me, for, in the King's name, I arrest you, your ship, and goods, and

---

[1] His son, Nathaniel, became Councillor of Maryland, and an island called Spesutia, at the head of the Chesapeake Bay, once belonged to him.

likewise your company, to answer such things as the Governor and Council shall object.'

"I obeyed; yet I conceived that I might use my own discretion, and most of his company being servants and ill-used, were willing to have followed me—yea, though it had been to have gone for England.

"The 29th of August we came to Patomack: here was I much tempted to take in corn, and then to proceed for New England; but wanting truck, and having much tobacco due to me in Virginia, I was unwilling to take any irregular course, especially in that I conceived all my hopes and future fortunes depended upon the trade and traffic that was to be had out of this river.

"I took in some provisions, and came down to a town called Patobanos,[1] where I found that all the Indians below the cannibals, which are in number five thousand persons in the river of Patomack, will take pains this winter in the killing of beavers, and preserve the furs for me now that they begin to find what benefit may accrue to them thereby. By this means I shall have in readiness at least five or six thousand weight against my next coming to trade there. Thursday, the 6th of September 1632, we came to the river of James Town, and on the 7th day anchored at James Town, and I went ashore the same night.

"The Governor, bearing himself like a noble gentleman, showed me very much favour, and used me with unexpected courtesy. Captain Utye did acquaint the

---

[1] Also called Potopaco and Portobatto, and now corrupted into Port Tobacco.

Council with the success of the voyage, and every man seemed to be desirous to be a partner with me in these employments. I made as fair weather as might be with them, to the end I might know what would be the business in question, and what they would or could object, that I might see what issue it would come to.

"The Court was called the 14th of September, where an order was made, which I have here enclosed, and I find that the Governor hath favoured me therein. After this day, I had free power to dispose of myself. Whereupon I took into consideration my business, and what course would be most for mine advantage, and what was fittest for me to resolve upon. I conceived it would be prejudicial to my designs to lose the advantage of the spring, because of the infancy of this project, considering how needful it was to settle this course of trade with the Indians so newly begun, and now that I had gotten £200 worth of [beaver] in readiness, and some of it very good.

"And I having now built a new barque of sixteen tons, and fitted myself with a partner that joineth with me for a moiety in that vessel, which we have sent to the Cannadies with provisions, and such merchandise, are there good commodities, and so to the Medeiras and Tenariffe. The loading is corn, meal, beef, pork, and clapboard. For myself, I hope to be gone up the river within the six days.

"And so, beloved friends, that shall have the perusal of this journal, I hope that you will hold me excused in the method of this relation, and bear with my weakness in penning the same. And consider that time would not permit me to use any rhetoric in the form of this discourse, which, to say truly, I am but a stranger unto as yet, considering that in my infancy and prime time of youth, which might have advantaged my study that way, and enabled me with more learning, I was for many years together compelled to live amongst these people, whose prisoner I was, and by that means am a better proficient in the Indian language than mine own, and am made more able that way.

"The thing that I have endeavoured herein is, in plain phrase, to make such relation of my voyage as may give some satisfaction to my good friends, whose longing thoughts may hereby have a little content, by perusing this discourse, wherein it will appear how I proceeded, and what success I have had, and how I am like to speed if God permit.—All which particulars, the whole ship's company are ready to testify on behalf of this Journal."

Governor Harvey appears to have colluded with Fleet in defrauding Griffith and Co. of London, the owners of the "Warwick." On July 10, 1634, in a communication to the Admiralty, the owners stated that three years before they had sent a ship to Virginia for trade and discovery, of which Henry Fleet was factor, with commission to return in a year, but that, by authority of Governor Harvey, Fleet had restrained the vessel and the profits, to their great loss.[1]

After the Maryland colony was planted, Fleet became a member of its Assembly and a man of some influence.

[1] *Cal. State Papers*, Col. series.

CHAPTER XIII.

CECILIUS, SECOND LORD BALTIMORE, AND THE SETTLEMENT OF MARYLAND.

THREE months after the death of the first Baron of Baltimore, the grant for the province of Maryland was issued in the name of Cecilius, his son and successor. By its provisions he was empowered to settle a colony in a country hitherto uncultivated, extending from Watkin's Point, near the river Pocomoke, to part of Delaware Bay, at the fortieth degree of latitude, "where New England is terminated."

Members of the old Virginia Company immediately offered objections on grounds of law, equity, and inconvenience, and this was followed by a remonstrance from the planters in Virginia; but on July 3, 1633, the Privy Council, by a diplomatic evasion, left Lord Baltimore to his patent, and the other parties to the course of law according to their desires, and a few days after the colonial authorities at Jamestown were notified that Lord Baltimore intended to transport a number of persons "to that part called Maryland, which we have given him," and they are directed to give him friendly assistance.

With the aid of a number of other persons, the "Ark," a ship of four hundred tons, and the "Dove," a pinnace of fifty tons, were obtained for carrying over the colonists. In October the party embarked, consisting not of two hundred gentlemen of good Catholic families, as many historians state, but of three hundred labouring men, chiefly Protestant, with about "twenty other gentlemen of very good fashion,"[1] two of whom were Leonard and George Calvert, brothers of Lord Baltimore.

After they left Gravesend, it was reported that the "Ark" of London, Richard Lowe, Master, and the "Dove," in charge of Captain Winter, had departed for Lord Baltimore's plantation "in or about New England," contrary to orders, and that the Company in charge of Captain Winter had not taken the oath of allegiance. Admiral Pennington immediately ordered the vessels to be brought back, and the oath having been duly administered, on the 30th of October 1633, a license was granted for them to sail.[2]

About the same time complaint was made against Lord Baltimore and his agent, Gabriel Hawley, that the latter had billeted men and women for Maryland, at twelve pence a day, in the houses of the complainants, and then took them away without paying the bills,

---

[1] Among these few were the councillors Hawley and Cornwallis, and Richard, son of Sir Thos. Gerard of Lancashire, Knight Marshal of the Palace.

Lord Baltimore, in a letter to the Earl of Strafford, says: "I have, by the help of some of your Lordship's good friends and mine, overcome these difficulties, and sent a hopeful colony into Maryland, with a fair and favourable expectation of good success, however without any danger of any great prejudice to myself, in respect that many others are joined with me in the adventure. There are two of my brothers gone, with very near twenty other gentlemen of very good fashion, and three hundred labouring men, well provided in all things."—Strafford's *Despatches*.

[2] Sainsbury's *Cal. of State Papers*.

amounting to about £60, for their entertainment. After various difficulties the ships left the Thames and went to Cowes. On the 22d of November they departed from the Isle of Wight, and by way of the West Indies, on the 24th of February 1633-34, anchored at Point Comfort, Virginia.

It had been arranged that Leonard Calvert should be Governor of Maryland, assisted by two councillors, Thomas Cornwallis and Jerome Hawley, both of whom were Protestants. On the 5th of March the expedition reached the mouth of the Potomac, which they ascended fourteen leagues, and came to St. George's isle, and anchored near to it, at another island which they called St. Clements. From this point, Calvert in the "Dove," ascended to Paschatoway, a few miles below the site of Washington city, to confer with Henry Fleet, who had lived many years in the country. Under Fleet's guidance he descended the river, and was conducted to one of Fleet's trading posts, at Yoacomaco, an Indian village upon a small tributary of the lower Potomac river. The position being pleasant, it was purchased of the Indians, and on the 27th of March 1634 Calvert took possession and named the place Saint Mary. Three days later the "Ark" and the "Dove" anchored in front of the spot, and the colonists immediately began to erect a stockade and storehouse.

Before Governor Calvert purchased St. Mary, William Clayborne appeared before the Council of Virginia, and stated that Governor Calvert told him that he was no longer a member of the Virginia colony, but belonged to his plantation, and he desired their advice as to the proper course for him to pursue.

It was answered by the Board that they wondered why such question was made, that they knew no reason why they should render up the right of the Isle of Kent, more than any other formerly given to this colony by his Majesty's patent, and that the right of Lord Baltimore's grant being yet undetermined in England, "we are bound in duty and by our oaths to maintain the rights and privileges of the colony."

The Privy Council of England, on the 22d of July 1634, also stated that "it is not intended that the interests which men have settled when you were a corporation should be impeached." While the citizens of Virginia sided with Clayborne, Sir John Harvey, appointed Governor by King Charles, was ready by every means to sustain the claims of Lord Baltimore. Windebank, Secretary of the Privy Council in England, a Roman Catholic in sympathies, was also friendly. Lord Baltimore, on the 15th of September, then staying at Warder Castle, the seat of Earl Arundel, his father-in-law, sent William Peasley, his sister's husband, to beg Windebank to procure a letter from the King to Governor Harvey, thanking him for the assistance he had given to the Maryland plantation against "Clayborne's malicious behaviour," and that if the letter was not sent by a ship about to sail, he feared his plantation would be overthrown. Windebank, three days after, sent a flattering note to Harvey, and on the 29th the King also wrote that he had given the grant to Lord Baltimore.

"there being land enough for the entertainment of many thousands, and the work more easily overcome by multitudes of hands and assistance," and then thanked the Governor for the ready assistance to the plantation begun in Maryland, and required him to continue the same. But the sturdy people of Virginia could not be made to believe that the usurpation was lawful, although sanctioned by an arbitrary King. The settlers of Kent Island had been represented by delegates in the Virginia Assembly, and they did not wish these relations surrendered. Governor Harvey discovered that though he had received flattering letters from England it did not give him influence, and on the 16th of December he despondingly wrote to Windebank:—

"Desirous to do Lord Baltimore all the service he is able, but his power is not great, being limited by his commission to the greater number of voices at the Council table, where almost all are against him, especially when it concerns Maryland. Many are so averse to that plantation that they proclaim and make it their familiar talk, that they would rather knock their cattle on the head than sell them to Maryland. He suspects the faction is nourished in England, and also by Capt. Sam. Matthews, who scratching his head, and in a fury stamping, cried out, 'a pox upon Maryland.'"

It was unfortunate for Leonard Calvert, upon his arrival at Saint Mary, to be associated with one so indiscreet as Harvey, for with prudence Clayborne and the other old settlers within the new province of Maryland might have been conciliated.

In the spring of 1635, Clayborne, who had a plantation in Accomac, despatched, as was his custom, a pinnace, called the "Long Tail," to trade with the Indians, which, on the 23d of April, was seized by the Marylanders. Indignant at this, Clayborne sent a vessel, in command of Ratcliff Warren, to recover the captured pinnace. In the harbour of great Wiggomoco, Warren met Captain Cornwallis in the pinnace "St. Margaret," and, on the 10th of May, a fight occurred, in which Warren and two others of the Virginia party were killed, while the Marylanders lost but one man.[1]

The seizure of the pinnace led to a revolution in Virginia. A meeting was held, on the 27th of April, at York, in the house of William Barrene, Speaker of the Virginia House of Burgesses, to take steps to redress their grievances, and Captain Matthews, on the next day, with forty musketeers, surrounded the Governor's residence, while John Uty, one of the Council, placing his hands upon him, said, "I arrest you for treason." Perfectly powerless in the face of an overwhelming public sentiment, he quietly submitted, and, on the 7th of May, a special meeting of burgesses chose as acting governor, John West, a brother of Lord Delaware,[2] and sent Harvey to England for misdemeanour. On the 23d of May Clayborne wrote to England, from Elizabeth City, that all his rights had been trampled upon, and

---

[1] At a meeting of the Privy Council of England it was stated that Lord Baltimore's men had slain three men at the entrance of Hudson's River, which is between the Choptank and Nanticoke river, Maryland.—*Cal. State Papers.*

[2] Sainsbury *Cal. State Papers.*

Captain Matthews, of the Virginia Council, informed Sir John Wolstenholme that he believed that the Marylanders seized the pinnace at Harvey's instigation, and concluded by the "hope that Sir John Harvey's return [to England] will be acceptable to God, not displeasing to his Majesty, and an assured happiness unto the colony."

Jerome Hawley, one of the councillors of Maryland, arrived at London early in June, for the purpose of defending the action of his fellow-councillor Thomas Cornwallis, and Thomas Harwood went as agent of the Virginians. On the 16th of December 1635 the Privy Council assembled at White Hall, both the King and Archbishop Laud being present, to inquire into the dismissal of the Governor.

The agent for Virginia charged that one Rabnet[1] said it was lawful to kill a heretic king, and that Harvey countenanced the "Romish religion" in Maryland, and that Hawley said Calvert went there to plant the same. Hawley positively denied this, but admitted that there was "public mass in Maryland," which was contrary to the laws of England, as well as the charter of the province. Governor Harvey characterized the legislative Assembly of Virginia as composed of "a rude, ignorant, and ill-conditioned people."

Charles the First, after hearing these statements, declared that it was an assumption of sovereignty for the people of the colony to send home their Governor, and that he should go back "if it was only to stay for a

---

[1] Francis Rabnet, of St. Mary, was a member of the first Maryland Assembly, and in the employ of a Mr. Winter.—*Maryland MSS.*

day." Lord Baltimore, finding the King in this temper, requested that John West, Samuel Matthews, and John Uty, might be arrested and brought to England to answer for insubordination; and further, that the Attorney-General might draw out a new commission for Harvey, with enlarged powers, and that Secretary Windebank prepare his instructions.

The grasping Baltimore, on February 25, 1637, through his brother-in-law, sends a letter to Secretary Windebank, in which he asserts that he is able to advance the King's service in Virginia, and is well assured of his own ability to perform with ample satisfaction what he undertakes, and proposes a way of serving the King which is most likely to take effect. The proposition, as it appears from a memorial in file, was to increase the revenue from Virginia £8000, on condition that he was made governor of that colony, with a salary of £2000 per annum.

The efforts of Baltimore resulted in the re-appointment of his friend Harvey as Governor of Virginia, with increased powers, and Jerome Hawley, one of the Councillors of Maryland, was also made Treasurer, with instructions to examine all land patents, and demand thereupon a yearly rental for the use of the Crown.

In October 1636 Harvey and Hawley sailed for Virginia in a Government vessel, called the "Black George," which proved "a most crazy old ship," and, when twenty leagues from the English coast, leaked so badly that the captain brought her back to Portsmouth. In April 1637 Hawley again sailed in the "Friendship," and safely arrived at Jamestown. Although Treasurer of Virginia, he did not sever his connection with the Maryland colony, but sat, in January 1638, as a Member of the Assembly, convened at Saint Mary."[1]

In this Assembly considerable difference of opinion was manifested. Leonard Calvert, Governor, and John Lewger, Secretary, although but few members of the House of Delegates were present, desired that the laws that had been prepared in England by Lord Baltimore should be assented to after a first reading, but Thomas Cornwallis, son of Sir William Cornwallis,[2] one of the two Councillors of the Province, a strong-minded and straight-forward Englishman, objected, because so few members were present. The brother of the proprietor, however, pressed the question, and the delegates, by a large majority, refused to accept the laws at that time. After a brief adjournment the Assembly again met, in February, and the delegates then resolved that all proposed laws should be read three times on three several days before the vote on their approval or rejection should be taken, and they also expressed a wish

---

[1] In July 1638 Hawley died, leaving Eleanor, his wife, and a daughter, who afterwards was living at Brabant. His will was dated in October 1633; and William Arthur Dodington, Groom of the King's Privy Chamber, and James Lisle, of the Inner Temple, were named therein executors.

Among those who certified to his death was Thomas White, aged sixty years, probably the Rev. Thomas White, sent out by the Virginia Company in 1621. Thomas Cornwallis was administrator of the estate. William Hawley, one of the Protestant members of the Maryland Assembly in 1650, and Henry Hawley, Governor of Barbadoes, were his brothers.

[2] Sir William Cornwallis was the son of Sir Charles, sent ambassador to Spain, and grandson of Sir Thomas Cornwallis, Treasurer of Calais and Comptroller of the Household of Queen Mary.

that all bills might emanate from a committee of their own choice.

Governor Calvert was very uneasy at the independence of the freemen, and proposed to adjourn; but "Captain Cornwallis," described in a pamphlet of the day as "that noble, right valiant, and politick soldier," opposed, and said "that they could not spend their time in any business better than this, for the country's good." The Governor, chagrined, replied that he would be accountable to no man, and adjourned the Assembly until the 5th of March.

Cornwallis was the most substantial man of the province, and in 1640 built a brick house, the first of which we have any record, and about this period visited England, and the next year he returned in the ship of Captain Richard Ingle.[1]

By order of Lord Baltimore, there was a re-organization of the colonial government in 1642, and Cornwallis was again nominated as councillor, but when, on the 16th of September, the new commission was tendered, "he absolutely refused to be in commission or to take the oath," probably because the new oath, swearing fealty to the proprietor, omitted the clause in the old form, "saving my allegiance to the Crown of England."

Being a royalist, after the troubles commenced between the King and his people, he appears to have again visited his native land, probably in company with Governor Calvert, who went to confer with his brother as to the position to be assumed in the crisis.

[1] Maryland MSS.

In October 1643, Charles the First, then at Oxford, granted letters of marque to Governor Calvert of Maryland and his deputies to seize upon all ships belonging to London, and the next month Parliament also passed an ordinance making the Earl of Warwick Governor-in-Chief, and Lord High Admiral of the Colonies, and he and his associates were empowered to take all necessary steps "to secure, preserve, and strengthen the said plantations."

Not many days after Warwick's appointment, Captain Richard Ingle sailed for Maryland, and on his arrival his crew and vessel were seized by the acting Governor, Brent, but he succeeded in escaping to England. Parliament, in August 1644, commissioned eight vessels to cruise in the waters of the Chesapeake, one of which was the "Reformation," in charge of Ingle,[1] and Governor Calvert hastened to Maryland to organize resistance.

In February 1645 Ingle appeared at the mouth of St. Inigo's creek, Maryland, and there was a general uprising in favour of Parliament, among others, all the servants of the absent Cornwallis, except some negroes, and one Richard Hervey, a tailor. A party under the leadership of a settler named Steerman seized the comfortable brick house of Cornwallis, "with the plate, linen-hangings, brass, pewter, and all household stuff, worth £1000,"[2] and also captured cattle, a shallop and pinnace, "worth twice as much more." Governor Calvert fled into Virginia, but the Jesuit Father White was taken prisoner.

Ingle returned to England with the property he had

---

[1] *Journals of Parliament.*   [2] MS. Maryland Records.

captured from those who opposed Parliament, but Cornwallis, who was there, instituted a suit against him, and in February 1646 Ingle made the following appeal to the House of Lords :—

"To the Right Honourable the Lords now in Parliament assembled :—

"The humble petition of Richard Ingle, showing— That whereas the petitioner, having taken the covenant, and going out with letters of marque, as Captain of the ship the 'Reformation' of London, and sailing to Maryland, where, finding the Governor of that Province to have received a commission from Oxford to seize upon all ships belonging to London, and to execute a tyrannical power against the Protestants, and such as adhered to the Parliament, and to press wicked oaths upon them, and to endeavour their extirpation, the petitioner, conceiving himself, not only by his warrant, but in his fidelity to the Parliament, to be conscientiously obliged to come to their assistance, did venture his life and fortune in landing his men and assisting the said well-affected Protestants against the said tyrannical government and the Papists and malignants. It pleased God to enable him to take divers places from them, and to make him a support to the said well affected. But since his return to England, the said Papists and malignants, conspiring together, have brought fictitious acts against him, at the common law, in the name of Thomas Cornwallis and others, for pretended trespass in taking away their goods in the parish of St. Christopher's, London, which are the very goods that were by force of war justly and lawfully taken from these wicked Papists and malignants in Maryland, and with which he relieved the poor distressed Protestants there, who otherwise must have starved, and been rooted out.

"Now, forasmuch as your Lordships in Parliament of State, by the order annexed, were pleased to direct an ordinance to be framed for the settlement of the said province of Maryland, under the Committee of Plantations, and for the indemnity of the actors in it, and for that such false and feigned actions for matters of war acted in foreign parts, are not tryable at common law, but, if at all, before the Court and Marshal; and for that it would be a dangerous example to permit Papists and malignants to bring actions of trespass or otherwise against the well affected for fighting and standing for the Parliament:

"The petitioner most humbly beseecheth your Lordships to be pleased to direct that this business may be heard before your Lordships at the bar, or to refer it to a committee to report the true state of the case, and to order that the said suits against the petitioner at the common law may be stayed, and no further proceeded in. "RICHARD INGLE."

In September 1647 the difficulty was compromised by Ingle appointing Cornwallis to collect certain moneys due to him in Maryland and Virginia, to be applied to the settlement of the claim. In 1654 Cornwallis authorizes an agent to dispose of all his property in Maryland, with the exception of 100 acres, which he wishes reserved for his negroes Peter and John, but in 1657 he was still in the province. It is probable that after the revolution under Governor Fendall, he went to England. A neck of land on the Potomac, nearly opposite to the tomb of Washington, to this day bears his name, and many miles below at Yorktown is the field where Lord Cornwallis, of the same ancestry, in 1781 surrendered his army to General George Washington.

At the age of seventy-two, in the year 1676, Thomas Cornwallis, then of Burnham Thorpe, Norfolk, died. His wife, Penelope, daughter of John Wiseman of Tyrells, Essex, and of the Inner Temple, at the age of fifty-seven, survived until 1693, and was buried at Ewarton, Suffolk. His second son, Thomas, was a clergyman, and for more than a hundred years, one of his direct descendants was a rector in the Church of England. The last representative of the Maryland pioneer, was the talented authoress of *Small Books on Great Subjects*, who died in 1858.[1]

Leonard Calvert in 1647 returned from Virginia, and with a small force regained possession of the Government, but on the 9th of June he died, leaving his house to Mistress Margaret Brent,[2] who was also named as his

---

[1] Rev. Thomas Cornwallis, son of the first Councillor of Maryland, born 1662, rector of Ewarton, Suffolk, died A.D. 1731.

Rev. William Cornwallis, son of preceding, born 1708, rector of Chelmondester, Suffolk, died 1786.

Rev. William, his son, born 1751, rector of Wittersham and Elam, Kent, died 1827.

Caroline Frances, his daughter, the talented authoress, born 1786, died unmarried in 1858.

[2] After Governor Stone came to Saint Mary, she claimed the residence of late Governor Calvert.—(Maryland MSS.)

Leaving Saint Mary she went to reside with her brother, Giles Brent, who

attorney. He was succeeded by Thomas Green in the governorship, and as the attorney of Calvert she asked for a vote in the Maryland House of Delegates, which Governor Green refusing, she formally protested. Lord Baltimore appears to have disapproved of Margaret Brent's course, but the Assembly of 1649 right gallantly defended her. They wrote to the proprietor of the province as follows:—

"As for Mistress Brent's undertaking and meddling with your estate, we do verily believe, and in conscience report, that it was better for the colony's safety at that time in her hands *than in any man's else*,[1] in the whole province after your brother's death, for the soldiers would never have treated any other with that civility and respect, and though they were even ready at several times to run into mutiny, yet she still pacified them, till at last things were brought to that strait, that she must be admitted and declared your Lordship's attorney by order of Court, or else all must go to ruin again, and the second mischief had been doubtless far greater than the former. .... Then we conceive from that time she rather deserved favour and thanks from your Honour, for her so much concurring to the public safety, than to be justly liable to all those bitter invectives you have been pleased to express against her."

After the reverses of King Charles at Marston Moor and Naseby, Lord Baltimore became increasingly politic,

---

lived on the Virginia shore of the Potomac. William, the grandson of Giles, died in 1709 in England, at the age of twenty-five.

[1] This could not have been irony, but rather an "Irish bull."

and sought the favour of Parliament, especially as in the House of Lords the Committee on Plantations, on November 28, 1645, had reported that it would be very proper that the government of Maryland should be settled in Protestants' hands by order of Parliament. To conciliate the opposition, and save his rental, he therefore, in 1648, appointed William Stone of Virginia, a Protestant, and "well affected to Parliament, Governor of Maryland."

Notwithstanding this compromise, in 1650 the Attorney-General was directed to consider the validity of the Maryland patent, and in September 1651 Parliament appointed Captain Robert Dennis, Richard Bennett, Thomas Stagg of Westover, and Captain William Clayborne, commissioners to reduce the people "in all the Plantations within the Bay of Chesapeake." Owing to Captain Dennis and the frigate "John" being lost at sea, Captain Edward Curtis of the "Guinea," a ship of twenty-eight guns, co-operated with Clayborne and Bennett. Sir William Berkeley[1] readily surrendered the government of Virginia, and the best men of the colony rejoiced in the establishment of Parliament rule, among others Colonel Richard Lee,[2] the ancestor of the Richard Henry Lee, who in the Continental Congress, offered the resolution declaring the freedom of the thirteen American colonies.

---

[1] Robertson's History erroneously states the position of Virginia at this period.

[2] Richard Lee, and Anna, his wife, came to the Potomac in 1638.—(Maryland MSS.) He was described during the English civil war as "being faithful and useful to the interest of the Commonwealth."— *Cal. State Papers, Col. Ser.* 1574-1660.

Passing from Virginia to Maryland, the commissioners told Governor Stone that they did not come to infringe Lord Baltimore's rights, but only desired conformity to the Commonwealth of England. Stone at first refused to accept the terms offered, but at length consented, and he was continued as Governor.

Matters now remained quiet in Maryland until Stone, under instructions from Lord Baltimore, issued an order that no person should hold lands that did not take the oath of fidelity to Baltimore as the proprietor of the province, and the most substantial citizens petitioned the commissioners for relief. About this time, fearing that Maryland would be restored to Virginia, from which it had been so arbitrarily severed, the time-serving Baltimore presented a paper to the authorities in England showing the importance of not uniting the two; and strange it seems, to see the old friend of the beheaded Charles, writing about the cavalier tendencies of Virginia, and claiming that Maryland and New England had remained true to the Parliament.

In 1654, Governor Stone, by proclamation, acknowledged Cromwell as Protector, but ignored the authority of the Parliament Commissioners, when he was made to resign, and a provisional government was established, of which William Durand was made Secretary. The new government had no difficulties until the arrival, in January 1654-5, of one Eltonhead, in the "Golden Fortune," Captain Tilghman, who seems to have brought instructions from Lord Baltimore, who was dissatisfied. Stone now began to organize an armed force against the existing authorities, and, sending a party to the house of Richard Preston, situated on the Patuxent river, seized the public records. He then, on the 12th of March, started with twelve boats and two hundred men to reduce the settlements on the Severn river. Before they reached Herring Bay they were met by messengers in a boat from Providence, with a letter to Stone asking under what instructions he acted, and telling him "they were resolved to commit themselves into the hands of God, and would rather die like men, than live like slaves."

Stone did not heed the remonstrance, and chased the vessel of a Captain Gookin and fired several shots. About sunset, on the 24th of March 1654-5, he neared the Severn river, and found in the harbour the ship "Golden Lion," commanded by Captain Roger Heamans, and a small vessel from New England in charge of Captain John Cutts. As Stone's flotilla approached, a shot was fired from the "Golden Lion," with an order to stop, but he moved on toward Horn Point, and began to land his men on the neck, which is now a suburb of Annapolis, the present capital of Maryland.

On the next morning, which was Sunday, Stone found that the creek where his boats lay was blockaded by the "Golden Lion," and, forced to move up the peninsula, drew up in line of battle, and unfurled the colours of Lord Baltimore. The Severn planters, one hundred and twenty in number, under Captain Fuller, marched around the peninsula with the colours of the Commonwealth of England, and attacked. After a sharp and brief contest, Stone's party was routed, and sued for mercy. A court-martial was held, and Lieutenant William Lewis and two others who had made themselves especially obnoxious, were executed for treason. The wife of Stone, in a letter to Lord Baltimore, says: "They tried all your councillors by a council of war, and sentence was passed upon my husband to be shot to death, but was after saved by the enemy's own soldiers, and so the rest of the councillors were saved by the petitions of the women, with some other friends they found there." In 1655, Richard Bennett, one of the commissioners, was in England to explain the reasons for their resistance to Stone's party, and on the 26th of September Cromwell wrote to parties in America: "It seems to us, by yours of the twenty-ninth of June, and by the relation we received by Colonel Bennett, that some mistake or scruple hath arisen concerning the sense of our letter of the twelfth of January last, as if by our letter we had intimated that we could have a stop put to the proceedings of those commissioners who were authorized to settle the civil government of Maryland, which was not at all intended by us, nor so much as proposed to us, by those who made addresses to us to obtain our said letter."

After many interviews between Commissioners Bennett and Lord Baltimore, on November 30, 1657, articles of agreement were signed, in which Baltimore pledged himself that he would never consent to the repeal of the law of the Maryland Assembly, enacted under Puritan influence, whereby all persons professing to believe in Jesus Christ should have freedom of conscience.

The Commissioners formally surrendered the province

on March 24, 1657-8, and Lord Baltimore made Josias Fendall Governor, and Philip Calvert, illegitimate son of his father, Secretary of the province.[1] The only mention of Lord Baltimore after this, previous to the restoration of Charles the Second, is an order of the Council of State to apprehend Cecilius Lord Baltimore and associates, suspected of making and exporting great sums of money, and to seize all money stamps, tools, and instruments for coining.[2]

The Commissioners Clayborne and Bennett quietly retired to Virginia. Clayborne settled at Candayack, at the mouth of the Pamunkey, the point where in 1629 he had defeated the Indians, and when Sir William Berkeley was again made Governor by the Virginia Legislature, he was chosen Secretary of Virginia, and as late as 1666 was a member of the House of Burgesses.[3]

When Edmundson, the Irish Quaker preacher, was in America, he visited Governor Berkeley, whose brother was Lord Lieutenant of Ireland, and then went to one William Wright's in the neighbourhood to hold a religious meeting, at which Major-General Bennett and some other influential men were present. In his journal Edmundson quaintly writes:—

"They said he spoke the truth, and they were courteous. The Major-General replied he was glad to hear

[1] He afterwards was Governor. Hildreth erroneously states that Leonard Calvert was illegitimate.

[2] The coins issued by Baltimore had on one side his coat of arms, with the motto, "Crescite et multiplicamini;" upon the reverse his image, with the circumscription, "Cæcilius Dominus Terræ Mariæ."

[3] M'Sherry, in his *History of Maryland*, erroneously states that Clayborne was killed by the Indians. His son Thomas thus died.

that there was such order among us, and would it had been so with others. He further said he was a man of great estate, and many of our friends poor, and therefore he desired to contribute. He likewise asked me how I was treated by the Governor [Berkeley], having heard I was with him. I told him he was brittle and peevish, and I could get nothing further on him. He asked me if the Governor called me dog, rogue, etc. ? I said, No. Then, said he, you took him in the best humour, those being his usual terms when he is angry, for he is an enemy to every good."[1]

Speaking of Bennett, the journal says: "He was a solid wise man, received the truth, and died in the same, leaving two friends his executors."

About this period, November 19, 1675, Cecilius the second Baron of Baltimore died, one whose whole life was passed in self-aggrandizement, first deserting Father White, then Charles the First, and making friends of puritans and republicans to secure the rentals of the province of Maryland, and never contributing a penny for a church or school-house.

[1] Sir William Berkeley came to Canada in 1631. He was twice Governor of Virginia. After the Bacon rebellion he went to England, but he was so censured for his cruelty to the insurgents that he soon died.

CHAPTER XIV.

ROBERT EVELYN AND EARLY EXPLORERS OF DELAWARE RIVER.

ARGALL, in 1610, entered and named the Bay of Delaware after his commander, and as early as the year 1613 it had been discovered, that by a short cut, a passage for boats could be made from the tributaries of the Chesapeake to the waters of the Delaware. Dermer, in 1619, coasted from Cape Code to Cape Henry, examining the Delaware and Hudson rivers, and saw that ships of Horn and Amsterdam had opened a trade for furs with the Indians of that region. In November 1621 the London Company despatched the "Discovery," Captain Thomas Jones, late of the "May Flower," to engage in the fur trade at Manhattan, and a few days after he sailed they "received certain advices that there was newly gone from Amsterdam for the same trade of furs, and the self-same place, two private pinnaces, the one of forty tons, and the other of eighty tons, with six pieces of ordnance, double manned, and exceedingly well provided."[1]

The Dutch, notwithstanding these efforts, secured a

[1] MS. Records Va. Company.

foothold at Manhattan, and obtained the trade of the Hudson. About the year 1619, Ensign Savage explored the Chesapeake Bay. In June of that year, a few days after the London Company granted a patent for the benefit of the Leyden Puritans, it was ordered that "sundry Kentish men who would seat and plant themselves in Virginia, should have as large privileges and immunities as is granted to any others in that land," and as Purchas, in his work published in 1625, speaks of, there settled "near one hundred English very happily, with hope of a very good trade of furs," it may be that these Kentish men gave to the isle in the upper part of the Chesapeake Bay the name of Kent, and that they were English Puritans. Fuller, in his *Worthies of England*, states that Edward Palmer of Leamington, a man of wealth and learning, who died before 1625, resolved to found an academy in Virginia, "in order whereunto he purchased an island called Palmer's Island unto this day," but that he failed in the enterprise owing to the faithlessnesses of some of his agents.[1]

In 1631 Nathaniel Basse, a councillor of Virginia, was authorized to invite those of New England that "disliked coldness of climate or barrenness of soil, to settle in Delaware Bay."[2] In September 1632 some Englishmen ascended the Delaware, and were murdered by the Indians near Fort Nassau, now Gloucester, New Jersey.

Before the patent for Maryland was issued, Sir John Lawrence, Sir Edmund Plowden, and others, petitioned

---

[1] See p. 220.　　　　　　　　[2] MS. Va. Records.

for a grant of Long Island and thirty miles square, to be called Syon. After the death of the first Lord Baltimore, they again petitioned for Isle Plowden or Long Isle, and the small isles between thirty and forty degrees of latitude, six leagues from the main, near Delaware Bay, and forty leagues square of the adjoining coast, to be held as a county palatine, and called New Albion, with the same privileges "as heretofore granted to Sir George Calvert, late Lord Baltimore, in New Foundland."

One month after the patent for Maryland received the great seal, the King, on July 24, 1632, ordered Secretary John Coke to direct the Lords Justices, Ireland, to issue a patent for Long Isle and adjacent country to Plowden and associates.

Before Leonard Calvert and colony sailed for the Chesapeake, Captain Thomas Young, who was a gentleman of influence in London, received a special commission from the King, which is printed in the nineteenth volume of Rymer's *Fœdera*, and dated September 23, 1633, authorizing him to fit out ships, appoint officers, to explore all territories in America that he wished, and commanding all English subjects not to impede his movements, notwithstanding they had received patents, before the date of his commission.

In the spring of 1634 the exploring expedition departed, the Lieutenant of which was Robert Evelyn,[1] a nephew of Young, and cousin of John Evelyn, the

---

[1] His father was Robert Evelyn of Godstone, Surrey. His mother's name before marriage was Susan Young, daughter of Gregory Young of York. His brother George was commander at Kent Island, and, in a controversy with Leonard Calvert, sneeringly said that the first Lord Baltimore was only

celebrated author of *Sylva*. Among the officers appointed was a surgeon named Scott, and Alexander Baker of St. Holborn's parish, Middlesex, cosmographer, described by Young as "skilful in mines and trying of metals," who had been confined as a recusant. Early in the month of July, Young was at Jamestown[1] conferring, in the presence of Thomas Cornwallis, with Virginians, relative to a ship-carpenter whose services he desired, and after this, having constructed a shallop for small streams, appeared to have sailed up the Delaware and established a post at Eriwomeck, which on Speed's map is not far from the mouth of the Schuylkill, and perhaps at Fort Beversrede, within the limits of the present city of Philadelphia, which the year before had been secured but abandoned by the Dutch.

Early in 1635 Lieutenant Evelyn returned to England on special business, while Young continued to seek for a navigable inland passage for ships from the Atlantic Ocean to the South Sea. In September of this year, Captain George Holmes, and others from Virginia, historians tell us, seized Fort Nassau, now the site of Gloucester, on the New Jersey side of the Delaware, and were afterwards taken prisoners by the Dutch and carried to Manhattan, from whence they were returned in a vessel commanded by Captain De Vries, to Jamestown. This party probably had some connection with the explorations of Young.

---

the "son of a grazier." The Maryland Historical Society have published a sketch of the commander of Kent, written by S. F. Streeter.

[1] Harvey in *Sainsbury*, p. 184.

After eighteen months passed in discoveries, and seeking an inland water route through the American continent, supposed to be somewhere about the fortieth parallel of latitude, Young proceeded to England, and asked that the King would grant permission for him and his associates to enjoy the right to such inland countries as they might discover. In 1637 the Governor and Council of Virginia chose Robert Evelyn as surveyor of the colony, in the place of Gabriel Hawley, deceased, who was a relative of Jerome Hawley, councillor of Maryland, but the appointment does not appear to have been confirmed, as he was afterwards a proxy for St. George's Hundred in the Maryland Assembly.

The next year a party of Swedes entered the Delaware, of which Jerome Hawley writes to Secretary Windebank as follows :—" RIGHT HON^{ble}.—Uppon the 20th of March last, I took the bouldness to p'sent you wth my letters, wherein I gave only a tuch of the business of our Assembly, referring yor Hono^{r} to the general letters sent by Mr. Kemp from the Govern^{r} and Councell. Since wch tyme heare arrived a Dutch shipp wth comission from the young Queene of Sweaden, and signed by eight of the Cheife Lordes of Sweden, the coppe whereof I would have taken to send to yor Hono^{r}, but the Captayne would not p'mitt me to take any coppe thereof, except hee might have free trade for tobacco to carry to Sweaden, wch being contrary his Ma^{ts} instructions, the Govern^{r} excused himself thereof.

"The shipp remayned heare about 10 dayes to refresh wth food and water, during wch tyme the M^{r} of the said shipp made knowne that bothe himself and another shipp of his company were bound for Delaware Baye, wch is the confines of Virginea and New England, and there they p'tend to make a plantation, and to plant tobacco, wch the Dutch do allso already in Hudson's River, which is the very next river northard from Delaware Baye. All wch being his Ma^{ts} territorys I humbly conceive it may be done by his Ma^{ts} subjects of these parts making use only of some English ships that resort heather for trade yearly, and be no charge at all to His Ma^{te}."

In 1641 Evelyn was in England, and in a card published at that time, and signed by Captain Brown and Christopher Thomas, who had represented in 1638 the Isle of Kent, in the Maryland Assembly, as well as by Clayborne and Evelyn, the advantages of the country north of the entrance of Delaware Bay were set forth, and it was also therein stated that Clayborne had traded there since 1627, and that Evelyn had resided in the region four years, and traded near the Schuylkill with fifteen men.

On June 23, 1642, Evelyn had returned to America, and the authorities of Maryland commissioned him "to take charge and command of all or any of the English in or near about Piscattaway, and to levy, train, and muster them." Piscattaway was the point where Father White had laboured for the conversion of the Indians, a few miles below the city of Washington.

Sir Edmund Plowden, the descendant of the eminent jurist, whose wife Mabel, daughter of Peter Mariner of

Wanstead, Hampshire, had left him after being married twenty-five years, on account of bad treatment, came to Virginia, and in 1642 visited "Eriwomeck," near the Schuylkill, "the fort given over by Captain Young and Master Evelin." On May 23d the sloops "Real" and "St. Martin" were sent from Manhattan to Fort Nassau, near Gloucester, New Jersey, with orders to the commissary there to enter the Schuylkill and approach the place where the English had taken possession.

Plowden this year visited the Dutch at Manhattan, and returned to Virginia. In 1648, by way of Boston, he went to England, and in 1652 there is a record of Marylanders visiting him at his lodgings in London. Eventually he was led to the debtors' prison, and in 1655 died,[1] and the Swedes and Dutch remained in possession of the Delaware until they capitulated to the English under Sir Robert Carr.

[1] In a map compiled by John Ferrar, late Deputy of Virginia Company, of the American colonies, the province of Nova Albion is marked as belonging to Plowden.

CHAPTER XV.

FATHER ANDREW WHITE, S.J.

THE "Ark" and "Dove" had been searched in the river Thames, and all the passengers for the new province of Maryland, in accordance with the law, took the oath of allegiance, but it was arranged that, at the Isle of Wight,[1] there should quietly embark Father Andrew White, of the Society of Jesus, with his colleague, John Altham *alias* Gravener, and two lay brothers, John Knowles and Thomas Gervase.[2]

No class of religionists have been more zealous and untiring than the Jesuits, and Father Andrew White was second to none of his order. Born in the city of London about the year 1569, he pursued his studies at Douay, and, after becoming a priest, returned to England. On account of his proselytizing efforts, in 1606, he was banished. It was not until 1619 that he was fully admitted as a member of the Society of Jesus, and then passed several years as a professor at Liege and Louvain.

[1] White's *Journal. Force*, vol. iv.
[2] Gravener and Gervase were members of the Clerkenwell College, London, disbanded by the Government in 1627.—Heath's *Narrative in Camden Soc. Pub.*

Although more than threescore years of age when he engaged in the Maryland mission, his natural force was not abated. The passengers on board of the ships were largely Protestant, two only out of twelve of those that died at sea professing adhesion to the Church at Rome; and no effort was spared by the Jesuit to lead the colonists to embrace what he deemed was the true religion.

When the expedition reached the island, which they called Saint Clements, a cross was set up, and the country was taken possession of, with religious ceremonies resembling those which a poet has described in connection with the planting of Christianity in England—

> " In the bright
> Fringe of the living sea, that came and went,
> Tapping its planks, a great ship sideways lay,
> And o'er the sands a grave procession passed,
> Melodious with many a chanting voice;
> Nor spear, nor buckler had these foreign men,
> Each wore a snowy robe, that downward flowed;
> Fair in the front a silver cross they bore,
> A painted Saviour floated in the wind,
> The chanting voices, as they rose and fell,
> Hallowed the rude sea air."[1]

After the colonists landed at the village of Yowcomaco, the settlement was called Saint Mary; and although contrary to the laws of England, White and his coadjutors immediately fitted up a rude Indian hut, and consecrating it for a chapel, celebrated mass.

At once steps were taken to secure property for the

---

[1] Alexander Smith's *Edwin of Deira*.

Church, and a Jesuit, called Thomas Copley, Esq.,[1] in the early records, entered lands for Fathers White and Altham, and thirty other settlers, among others, Francisco, a mulatto.

In 1635 Jerome Hawley, one of the councillors of Maryland, told Charles the First and Archbishop Laud that mass was celebrated in the province. When the settlers held the first legislative Assembly, they expressed their adhesion to the Church of their native land, and re-enacted the formula of the Statute Book of England, "That Holy Church shall have and enjoy all her rights, liberties, and franchises, wholly and without blemish."

Owing to the hostile disposition of the natives, the Jesuits were prevented from attempting their conversion, but, says White in his Journal:—

"In the interim we are more constantly intent on the English, and since then on Protestants as well as Catholics we have laboured, and God has blessed our labours, for of the Protestants who came from England this year almost all have been converted to the faith, besides many others, with four servants that were brought for necessary use in Virginia. And of five workmen we hired we have in the meantime gained two."

Late in the month of November 1637 Father White was strengthened by the arrival at Saint Mary of John

---

[1] There also appears this entry in the Maryland MS. Records:—"Thomas Copley, Esq., demandeth 4000 acre of land, due by conditions of plantation, for transporting into this province himself and twenty able men, at his own charge, to plant and inhabit, in the year 1637."

Lewger, wife, and family.[1] On the previous 15th of April he had been commissioned as Secretary of the province, and was subsequently Councillor, Attorney-General, and Judge of all causes testamentary and matrimonial. He had been a college friend of Lord Baltimore, and in 1622 received the degree of Master of Arts at Oxford.

In 1632 he became rector of a parish in Essex, but by the arguments of the acute disputant William Chillingworth, he became a Roman Catholic, and by a singular coincidence, his proselyter soon returned to the Church of England, and wrote the well-known sentence, "The Bible, and that only, is the religion of Protestants, and every one, by making use of the helps and assistances that God had placed in his hands, must learn and understand it for himself, as well as he can."

Lewger was chagrined when he heard that Chillingworth had reverted to the Church of England; but the latter answered his wrath in a kind letter, entitled, "Reasons against Popery, in a letter from Mr. William Chillingworth to his friend Mr. Lewger, persuading him to return to his mother, the Church of England, from the corrupt Church of Rome." The letter had a softening influence, and Lewger was willing to have a conference with his old friend, but clung to the Church into which he had been led.

---

[1] He arrived, November 28, 1637, in the ship "Unity," from the Isle of Wight, with Ann, his wife, John, his son, aged nine years; maid-servants, Martha Williamson, Ann Pike, Mary Whitebead; men-servants, Benjamin Colby, Philip Lines, Thomas Thurston, and a boy, Robert Serle, aged twelve years.

Deprived of his benefice, a married man, and with no means of living, Lord Baltimore made him Secretary of the province of Maryland, and confidential adviser of his brother Leonard, the Governor.

With the arrival of Lewger in Maryland, there was increased zeal upon the part of the Jesuits, and mission stations were established among the Indians. On the 5th of July 1640, Father White, in the presence of his colleague Altham, Governor Calvert, and Secretary Lewger, baptized the family of the chief of the Piscattaway village, which was nearly opposite to Mount Vernon, the home of Washington, the first President of the United States of America. The chief was christened Charles, the wife Mary, and the child Anna, in compliment to the royal family of England, and on the afternoon of the same day the chief was married according to the rites of the Church of Rome, and a cross was planted commemorative of the event, the priests chanting the litany, and Calvert, Lewger, and other sympathizers, following in solemn procession. Tanner, in his *Gesta Præclara*, published in the city of Prague, nearly two centuries ago, gives a rude engraving of the baptismal scene, but this and the marriage ceremony remain yet to be coloured in poetry, as Longfellow has embalmed the myths of the Indians about Lake Superior and the Falls of Saint Anthony in the legend of *Hiawatha*.

Father White in his journal states that the reason the Piscattaway chief loved him was on account of a dream. The savage told him that one night he had a vision, in which he saw his deceased father worshipping a dark and hideous god; at a little distance was a most ludicrous demon, with a colonist named Snow,[1] "an obstinate heretic from England; by his side, after which Governor Calvert and Father White appeared in the company of a beautiful god of exceeding whiteness, who with gentleness beckoned unto him, and from that hour he had been drawn by cords of affection toward the black robes."

According to their prejudices, those who read this story will call it a wonderful providence, an Indian superstition, a Jesuit fiction, or will say, *Credat Judæus Apella;* but whatever the conclusion, it shows that some one had impressed the ignorant savage with the belief that those were heretics, who were not Roman Catholics.

Unpleasant differences at times occurred between the early colonists. The first settlers were largely indented white servants and poor young men who came to seek their fortunes. They had no clergy of the Church of England furnished by the proprietor for the cure of their souls; but in their chests a few books had been placed by anxious parents and friends, that might prove sources of comfort in hours of doubt, loneliness, and temptation.

Thomas Cornwallis, himself a Protestant, and the leading Councillor of the province, had a number of indented white servants, in care of an overseer named

---

[1] Marmaduke Snow was the early merchant at Saint Mary, a brother of Abel Snow of the Cursitor's Office, London.—*Maryland MS. Records.*

William Lewis. One day, in the year 1638, these servants were listening to the reading of sermons[1] written by the eloquent Puritan divine known as the "silver-tongued Smith," when the overseer appeared and said in a rage that "the book came from the devil, as all lies did, and that he that wrote it was an instrument of the devil, and that they should not keep nor read such books." But Cornwallis protected the rights of his servants, and Lewis was fined for his offensive and indiscreet speech.

The journal of Father White abounds in religious sentiment. Shortly after the marriage of the Piscattaway chief, Father Altham died at Kent Island, and White, asking his Superior for more men, wrote:—" Those who are sent need not fear lest the means of support be wanting, for He who clothes the lilies, and feeds the birds of the air, will not suffer those who are labouring to extend His kingdom to be destitute of necessary sustenance." Father Brock, whose real name was Morgan, a relative of Father Thomas FitzHerbert, rector of the English College at Rome, died in July 1641, but about a month before wrote:—" For my part I would rather,

---

[1] The sermons of Dr. Henry Smith were very practical, and much read in Puritan households. Mary, the orphan daughter of Sir John Proude, wife of Sir William Springett, and mother-in-law of William Penn, in 1635 was residing with her guardian, Sir Edward Partridge, and in one of her letters alludes to his Puritan household in these words:—

"They would not admit of sports on the first day of the week, calling it the Sabbath. . . . . When I was about eleven years of age, a maidservant who tended on me and the rest of the children, and was zealous in that way, would read *Smith's* and *Preston's* sermons on the first day between the services."—*Penns and Penningtons of* 17*th Century*. London, 1847.

labouring in the conversion of the Indians, expire on the bare ground, deprived of all human succour, and perishing from hunger, than ever think of abandoning the holy work of God for fear of want."

The Jesuit enjoyed his work. "God now imparts to us," said one, "a foretaste of what he is about to give to those that live faithfully in this life, and mitigating all hardship with a degree of pleasantness, so that his Divine Majesty appears to be present with us in an external manner." In 1639 Father Philip Fisher officiated at Saint Mary. He had been connected with the Clerkenwell College, and in England went under the assumed name of Musket. For a time he was in Newgate prison, but by the influence of Secretary Windebank was released and harboured,[1] until he found an opportunity to go to America.

The open efforts to proselyte the early settlers of Maryland, in the face of the charter of the province forbidding the erection of places of worship not in connection with the Church of England, at length attracted the attention of Parliament, and on December 1, 1641, a remonstrance of the House of Commons was presented to Charles at Hampton Court, in which they complained that he had permitted "another State, moulded within this State, independent in government, contrary in interest and affection, secretly corrupting the ignorant or negligent professors of religion, and clearly uniting themselves against such."[2]

Lord Baltimore now became alarmed lest the grant

[1] Rushworth, vol. iv. pp. 44, 68. [2] *Ibid.* vol. iv.

might be annulled, which was a source of profit, and on October 7, 1642, wrote to the Jesuit Fathers in Maryland :—

"Considering the dependence of the State of Maryland on the State of England, unto which it must, as near as may be, be conformable, no ecclesiastic in the province ought to expect, nor is Lord Baltimore nor any of his officers, although they are Roman Catholics, obliged in conscience to allow such ecclesiastics any more or other privileges, exemptions, or immunities for their persons, lands, or goods than is allowed by his Majesty or officers to like persons in England."

This unexpected communication was exceedingly depressing to Father White, penned as it was by one who had assisted them in settling in Maryland, and with a sorrowing heart the aged Father thus records the circumstance in his journal :—

"Occasion of suffering has not been wanting from those from whom rather it was proper to expect aid and protection, who, too intent upon their own affairs, have not feared to violate the immunities of the Church."

Perceiving the thrift of the Puritans of Plymouth and Massachusetts Bay, and that their political power was on the increase in England, Lord Baltimore, the year after he wrote the cold letter to Father White, deputed his brother, Governor Calvert, to write to Captain Gibbons, of Boston, offering him a commission if he would settle a colony in Maryland; but, says Winthrop, "our captain had no mind to further his desire, nor had any of our people temptation that way."

Soon after this the civil war in England began, and on the 26th of August 1644, eight vessels, one of which was the "Reformation," Captain Ingle, were commissioned by Parliament to transport ammunition, clothing, and supplies to the settlements of Chesapeake Bay.

In February 1645, Ingle appeared at Saint Mary, and Leonard Calvert, the Governor, and others, refusing to recognise the authority of Parliament, were driven to Virginia, and Father White was taken prisoner, and sent to England, tried, and found guilty of teaching doctrines contrary to the Statutes of England, but on the 4th of July 1644 judgment was stayed. After this he remained in Newgate prison for eighteen months, but on January 7, 1648, the House of Commons "did concur with the Lords in granting the petition of Andrew White, a Jesuit, who was brought out of America into the kingdom by force, upon an English ship," and ordered him to be discharged, provided he left the kingdom within fifteen days.[1] In accordance with the order he retired, but, after a prolonged absence, returned to England, where he died December 27, 1656, more than fourscore years of age.[2]

After Leonard Calvert resumed the governorship of Maryland, Father Fisher came back to the province from which he had fled, and on March 1, 1648, wrote to his superior:—

"OUR VERY REVD. FATHER IN CHRIST,—Although my companion and myself reached Virginia on the 7th of January, after a tolerable journey of seven weeks,

[1] *House of Commons Journal.*   [2] Oliver.

there I left my companion, and availed myself of the opportunity of proceeding to Maryland, where I arrived in the course of February. By the singular providence of God I found my flock collected together, after they had been scattered three long years. . . . Truly flowers appear in our land; may they attain to fruit.

"A road by land through the forest has just been opened from Maryland to Virginia. After Easter I shall visit the Governor of Virginia on momentous business; may it tend to the praise and glory of God. My companion,[1] I trust, still lies concealed, but I hope will soon commence his labour under favourable auspices."

The Jesuit mission was not very successful, as will be seen from the statement of its strength for several years:[2]—

In 1635 there were 3 priests, 2 lay brothers.
,, 1636 ,, ,, 4 ,, 1 ,, ,,
,, 1638 ,, ,, 4 ,, 1 ,, ,,
,, 1639 ,, ,, 4 ,, 1 ,, ,,
,, 1640 ,, ,, 4 ,, 1 ,, ,,
,, 1642 ,, ,, 3 ,,
,, 1669 ,, ,, 3 ,,
,, 1670 ,, ,, 3 ,, 3 ,, ,,
,, 1671 ,, ,, 2 ,, 2 ,, ,,
,, 1672 ,, ,, 2 ,,
,, 1673 ,, ,, 2 ,, 1 ,, ,,
,, 1674 ,, ,, 2 ,, 1 ,, ,,
,, 1675 ,, ,, 2 ,, 2 ,, ,,

A few of the names of the Fathers of the Maryland Mission are preserved in Oliver's *Dictionary of the*

---

[1] Probably Lawrence Sankey, S.J., who came to Maryland in 1649.
[2] These statistics are appended to White's *Narrative*.

Jesuits:—Laurence Sankey was born in Lancashire in 1606, became a Jesuit in 1636, came to Maryland in 1649, and died in Virginia, February 13, 1657, aged fifty-nine years. Father Pelham, born in 1623, came to Maryland in 1653, and died in 1671. Father Peter Manners came in 1663 and died in 1667. Father Fitz-Herbert came in 1654 and died at St. Omer, May 22, 1687.

Upon John Lewger's return to England, his wife having been buried in Maryland, he became a priest of the Church of Rome, and lived at Lord Baltimore's house in Wild Street, London. In 1659 he published a work entitled "Erastus Junior, a solid demonstration by principles, forms of ordination, common laws, Acts of Parliament, that no Bishop nor Presbyter hath any authority to preach from Christ, but from Parliament."

The Earl of Winchester's chaplain, Benjamin Denham, writes from Pera, near Constantinople:—

"All that is treated of in the Privy Council about Roman Catholics is discovered to Lord Brudenell, and Lord Baltimore, Governor of Maryland, whose chaplain, an English recusant, now a Romish priest, was one of the vicegerents there in Charles the First's time."[1]

True to the last to the Church of Rome, Lewger died in 1665, from the plague, caused by visiting the sick poor of his communion, and was buried at St. Giles-in-the-Fields.

[1] *Cal. State Papers.*

CHAPTER XVI.

DR. THOMAS HARRISON AND THE VIRGINIA PURITANS.

FROM the first settlement Nonconformists had been in Virginia, and as some of the colonists were Hollanders there was a disposition to allow liberty in worship.

The first minister at Henrico was Alexander Whitaker, son of the distinguished Calvinist, Dr. Whitaker, who had been Master of St. John's College, Cambridge, and cousin of Rev. William Gouge, for many years the Puritan preacher at Black Friar's, London. His services in Virginia were modified by the circumstances of the new settlement. Every Saturday night he held a religious meeting in a private house, the communion was administered every month, once a year there was a solemn fast, and the affairs of the church were administered by a council composed of the minister and four of the most religious men. Questions concerning subscription and the wearing of the surplice, then so rife in the parishes of England, were never mooted in Virginia when Whitaker was alive. While he was minister at Bermuda Hundred, on the lower side of the James River, and five miles by water from Henrico, the minister at the latter place was William Wickham, respected for his pure life and sound doctrines, who had never received Episcopal ordination; and after Whitaker was drowned, in 1617, he was the only religious teacher above Jamestown, and almost blind. In the year 1618, Captain Christopher Lawne[1] established a plantation upon the lower side of the river, not far from Jamestown, the settlers of which were Puritan in their sympathies. Lawne was a member of the first American Legislature that met on July 30, 1619, but soon after died; and on the 3d of November 1620, upon the petition of Nathaniel Basse, gent., and fellow-adventurers, the Virginia Company agreed that hereafter the Lawne Plantation should be known as the Isle of Wight Plantation.[2]

The next year Edward Bennet, who had been Deputy-Governor of Merchant Adventurers of England resident at Delft,[3] and now an influential citizen of London, who, upon motion of Sir Edwin Sandys, had been made a free member of the Virginia Company, on account of a paper which he had submitted to the House of Commons, urging the prohibition of Spanish tobacco, determined to make a plantation near the Isle of Wight settlement. Associated with Richard Wiseman, Thomas Ayres, and others, in the summer of 1621, he, at great expense,

---

[1] He may have been Christopher Lawne who had been prominent among the English Separatists in Holland, or his son.

[2] In Isle of Wight Co., Virginia, Lawne's Creek preserves the name of the first plantation.

[3] Wing's *Discourse*. Flushing, 1622.

sent a colony to Virginia, who were settled at Warrosquoyak, on the Nansemond River.

The minister who accompanied them was the Rev. William Bennett, who remained for two years. It is probable that he was succeeded by the learned divine Henry Jacob, who was in his youth precentor of Christ Church College, Oxford,[1] but visiting Leyden became a *jure divino* Congregationalist, and when he returned, established the first Independent Church in England. He died after a brief residence in Virginia, and there is no record as to the precise time or place of his burial.

The Nansemond parish having increased in population, in 1642 an Act was passed by the Virginia Assembly authorizing its division.[2]

On May 24, 1642, Richard Bennet, a nephew of Edward Bennet, Daniel Gookin, late of Ireland, John Hill, and others, of the county of Upper Norfolk, wrote a letter to the "Pastors and Elders of Christ Church in New England," in which they alluded to the late law, by which their old parish was divided, and stated that each of the three new parishes was "entire within itself, and the inhabitants willing to maintain a pastor."

William Durand also wrote to Rev. John Davenport of

---

[1] Wood, in *Athenæ Oxonienses*, says he "entered college at fifteen, and was excellently well read." His son Henry also became a fine scholar, and assisted the learned Selden.

[2] The law in Hening's *Statutes* has the following preamble:—" For the better enabling the inhabitants of this colony to the religious worship and service of Almighty God, which is often neglected and slackened by the inconvenient and remote vastness of parishes : Resolved that the county of Upper Norfolk be divided into three distinct parishes."

New Haven, Connecticut, formerly Vicar of St. Stephens, Coleman Street, London, that he and others, of Upper Norfolk or Nansemond County, had heard him preach in England, and requested him to assist Mr. Philip Bennet, who had gone to Boston to procure ministers. He also stated that they had once thought of sending to England, but at last concluded that a ministry better adapted for them could be obtained in New England.

The letter from Virginia was read in September at a public religious meeting in Boston, and the ministers set apart a day for its consideration, after which three were selected for the Virginia parishes lately established. They were all men of education and experience,—John Knowles, a ripe scholar, of Immanuel College, Cambridge, who had been preacher at Watertown, near Boston, William Tompson, who had been a student of Oxford, and had been Rector of Winwick, and Thomas James, who had been ten years minister at Charlestown, the adjoining parish to Boston, but then living at New Haven, Connecticut. In October they sailed from New Haven, but in a few days their pinnace was wrecked at Hell Gate, in Long Island Sound. Procuring at Manhattan another vessel they re-embarked, and, after exposure to the storms of winter, reached Jamestown eleven weeks after they left New England. Letters of commendation from Governor Winthrop were presented to Governor Berkeley, but he was churlish and unsatisfactory; and under his influence the House of Burgesses, the next spring, March 1644, passed a law forbidding any to officiate in the churches who did not conform to the Book of Common Prayer. Although the church doors were closed against them they found opportunities to preach. "Though the State did silence the ministers," says Winthrop, "because they would not conform to the order of England, yet the people resorted to them in private houses, to hear them as before."

On the 20th of June Knowles returned to Boston, but Tompson remained preaching in Virginia and Maryland with much success. Mather, in a commemorative poem, writes—

> "Hearers, like doves, flocked with contentious wing,
> Who should be first, feed most, most homeward bring,
> Laden with honey, like Hyblæan bees,
> They knead it into combs upon their knees.
>
> . . . . .
>
> A constellation of great converts there
> Shone round him, and his heavenly glory wear,
> Gookin[1] was one of them, by Tompson's pains,
> Christ and New England, a dear Gookin gains."

At the time that Knowles[2] and his associates left Virginia party feeling ran high, and the community were divided into adherents of Charles the First and the

---

[1] Gookin was the son of Daniel Gookin, who came with a colony from Ireland to Newport News, in 1621, and the nephew of Sir Vincent Gookin. After he went to Massachusetts he became superintendent of Indian affairs and the friend of the missionary John Eliot.

[2] Knowles did not remain in America. After his return to England he was preacher at Bristol Cathedral, and then was sixteen years at Pershore, in Worcester. On April 9, 1665, his house was searched, and he imprisoned, because he had collected money for the suffering Polanders, which in his petition he says "he did not know was unlawful, but thought them an object of pity." He died April 10, 1685, at the advanced age of eighty-five years.

Parliament, the former called Bristolers and the latter Londoners.

On the 13th of April 1644, at the mouth of Warwick Creek, a small tributary of the James, near Newport News, a fight occurred between a twelve-gun ship of the former and two vessels of the latter. The Indians perceiving the strife among the whites seized the opportunity to gratify their revenge, and, on the 18th of the month—a black Good-Friday in the Colonial calendar—suddenly swarmed around the feeble settlements, and with a yell filled their hands with reeking scalps, and quickly disappeared in the woods.

Strong men were appalled, women mourned and refused to be comforted, for their children were not. The rich and the poor felt they were stricken by God; and the Legislature, when it assembled, enacted, " to the end that God mayeth avert his heavy judgments that are upon us, that the last Wednesday in every month be set apart for fasting and humiliation, and that it be wholly dedicated to prayers and preaching."[1]

Among those upon whom the massacre made a deep impression was the Rev. Thomas Harrison, the chaplain of Governor Berkeley. He had been a bigot before, and he now confessed that although he had kept a fair exterior to the scholarly Knowles and companions, still he had used his influence with the Governor to have them silenced.[2] His style of preaching became more earnest and practical, which was displeasing to his patron, who said he did not wish so grave a chaplain.

[1] Hening's *Statutes*.   [2] Calamy.

Not discouraged by the censure of the Governor, he crossed the river, and preached to the planters of Nansemond and Elizabeth River, in the parishes made vacant by the ejection of the three New England ministers.

In little more than a year after this, on October 27, 1645, the House of Commons "ordered that the inhabitants of the Summer Islands, and such others as shall join themselves to them, shall, without any molestation or trouble, have and enjoy the liberty of the conscience in matters of God's worship, as well in those parts of America where they are not planted as in all other parts of America where hereafter they may plant."[1]

About this period Governor Sayle of Eleuthera, a small isle of the Bahamas,[2] visited the Nansemond people, and invited them to go to his plantation, the charter of which provided that in matters purely religious the civil magistrate should exercise no jurisdiction. Harrison wrote to Governor Winthrop of Massachusetts relative to the proposal, and he advised them not to leave Virginia.

In another letter to Winthrop, dated Elizabeth River, November 2, 1646, and sent to Boston by Captain Edward Gibbons, "the younger brother of the house of an honourable extraction,"[3] Harrison remarks, "Had your proposition found us risen up in a posture of removal, there is weight and force enough [in yours] to have staked us down again."

The House of Commons, in October 1647, passed an

---

[1] *House of Commons Journal.* [2] See page 180.
[3] Scottow in *Mass. Hist. Coll.*, 4th Series, vol. iv.

ordinance of toleration,[1] of which Harrison, writing to Winthrop in the following February, says:—

"That golden apple, the ordinance of toleration, is now fairly fallen into the lap of the saints, no more compelling men to go to the parish churches. . . . Concerning ourselves we have received letters full of life and love from the Earl of Warwick, who engageth himself to the uttermost to advance the things of our peace and welfare, and the Prince of Peace himself hath hitherto been so tender to us, that He hath not suffered the least cold air, or breathing of any opposition, yet to fall amongst us, a matter of no small admiration, considering where we dwell, even where Satan's throne is."[2]

At that time there were seventy-four communicants in Harrison's parish, who in a few months increased to one hundred and eighteen, and about one thousand of the colonists were Nonconformists in sympathy.[3]

Opposition was soon after this manifested toward the Nonconformists, and on the 3d of November the Virginia Assembly, at the instigation of the Governor, enacted the following:—

"Upon divers informations presented to this Assembly against several ministers for their neglect and refractory

---

[1] In the Act of Parliament settling Church government was the following clause:—

"And that such as shall not voluntarily conform to the said form of government and divine service, shall have liberty to meet for the service and worship of God, and for exercise of religious duties and ordinances in a fit and convenient place, so as nothing be done by them to the disturbance of the peace of the kingdom."

[2] *Winthrop Papers.*   [3] *Hawks, Anderson, Winthrop.*

refusing, after warning given to them, to read common prayer in Divine service upon the Sabbath-days, contrary to the canons of the Church, and the Acts of Parliament therein established: for future remedy hereof;

"Be it enacted, by Governor, Council, and Burgesses of this Grand Assembly, That all ministers in their several cures throughout the colony do duly upon every Sabbath-day read such prayers as are appointed and prescribed unto them by the said Book of Common Prayer;

"And be it further enacted, as a further penalty to such as have neglected or shall neglect their duty herein, that no parishioners shall be compelled, either by distress or otherwise, to pay any manner of tithes or duties to any Nonconformist aforesaid."

The ill-tempered Governor Berkeley a few weeks later notified Harrison that the Nonconformists must leave Virginia. In company with elder William Durand he went to Boston, and consulted with the Puritan ministers, and soon after sailed for England, to complain of Berkeley's arbitrary conduct, and appears to have then conferred with Lord Baltimore, who appointed a Protestant Governor for Maryland, William Stone of Virginia, under whose auspices William Durand, and the Nonconformists of James River, settled on the shores of the Chesapeake Bay, where is now Annapolis, the capital of Maryland. At the same time the Proprietor was induced to send "that golden apple, the ordinance of toleration," to be in all its substantial features enacted by the Maryland Assembly of 1649, under the title of "An Act concerning Religion."

It declared that any one that should deny the Holy Trinity should be punished with death and confiscation of goods. It further provided, "That every person or persons within this province that shall at any time hereafter profane the Sabbath or Lord's-day, called Sunday, by frequent swearing, drunkenness, or by any uncivil or disorderly recreation, or by working on that day when absolute necessity doth not require," shall be fined, and for the third offence they were to be publicly whipped.

It also prohibited the use of any reproachful words concerning the Blessed Virgin Mary, the mother of our Saviour, or the holy apostles, or evangelists, and the calling of any one in a reproachful way heretic, schismatic, idolater, Presbyterian, Independent, Popish Priest, Jesuit, Jesuited Priest, Lutheran, Anabaptist, Brownist, Antinomian, Barrowist, Roundhead, and Separatist, or any other name."

Harrison and Lord Baltimore continued on friendly terms in England, where he was for some time the minister of St. Dunstan's East, London.

When the mild Henry Cromwell, son of the Protector, became Lord-Lieutenant of Ireland, Harrison went with him to Dublin as chief chaplain, and there he " rather desired to serve in love and pity, than censure those "[1] who differed in points of doctrine and forms of worship. Refined in manners, a graceful speaker, and earnest Christian, he was greatly admired, and the Earl of Thomond used to say, "he had rather hear Dr. Harri-

[1] *Thurloe State Papers.*

son say grace over an egg, than hear the bishops pray or preach."

In the year 1659 a solemn procession, preceded by men in black gowns and hoods, and soldiery with hautboys and trumpets sounding a funeral march, emerged from the gate of Dublin Castle, and wended its way through the narrow street to the historic Christ Church Cathedral, whose foundations had been laid by the Danes, within whose walls also was the tomb of the Anglo-Norman warrior, Richard Earl of Chepstow, surnamed Strongbow, who had expelled the Danes, and where on Easter Sunday in 1550 the liturgy was read in the English language, for the first time in Ireland, and soon after this a Parliament had assembled beneath its roof.

After the nobles and dignitaries had entered the ancient cathedral and seated themselves in their closets of carved wood, with panelling painted in heraldic colours and devices, Dr. Harrison, the chief chaplain of the Lord Lieutenant, delivered a funeral sermon from Lamentations, chap. v., ver. 16, "The crown is fallen from our head: wo unto us that we have sinned,"[1] occasioned by the death of the Protector, Oliver Cromwell.

[1] THRENI HYBERNICI;
OR
IRELAND
SYMPATHIZING WITH
ENGLAND AND SCOTLAND
IN A SAD LAMENTATION FOR LOSS OF THEIR JOSIAH.

Represented
In a Sermon at Christ Church in Dublin,
before his Excellency the Lord Deputy,
with divers of the Nobility, Gentry, and Commonalty

One who was present, wrote, that the discourse was delivered in the most pathetic manner, and that the breathless silence in the cathedral was only disturbed by the sighs of those in tears.

Upon the accession of Charles the Second, Harrison was unable to accept the terms of conformity, and he retired to Chester, and served God as he had opportunity. On the 3d of July 1665, a rough adherent of Charles made a report of his work, of which the following is the substance:[1]—" A conventicle of one hundred persons was appointed at the house of Dr. Thomas Harrison, late chaplain of Harry Cromwell; broke open the house, found some under the beds, others in the closets, and thirty were taken before the Mayor."

After this there is no record of his life to be found, and it has been supposed that he died of the plague.

<blockquote>
there assembled to celebrate a funeral solemnity,
upon the death of the late Lord Protector.

By Dr. HARRISON, Chief Chaplain to his said Excellency.

* * * * * * * .

London
Printed by E. Cotes, and are to be sold by John North Bookseller, in Castle Street at Dublin in Ireland, 1659.
</blockquote>

---

[1] *Cal. State Papers.—Domestic Series.*

CHAPTER XVII.

FRANCIS HOWGILL AND EARLY QUAKERS.

IT cannot be denied that some of the people called "Friends of Truth" made themselves ridiculous during the Cromwellian era. That once sturdy soldier, James Nayler, led captive by silly women, and addressed as the "fairest among ten thousand," when he rode into Bristol, preceded by female devotees strewing the road with their scarfs, shawls, and handkerchiefs, was of course laughed at by thoughtless boys, insulted by foul-mouthed men, and pitied by charitable citizens.

A daughter of an honourable family, Elizabeth Fletcher, "drunk with imagination," was impelled to visit Oxford University, to exhort the students to repentance. The young men did not throw down their cloaks for her to walk upon, as Sir Walter Raleigh did for Queen Elizabeth, but, turning the fair enthusiast upon her head, disgraced themselves by ribaldry and "ducking" her at the college pump, almost to suffocation. William Penn states that another of the gentler sex divested herself of the garments of delicacy, to symbolize the nakedness of the world, where "all is show and counterfeit," but no one ever thought she was not "clothed on with chastity," as much as the pure woman of the legend, who rode naked through the town,

> "Godiva, wife to that grim Earl, who ruled
> In Coventry."[1]

The representative men of the Society of Friends condemned these irregular manifestations as pointedly as their most bitter opponents. Long ago the fanatical movements of those, whose zeal was not according to knowledge, have passed into comparative oblivion, and the Quakers are justly honoured by reflective persons as a society that have done much in promulgating the Christian doctrine of toleration, which at the time of their origin was greatly obscured, the doctrine which renders it proper for a man of Galilee to ask drink even of a woman of Samaria. In America especially, by their efforts, liberality of feeling has been increased among all who profess and call themselves Christians, and it is therefore instructive to note the advent and trials of Quakerism on the other side of the Atlantic.

On a quiet Sabbath-day there sat on a rock, contiguous to a chapel in Westmoreland, England, a man of plain but neat attire, who by the mellowness of his voice and the clearness of his statements attracted a large crowd. It was George Fox, the great expounder of the principles of the "Friends of Truth." As he urged, that a consecrated heart, speaking from love to Christ, was more acceptable in the sight of Heaven than a dead heart preaching in a so-called consecrated place, and

[1] Tennyson.

further taught that no man should preach for emolument, and no man be compelled to support a minister whom he did not acknowledge as a teacher of truth, the Rev. Francis Howgill, educated in the Church of England, and at this time a Nonconformist, who had been preaching that same day in the parish church near by, happened to be one of his hearers, and acknowledged that his assertions were scriptural, and shortly became his follower. Early in 1655 he accompanied Fox to London; and Lady Darcy, some of the nobility, clergymen, and army officers, attentively listened to the simple and heart-searching declarations of the new convert. Believing it was his duty, in a few months he crossed the sea to Ireland. At Dublin, described by a companion "as a bad place, a very refuge for the wicked," amid much opposition, he spoke, and Edward Cook, a strong-minded man, a cornet in Cromwell's own troop, was convinced.

Proceeding with Cook to the southern portion of the island, he, on the first day of the week, spoke in the parish church at Bandon. Throughout the neighbouring towns, disciples were obtained, among others, Susan, the wife of Rev. Dr. Worth, subsequently Bishop of Killaloe. Hodder, Governor of Kinsale Fort, and Phayre, Governor of Cork, were sympathizers, the latter declaring that "more was done by the Quakers, than all the priests in the country had done for a hundred years."

Enemies reported Howgill and his companion Burroughs as men of "counterfeit simplicity," and the Lord-Lieutenant of Ireland ordered them to be brought to Dublin, and, in the month of December 1655, they were banished. Howgill appears to have immediately sailed for America, and visited the shores of the Chesapeake Bay, where there were already some Quakers, one of whom, Dr. Peter Sharpe, who had in 1651 married Judith Gary, owned an island near the Choptanck river, Maryland, which still bears his name. In October 1647 the English House of Commons had passed the Ordinance of Toleration, which in all essentials was also enacted in 1649 by the Provincial Assembly of Maryland, and thus the colony became attractive to those who refused to recognise the clergymen of an Established Church.

The next year after Howgill's advent there appeared Elizabeth Harris of London, who had left her husband to persuade men to be spiritually-minded. With such mildness of manner, and yet earnestness of heart, she spoke to the colonists, who had not been accustomed to instructions from an ordained ministry since they settled in the wilderness, that numbers listened to her teachings and embraced her opinions. Even William Durand, the Secretary of the Province, who had sat under the preaching of the celebrated John Davenport in London, and had been an elder of the Puritan congregation at Nausemond, Virginia, before he settled near Annapolis, Maryland, began to attend the Quaker meeting. In 1657 she returned to London, and a few months after, one of her converts, named Robert Clarkson, wrote to her as follows :—

"DEAR HEART,—I salute thee in the tender love of the Father which moved thee towards us, and do own thee to have been a minister, by the good will of God, to bear outward testimony to the inward truth in me and others, even as many as the Lord in tender love and mercy did give an ear to hear. Praise be to His name for ever, of which word of life God hath made my wife partaker with me, and hath established our hearts in his fear: and likewise Ann Dorsey in a more large measure; her husband I hope abideth faithful, likewise John Baldwin and Henry Carline. Charles Balye, the young man who was with us at our parting, abides convinced, and several others in those parts where he dwells. Elizabeth Beaseley abides as she was, when thou wast here. Thomas Cole and William Cole[1] have made open confession of the truth, likewise Henry Woolchurch, and many others, suffer with us the reproachful name. William Fuller[2] abides unmoved. I know not but that William Durand doth the like; he frequents our meeting but seldom. . . . We have disposed of the most part of the books which were sent, so that all parts are furnished, and every one that desires it may have benefit by them, at Herring Creek, Roade River, South River, all about Severn, the Broad Neck, and thereabout, the Seven Mountains, and Kent. With my dear love I salute thy husband, and rest with thee and the gathered ones in the eternal world, which abideth for ever."

Toward the latter part of December 1657 a ship arrived in James River with Josiah Coale and Thomas Thurston, Quaker preachers, who were treated by the

---

[1] Cole died about 1678.   [2] Had been captain of the Severn men.

Virginians as disturbers of the peace, and confined. Released at the approach of spring, they went to Maryland, and were entertained by Richard Preston, on the Patuxent, William Berry,[1] and other respectable citizens. But unfortunately for them there was a change in the political authorities, and in the place of those who had been friendly, were those disposed to persecute. The new Governor Fendall, and the Secretary Philip Calvert, an illegitimate son of the first Lord Baltimore, although it had been stipulated by the Proprietor that he would see that "all persons believing in Jesus Christ should have freedom of conscience," became oppressors. Preston and others were fined for receiving the preachers into their houses, another was whipped for refusing to assist the sheriff in arresting Thurston. Peter Sharpe, a surgeon, was outlawed because he had conscientious scruples relative to taking oaths, and his debtors were released from obligations. The preachers finding that the arm of the Government was raised against them, were at length compelled to leave the province where they had hoped for liberty of conscience. Passing northward with another friend, Thomas Chapman of Virginia, they at length passed the last dwelling of a white settler, and walked through what was then a wilderness, but in which region are now Philadelphia and New York, among the largest and wealthiest cities of the world.

For food they at times depended upon the chestnuts and berries of the forest, but frequently they were fed by the Susquehannocks, a tribe whose wigwams they

---

[1] Berry lived at Choptanck, and was a Quaker preacher.

found. When Francis Howgill learned of the indignities heaped upon Josiah Coale and others by the authorities of Maryland, he wrote a pamphlet,[1] called "The Deceiver of the Nations discovered, and his Cruelty made manifest, more especially his Cruel Works of Darkness laid open and reproved in Mariland and Virginia." Therein he alluded to the journey of the banished in the wilderness, in these words:—" The Indians whom they judge to be heathen exceeded in kindness, in courtesies, in love and mercy, unto them who were strangers, which is a shame to the mad, rash rulers of Mariland, that have acted so barbarously to our people, and them that came to visit them in the name of the Lord, that instead of receiving them rejected them, and made order after order, and warrant after warrant, for pursuing, banishing, and whipping of them who came to them in the name of the Lord, in such haste, that I have seen fifteen warrants out against one man in a little time, and in one province."

It is painful in this age to contemplate the persecuting spirit of nearly every class in the seventeenth century, and to note how people were put to death upon mere suspicion or vague accusations. In the year 1654, a passenger, named Mary Lee, on the ship "Unity," Captain Bosworth, bound for Maryland, was suspected of witch-marks, tied to the capstan, examined, then hung to the yard-arm, and after life was extinct, tossed overboard. John Washington, the ancestor of the first President, in 1658, came to America in a vessel destined

[1] Published in 1660, at London.

for Maryland, and among the passengers was one Elizabeth Richardson, perhaps a Quakeress and preacher, who during the voyage was accused of witchcraft, and hung. Washington, indignant at what he felt was an outrage, upon landing preferred charges before the Governor of Maryland against Prescott, the captain.[1] When the Quakeresses, Anne Austin and Mary Fisher, came from Barbadoes to Boston the authorities there caused them to be imprisoned, and then stripped and examined, to discover if any witch-marks were on their bodies.

History clearly shows that Maryland and Massachusetts were twin-sisters in superstitious fear, and that the latter simultaneously with the former began to fine, whip, banish, and imprison the Quakers.

During the year 1658, William Robinson, a merchant of London, Robert Hodgson, and Christopher Holder, landed on the shores of the Chesapeake Bay, and after tarrying some time in the province of Maryland, found

---

[1] Washington, in September 1659, was summoned by Governor Fendall, of Maryland, to appear as a witness, but failed, as his letter from Westmoreland, written the next day, shows:—

"Honb'le S'r,—Yo^rs of this 29th instant this day I received. I am sorry y't my extraordinary occasions will not permitt mee to bee att ye next Provincial Court to be held in Mary-Land ye 4th of this next month. Because then, God willing, I intend to gett my young Sonne baptized. All ye company and Gossips being already invited. Besides, in this short time witnesses cannot be gott to come over. But if Mr. Prescott bee bound to answer itt ye next Provinciall Court after this I shall doe what lyeth in my power to gett them over. S'r, I shall desire you for to acquaint mee whither Mr. Prescott be bound over to ye next Court, and when ye Court is, that I may have some time for to provide evidence; and soe I rest

"Yo'r ffriend and serv't,

"John Washington."

"30 Sept. 1659."

their way to Massachusetts. In the month of September they were brought before the Boston magistrates Christopher Holder, John Copeland,[1] and John Rouse, as disturbers of the peace, and Endicott, in the name of his associates, pronounced the following sentence :— "It is the sentence of this Court that you three have each his right ear cut off by the hangman." After the bloody sentence was executed they said, "Those who do it ignorantly, we desire from our hearts the Lord to forgive them, but for them that do it maliciously let our blood be upon their heads, and such shall know in the day of account, that each drop of our blood shall be heavier than a mill-stone."

During the year 1659 William Robinson[2] was publicly whipped and banished, after which he tarried at Salem.

---

[1] Copeland, after the loss of his ear, still continued the work of preaching, but at length settled in Virginia, where he lived to an advanced age.

[2] Longfellow, in the "New England Tragedy of *Endicott*," alludes to the persecution of Robinson and associates :—

"ENDICOTT.
"Four already have been slain;
And others banished upon pain of death.
But they came back again to meet their doom,
Bringing the linen for their winding-sheets.
We must not go too far. In truth I shrink
From shedding of more blood. The people murmur
At our severity.
"NORTON.
"Then let them murmur!
Truth is relentless; Justice never wavers;
The greatest firmness is the greatest mercy;
The noble order of the Magistracy
Cometh immediately from God, and yet
This noble order of Magistracy
Is by these Heretics despised and outraged.
"ENDICOTT.
"To-night they sleep in prison. If they die,
They cannot say that we have caused their death.
We do but guard the passage, with the sword
Pointed towards them; If they dash upon it,
Their blood will be on their own heads, not ours."

For this delay he was brought to Boston, and there chained and imprisoned.

On the 20th of October, with Mary Dyer and Marmaduke Stevenson, he was arraigned before the Court, and after a short examination, with the others, condemned to death, and in seven days, the three, with the woman in the centre, calmly and joyfully walked to their execution, and died as martyrs die, while Massachusetts received a blot on her escutcheon, that will grow darker and darker, as the tolerant spirit of Christ increases in America, and the other nations of the world.

During the autumn of 1663 Mary Tomkins and Alice Ambrose were at the Cliffs[1] in Calvert County, Maryland, and wrote to George Fox: "We have been in Virginia, where we have had good service for the Lord. Our sufferings have been large. . . . We are now about to set sail for Virginia again."

Bishop, speaking of these persons, remarks :—" Mary Tomkins and Alice Ambrose, alias Gary, these two servants of the Lord having been at Virginia, whitherto they departed from New England, who had there suffered thirty-two stripes apiece with a nine-corded whip, three knots in each cord, being drawn up to the pillory in such an uncivil manner, as is not to be rehearsed, with a running knot about their hands, the very first lash of which drew the blood, and made it run down in abundance from their breasts."[2]

George Rofe of Halstead in Essex in 1661 visited

---

[1] Alice Ambrose appears to have married John Gary, who lived at the Cliffs of Calvert County.

[2] Bishop, p. 423, London, edition of 1703.

Maryland for the first time, and on a second visit, in 1663, was drowned by the capsizing of a small boat in one of the rivers.[1]

William Cole of Maryland, proceeding with George Wilson, a preacher from England to Virginia, was there imprisoned. The following letter, written by his companion, is an evidence of a common fault of the early ministers of the Society of Friends, who, in their desire to use plainness, descended to uncharitableness and coarseness of speech. It was dated, "From that dirty dungeon in James Town, the 17th of the Third Month, 1662."

"If they who visit not such in prison (as Christ speaks of) shall be punished with everlasting destruction, O what will ye do? or what will become of you, who put us into such nasty stinking prisons as this dirty dungeon, where we have not had the benefit to do what nature requireth, nor so much as air to blow in at a window, but close made up with brick and lime, so that there is no air to take away the smell of our dung and p——,[2] who, for all their cruelty, I can truly say, '*Father forgive them, for they know not what they do.*' But thus saith the Lord unto me, 'Tell them that because wilfully they are ignorant, I will strike them with astonishment, and will bring upon them the filth of their detestable things, and in that day they should be glad if they could eat their own dung, and drink their own p——, it shall so odiously stand before them, that it

---

[1] He had organized a society at Creisheim on the Rhine, whose members twenty years afterward, went to German-town, now part of Philadelphia.

[2] It is unnecessary to print this word in full, which is vulgar and offensive.

shall be an evil stink in succeeding generations. This you shall eternally witness, for I have spoken it with you in the name of the Lord, in whose authority this is to go abroad."[1]

The first published religious pamphlet written by a citizen of Virginia, appears to have been a poem by John Grave, a Quaker, and issued in 1662, with the title, " A Song of Sion, written by a Citizen thereof, whose outward habitation is in Virginia, and being sent over to some of his Friends in England, the same is found fitting to be published, for to warn the seed of Evil-doers."

John Burnyeat of Cumberland, after travelling on foot through Londonderry, Dublin, Galway, Cork, and other places in Ireland, was impelled by the Spirit, as he believed, to promulgate the truth in America, and in the year 1665 was in Maryland, and held large meetings, and "Friends were greatly comforted, and several were convinced." At this time a schism existed among the American Quakers, caused by the labours of John Perrot, who, after visiting Rome to convert the Pope, came to the New World, and introduced ritualism in worship, by insisting upon what Fox called "the evil and untimely practice of keeping on the hat in time of public prayer." In 1671 Burnyeat made a second visit to America, and on the 5th day of ninth month, accompanied by Daniel Gould of Rhode Island, arrived at the "Pertuxen," and in visiting the Friends, found a freshness among them.

One day in 1672, as he was about to sail for England,

[1] Besse, ii. 381.

unexpectedly to all, a ship from Jamaica, appeared in the Patuxent river, having on board George Fox, the spiritual iconoclast, whose name is identified with the religious history of the seventeenth century, and several other Quakers, one of whom was William Edmundson, a native of Westmoreland, once a soldier in Cromwell's army, and who had established the first settled meeting of Quakers in Ireland, at Lurgan.

Fox, feeling that his stay must be brief, and that time was precious, immediately began to preach. For four days he expounded his doctrines with singular clearness, and with a mellow voice prayed from the depth of his soul, and as a result, five or six Justices of the Peace, and many world's people who came from curiosity, went away from the meetings much interested.

Partly by land, and partly by water, he hastened to the Cliffs in Calvert County, and addressed a large assembly, and then, crossing the Chesapeake Bay, crowds gathered round him and listened gladly, and a judge's wife frankly said she "had rather hear him once, than the priests a thousand times." Recrossing the Bay, he next spoke at the river Severn, now the city of Annapolis, where the number of hearers was so great, that no building could contain them. The next day he spoke at a place six or seven miles distant, and there the Speaker of the Maryland Legislative Assembly was convinced. Then mounting his horse he rode to Dr. Peter Sharpe's, at the Cliffs, and here, he says "was a heavenly meeting," many of the upper sort of people present, and a wife of one of the Governor's councillors was convinced.

Some Roman Catholics came to deride, but their hearts also were softened.

From thence, he rode to the Patuxent, and spoke at the house of one James Preston, where an Indian chief and some of his tribe, came to see the strange man who was lifting up his voice in the wilderness, causing the hearts of his listeners to burn within them. His labours were incessant, and he stopped neither on account of the burning sun, nor fierce snow-storms. He forded swollen streams, slept in barns, passed a winter's night in the open air, without fire, with as much complacency as in the house of friends, and was truly a wonder unto many. In 1673, a short period before he returned to England, he went to Annapolis, and attended a meeting of the Provincial Legislature. On the 6th day, 4th month, 1674, William Cole, William Richards, and John Gary, on behalf of a general meeting of Quakers, held at West River, Maryland, addressed a letter to the meeting at Bristol, England, in which they write:—

"Much people there be in our country that come to hear the truth declared, which in its eternal authority is over all, and many by it are convinced. . . . And now, dearly beloved brethren, we may not forget to make mention of our dearly beloved George Fox, with the rest of the servants of the Lord who accompanied him in the service of the blessed God in our country."[1]

---

[1] Bowden, vol. i. p. 381.—After Fox went back to England he sent a copy of the works of Edward Burroughs to several gentlemen, among others, to the following:—Judge Stephens, Anamessex, Maryland; Justices Johnson and Coleman, do.; Major-General Bennett, Virginia; Lieut.-Col. Waters, Nansemond, do.; Col. Thomas Dew, do.

Wenlock Christopherson, or Christison, as he was often called, the distinguished preacher, who, when sentenced to death at Boston, uttered these memorable words:—
"For the last man that was put to death here are five come in his room. If you have power take my life from me, God can raise up the same principle in ten of his servants, and send them among you in my room," when pardoned came to Maryland, and in 1674, he was one of those who petitioned the Colonial Assembly that Quakers might be permitted to affirm, instead of taking the usual oaths of law.

The persecution of the Quakers in America caused sorrow among the few tolerant men of that age. The distinguished philosopher, Robert Boyle, President of the Society for Propagating the Gospel in New England, wrote, in 1680, to John Eliot, the zealous and gentle-spirited missionary to the Indians around Boston:—

"Of late I have to my trouble heard the government of the Massachusetts sharply censured for their great severity to some dissenters. This severe proceeding seems to be the more strange, and the less defensible, in those who, having left their native country, and crossed the vast ocean to settle in a wilderness, that they may there enjoy the liberty of worshipping God according to their own conscience, seem to be engaged more than other men, not to allow their brethren a share in what they thought was so much all good men's due."[1]

The steady progress of Quakerism in Maryland had been such, as at this period to cause the opinions of those

[1] Boyle's *Works*, vol. i. folio, 1744.

who belonged to the Society to be regarded. In reply to a petition that Quakers might be allowed to affirm in the place of taking the usual oath, the Upper House of the Assembly, on September 6, 1681, took the following action :—

"Upon reading the paper delivered yesterday by William Berry and Richard Johns, this House do say : That if the rights and privileges of a free born Englishman, settled on him by Magna Charta, so often confirmed by subsequent Parliaments, can be preserved by yea and nay in wills and testaments, and other occurrents, the Lower House may do well to prepare such a law, and then the Upper House will consider of it."

Following up this favourable action, they presented an able and logical paper giving six reasons for the proposed modification of the law of oaths. The preamble was dignified and eloquent. "We are Englishmen ourselves, and free born, although in scorn commonly called Quakers, and therefore, so far from desiring the least breach of Magna Charta, or of the least privilege belonging to a free-born Englishman, that we had rather suffer many degrees more than we do (if it was possible), than willingly admit of the least violation of those ancient rights and liberties, which are indeed our birthright, and so often confirmed to us by subsequent Parliaments. And had we not been full well assured that our sufferings may be redressed, and our request granted without the violating of Magna Charta in the least degree, we would not have desired it."

The arguments had a good effect, and the Lower House enacted that the law should be modified in accordance with their petition, but it failed to receive the approval of Lord Baltimore at that time.

The period was now coming when the Quakers in America were to have a realization of the promise, that they "who sow in tears shall reap in joy." The conversion of William Penn, the son of a distinguished Admiral, a student of Oxford and the University of Paris, to the belief of the Society of Friends, caused a stir and inquiry for the first time in higher circles, as to the designs of these hitherto despised people, and a reaction began in their favour. As Penn listened to the story of the shameful persecutions his fellow-religionists endured in Virginia, Maryland, and Massachusetts, he conceived the project of establishing "a free colony for all mankind," wherein entire liberty of conscience should be allowed.

His father, the Admiral, had been promised a grant of land, which at length, after urgent solicitation, was given to William Penn, and on the 4th of March 1680, the patent was issued. When the intelligence reached America, that another plantation was to be established under the auspices of the Quakers, it was equally distasteful to Lord Baltimore, then in Maryland, and to the Puritans of Massachusetts.

A letter,[1] dated September 15, 1682, addressed to

---

[1] This letter is said to have been recently discovered among some old papers, by an officer of the Massachusetts Historical Society. It would be a relief to the lovers of toleration if it should be proved to be spurious.

John Higginson, gives a sad exhibition of the intolerance of a good man :—

"There bee now at sea a shippe (for our friend Mr. Esaias Holcraft, of London, did advise me by the last packet that it wolde sail some time in August) called ye Welcome, R. Greenway, master, which has aboard an hundred or more of ye heretics and malignants called Quakers, with W. Penne, who is ye chief scampe at the hedde of them. Ye General Court has accordingly given secret orders to Master Malachi Huxett, of ye brig Porposse, to waylaye ye said Welcome as near the coast of Codde as may be, and make captive ye said Penne and his ungodlie crew, so that ye Lord may be glorified and not mocked on ye soil of this new countre, with ye heathen worshippe of these people. Much spoyl can be made by selling ye whole lotte to Barbadoes, where slaves fetch good prices in rumme and sugar, and we shall not only do ye Lord great service by punishing ye wicked, but shall make great gayne for his ministers and people.

"Master Huxett feels hopeful, and I will set down the news he brings when his shippe gets back.—Yours in ye bowells of Christ, COTTON MATHER."

From the hour that Penn made his treaty with the Indians under the old elm at Shackamaxon, society in the New World assumed a new form. The men that began to build on the rectangular streets of the newly surveyed city of Philadelphia, were industrious, and glad to welcome as sharers in the temporal government, the Jew or the Turk, the Calvinist or Roman Catholic.

Within a year the success of the city became certain; not only Quakers from the southern and northern colonies flocked thither, but money-loving men, who foresaw that these industrious heretics would create a great commercial mart, on the banks of the broad and placid Delaware. The people of Jamestown, Saint Mary, Manhattan, and Boston were astounded to see a town quietly building up, and each year, increasing more than other towns had in a decade, and the moment the Quaker began to have commercial credit, and some social prestige through the Penns and others, then weak human nature became "mealy-mouthed," and ceased to kick and scourge them, and call them scamps and vagabonds.

Shortly after his arrival at Philadelphia, William Penn proceeded to visit the "Friends" on the tributaries of the Chesapeake. Subsequently he made a second visit, and conducted Lord and Lady Baltimore to a Quaker meeting at Tredhaven. Richardson, who was one of the preachers at the time of the visit, describes Lady Baltimore[1] as "a notable, wise, natural, and courteously-carriaged woman." She was pleased with the simple services of the Friends, and told Penn that she did not wish to hear him, as he was a scholar, but she would like to listen to the exposition of some of the unlearned mechanics and husbandmen.

After Penn's return to England, Quakerism was strengthened in America by the arrival of Thomas Story, another man of cultivated intellect. He had received in

[1] The wife of Charles third Lord Baltimore was the widow of Henry Sewall of Mattapany on the Patuxent, eight miles from Saint Mary, Maryland.

England a complete education, and was not only a proficient in Greek and mathematics, but was skilled in the arts of music and fencing. His associations in youth were with ritualism. The church he then attended conformed to the "new fangleism" that crept back to the Church of England in the days of Laud. His brother also was chaplain of the Countess of Carlisle.[1]

For a period he was zealous in the observance of rites, but in time, doubts arose as to their propriety in the Church of Christ, and at length he bounded over to the Society, which, forgetting that man was a compound of flesh and spirit, and demanded a few expressive rites, had abnegated all ritualism.

Having studied law, he went to Pennsylvania, was made Master of the Rolls and Keeper of the Great Seal of the colony, and subsequently Mayor of the city of Philadelphia.

On the 27th day of the third month, 1699, o.s., he attended the yearly meeting of the Quakers, at West River, in Maryland, in company with Dr. Griffith Owen, a distinguished physician of Philadelphia. On the 13th, his journal tells us, " came one Henry Hall, a priest of the Church of England, and, with others of his notion, eves-dropped the meeting, but came not in." Richard Johns, a prominent member of the meeting, then arose and made a confession of faith, a slight modification of the Apostles' Creed :—

"We believe that the Lord Jesus Christ, who was born of the Virgin Mary, being conceived by the

---

[1] He was afterwards a dean in Ireland.

promise and influence of the Holy Ghost, is the true Messiah or Saviour; that He died upon the cross at Jerusalem, a propitiation and sacrifice for the sins of all mankind; that He rose from the dead on the third day, ascended, and seated on the right hand of the Majesty on high, making intercession for us; and in the fullness of time shall come to judge both the living and the dead, and reward all according to their work."

The next day the clergyman and his friends again lurked near the meeting, and Story says:—

"My companion in his testimony apprehending they were within hearing, cried aloud to them to come forth out of their holes, and appear openly like men, and if they had anything to say, after meeting was over, they should be heard."

Story next challenged them to prove their call to the ministry, "which they taking upon them to do, only told us that Christ called the apostles, and they ordained others, and they again others in succession to that time."

Then Story demanded proof "who they were that the apostles ordained, and who from age to age successors ordained, wherein if they justly failed they were to be rejected as no ministers of Christ, since they had rested the matter on such a succession." "Many people," continues the journal, "called out to the clergyman, 'We will pay you the tobacco, being obliged by law, that is, forty pounds of tobacco for every negro slave, but we will never hear you more.' While we were yet in the gallery one climbed up into a window, and cried out with a loud voice to Henry Hall, 'Sir, you have broken a canon of the Church; you have baptized several negroes, who being infidels, baptism ought not to have been administered to them.'

"At this the priest was enraged, but made no answer to the charge, only fumed and fretted and threatened the man to trounce him. Then I observed to the people that if these negroes were made Christians in this sense, members of Christ, children of God, inheritors of the kingdom of heaven, received into the body of the Church of Christ, as the language is at the time of sprinkling, how could they now detain them longer as slaves? Several justices of the peace being ashamed of their priest, slid out of the meeting as unobservable as might be, and the people in general contemned them as such, who behind the back of the Quakers had 'greatly reproached and belied them, but face to face were utterly subdued by them. That night several of the justices, lodging with our friend Samuel Chew, expressed their sentiments altogether in our favour, and that the priests were really ignorant men in matters of religion."

Sir Thomas Lawrence, the Secretary of the colony, wincing under the plain arguments of Story, complained of what he called the tart expressions of the Quaker, to the Lords of Trade and Plantations. William Penn being in England, his attention was called to the subject, to which he alludes in a letter to a friend:—

"A silly knight! Though I hope it comes of officious weakness the talent of the gentleman, with some malice. Matters there, are never attacked by Thomas Story, nor in irreverent tones.

"I never heeded it, only said, that if the gentleman had sense enough for his office he might have known this tale was no part of it, that Thomas Story was discreet and temperate, and did not exceed in his retorts or returns.

"But 'tis children's play to provoke a combat and then cry out that such a one beats them; that I hoped that they were not a committee of conscience and religion, and that it showed the shallowness of the gentleman that played the busybody in it."

At the commencement of the eighteenth century the Quakers exercised a powerful influence in the colonies. Men were forced to admit, that they were keepers at home, industrious, intelligent, not given to wine or brawling, cleanly in their habits, and honest in their commercial transactions.

The yearly meeting of the Society was eagerly looked for by all classes. Edmundson well observed, "Yearly meeting in Maryland, many people resort to it and transact a deal of trade with one another, so that it is a kind of market or change, where the captains of ships and the planters meet and settle their affairs, and this draws abundance of people." Occurring as it did near the Whitsuntide holidays, the black slaves flocked thither to enjoy rest for a few days from the exhausting labours of the tobacco field. Families from the different counties rolled there, in ponderous old-fashioned carriages for the purpose of social reunion, young men came on fine horses, to compare them and give a trial of their speed, and others went to confer with the beautiful and pure-minded maidens, who, in their plain drab dresses and scooped bonnets, were to them far more interesting than the angels, who seemed cold and distant, because they had neither flesh nor blood.

CHAPTER XVIII.

THE PLANTING OF THE CHURCH OF ENGLAND IN THE COLONIES.

IT appears strange that the ecclesiastical authorities of England should not at the beginning of the colonization of America made more earnest effort for supplying the plantations with clergymen.

With the first expedition to Virginia, the Rev. Robert Hunt sailed as Chaplain, and by his Christian demeanour won the confidence of the early settlers of Jamestown, but no record has been preserved of his labours or the time of his death.

The next clergyman who arrived was the Rev. Richard Buck,[1] who accompanied Sir Thomas Gates and Sir George Somers, and after passing the winter at Bermudas, where the vessel in which he left England was wrecked, arrived, in May 1610, at Jamestown, and found a rude log church ruined and unfrequented, which probably had been used by Hunt. He was esteemed "a very good preacher," and opened with prayer, the first legislative assembly in America, which met in the chancel of his church.[2] He died about the

---

[1] Strachey says that Stephen Hopkins, who used to act as a lay reader for Buck during the voyage, was a Brownist.

[2] This church was of logs twenty feet wide and fifty-eight in length.

year 1623, leaving several sons, one of whom, Benoni, was the first idiot of white parents, in America, of whom we have any account.[1]

In the year 1610, the Netherlands made an overture about joining in the plantation of Virginia,[2] and a number of Dutch accompanied Dale, an army officer in the service of the States-General, to the James River, and made a settlement at and near Henrico.[3] The minister who came with this expedition was the Rev. Alexander Whitaker, the son of the distinguished Puritan lecturer of Cambridge University. He was possessed of some estate, and had been settled in one of the north counties of England, "but," says Crashaw, "without any persuasion but God's and his own heart, did voluntarily leave his warm nest to carry the gospel to the heathen of America."[4] In the year 1613, there was published in London, "Good Newes from Virginia, sent to the counsell and Company of Virginia, resident in England. . From Alexander Whitaker, Minister of Henrico, in Virginia."

He was a blunt but graphic writer, as will be seen from the following extracts. Speaking of the colony he remarks:—

"I may fitly compare it to the growth of an infant, which hath been afflicted from its birth with some grievous sickness, that many times no hope of life hath remained, and yet it liveth still. Again, if there were

---

[1] *Cal. State Papers*, Col. series.
[2] Winwood.
[3] This neighbourhood is sometimes called "Dutch Gap."
[4] Preface to *Good News from Virginia*.

nothing else to encourage us, yet this one thing may stir us up to go on cheerfully with it, that the devil is a capital enemy against it, and continually seeketh to hinder the prosperity and good proceedings of it. Yea hath heretofore so far prevailed by his instruments, the covetous hearts of many backsliding adventurers at home, also by his servants here, some striving for superiority, others by murmurings, mutinies, and plain treasons, and others by fornication, profaneness, idleness, and such monstrous sins." In alluding to the Indians he called them "naked slaves of the devil," and adds:—

"I have sent one image of their God to the Council in England, which is painted upon one side of a toad stool, much like unto a deformed monster. Their priests, whom they call Quockosoughs, are no other but such as our English witches are. They live naked in body, as if the shame of their mind deserved no covering. Their manners are as naked as their bodies, and they esteem it a virtue to lie, as their master the devil teacheth them. Much more might be said of their miserable condition, but I refer to the particular mention of these things to some other season.

"Wherefore you wealthy men of the world, whose bellies God hath filled with this hidden treasure, trust not in the uncertain riches, neither cast your eyes upon them, for riches taketh to her wings as an eagle, and flieth into heaven. But be each in good works ready to distribute and communicate. How shamefully do the most of you either insensibly detain or wickedly misspend God's goods, whereof he made you his stewards! The prodigal men of our land make haste to fling away God's treasure as a grievous burthen which they desire to be eased of. Some make no scruple at it, to spend yearly an hundred pounds, two, three, five hundred, and much more, about dogs, hawks, and hounds, and such sports, which will not give five hundred pence to the relief of God's poor members. Others will not care to lose two or three thousand pounds in a night at cards and dice, and yet suffer poor Lazarus to perish in the street for want of their charitable alms. Yea, divers will hire gardens at great rates, and build stately houses for their whores, which have no compassion on the fatherless and widows. How much better were it for these men to remember the affliction of Joseph, to extend the bowels of their compassion to the poor, the fatherless, the afflicted, and the like, than to misspend that which they must give a straight account of at the day of judgment. Are not these miserable people here, better than hawks, hounds, whores, and the like?"

On September 22, 1612, about the time that Whitaker wrote his plea for the Indian, Cunega, the ambassador of Spain in England, in a despatch said:—"He is credibly informed that there is a determination to marry some of the people that go over to Virginians. Forty or fifty are already so married, and English women intermingle, and are received kindly by the natives. A zealous minister hath been wounded for reprehending it." The minister may have been the plain-spoken Whitaker. Rolfe speaks of him in 1616 as at Henrico, and the rough Argall, in a letter to the Virginia Company, dated 9th of June 1617, states that he was drowned, but gives no particulars as to time, place, or circumstances.

When Gates made his second voyage to Virginia in the summer of 1611, an aged minister, by the name of Glover, who had preached in Bedford and Huntingdonshire, accompanied him, of whom we have a bare mention,[1] in the preface written by Crashaw, to Whitaker's *Good News from Virginia*.

The first minister of Hampton, or Kecoughtan, was the Rev. William Mease, who came about the same time as Glover, and after ten years' residence returned to England.[2]

In 1615 Lewis Hughes was sent as a clergyman to Bermudas. In a short period he and a colleague, by the name of Keith, refused to use the service-book of the Church of England,[3] and introduced the liturgy of the churches of the Isle of Jersey.

When Governor Yeardley arrived in 1619 at Jamestown, he found there only the log church and a few houses, and at Henrico a poor frame church in ruins, and three old houses, and in the whole colony five ministers, two of whom were without orders. Those in

---

[1] He soon died.

[2] *London Company MSS.*

[3] The writer possesses a little work by Hughes, entitled—

"Certaine Grievances, or the errours of the service-booke, plainly layd open, with some reasons wherefore it may and ought to be removed, well worthy the serious consideration of the Right Honorable and High Court of Parliament. Set forth by way of Dialogue between a country Gentleman and a Minister of God's Word."

orders were probably Mease, Buck, and Thomas Bargrave, a nephew of Dr. Bargrave, Dean of Canterbury, who came in 1618 with Captain John Bargrave, also his uncle, and the first in the colony to establish a private plantation. The Rev. Mr. Bargrave died in 1621, and left his library, valued at 100 marks, to the projected college at Henrico. Those not in orders were Mr. William Wickham and Mr. Samuel Macock, for whom Argall had in 1617 desired ordination.

Sir Edwin Sandys, who became President of the London Company after its reorganization in 1619, was the son of the Archbishop who left the following sentences as his last testimony concerning the rites and ceremonies of the Church of England :—" I have ever been, and am presently persuaded, that some of them be not so expedient in this Church now, but that in the Church reformed, and in all this time of the Gospel (wherein the seed of the Scripture hath so long been sown), they may better be disused by little and little, than more and more urged." The son of such a father was not the man to press for a literal conformity to ecclesiastical canons, and was ready to encourage any sincere minister of Christ to take up his abode in Virginia.

Nor were the benefactors of the plantation men who despised Puritans. On November 15, 1620, after the minutes were read, a stranger stepped into the meeting, and presented " four great books, as the gift of one unto the Company, that desired his name might not be made known, whereof one book was a treatise of St. Augustine of the *City of God,* translated into English, the other three great volumes were the works of Mr. Perkins, newly corrected and amended, which books the donor desired might be sent to the college in Virginia, there to remain in safety to the use of the collegiates thereafter, and not suffered at any time to be sent abroad, or used in the meanwhile, for which so worthy a gift my Lord of Southampton desired the party that presented them to return deserved thanks for himself and the rest of the Company to him that had so kindly bestowed them.[1] On November 14th, 1621, a letter was received enclosing forty shillings for a sermon to be preached before the Company, with a promise that it would be given yearly for the same purpose, and with the request that the Rev. John Davenport of London, afterwards the Puritan pastor at New Haven, Connecticut, should preach the first sermon.[2]

[1] Perkins had been a Puritan lecturer at Cambridge. Robinson, pastor at Leyden, had been one of his pupils, and used his catechism in Holland. Leverett, and associates of Massachusetts, in a letter to Boyle the philosopher writes :—

"If Mr. Perkins and those good old Puritans in King Edward the Sixth and Queen Elizabeth's time, did, in their principles of religion, teach evil doctrine, then may we be rendered such."

In the *Manuscript Council Book* of Maryland, there is an inventory of goods of Clayborne, seized on Palmer's Island; in the list is "one folio volume of Mr. Perkins' works." As Clayborne was secretary of the Virginia Colony at the time the present was made, may this folio not have been one of the three great volumes of Perkins that were sent over?

[2] The manuscript transactions of London Company, under date of October 23, 1622, has the following entry :—

"Mr. Deputy signified unto the Companie it was not unknowne unto them that amongst the many worthy guifts bestowed on the Plantacon, there was the last yeare giuen by a person, refusinge as yet to be named, 40s. p. ann. for euer (and thereupon an order established), for a sermon to be preached before the Virginia Companie euery Micha⁸ Terme, on Wednesday

After Sir Francis Wyatt was elected Governor, the Virginia Company sent over several clergymen. At a meeting held on the 16th of July 1621, "it was signified that Sir Francis Wyatt's brother, being a Master of Arts and a good divine, and very willing to go with him this present voyage, might be entertained and placed as minister over his people, and have the same allowance towards the furnishing of himself as others have had, and that his wife might have her transport free, which notion was thought very reasonable." A few days before the Earl of Southampton recommended

fortnight before the last Wednesday in the said Terme, Hee therefore moued to know their pleasure whome they would entreate to preach the said sermon: Whereupon some proposinge the Dean of Paules, the Court, without naming any other, did verie much desire he might be entreated thereunto, hoping he would please upon their general request signified unto him to undertake, and the rather for that he was a Brother of this Companie, and of their CounselL In considrance wherof the Court praid S^r Jo. Dauers, Sr Phil. Cary, Mr. Binge, and Mr. Deputy, to solicite him earnestly hereunto in the name of the Companie, wch. they promised to performe, and for the place where the sermon is to be preached, the Court haue made choise of St. Michaell's Church in Cornehill as the most conuenient.

"After wch. sermon ended, it is also thought fitt and agreed, the custome they began the last yeare shal be continued, namely to supp together, and for that cause haue entreated Mr. Caswell and Mr. Mellinge (who last time so well performed it, to all the Companies, being assigned with Mr. Bennett and Mr. Rider to be Stewards this yeare also, for prouidinge and orderinge of the supper and bussiness thereunto belonging, and of the place where it shall be kept, and accordingly to giue notice thereof unto all the Companie, by sending the officer with ticketts that are to be printed for this purpose, notifyinge the time and place, and what each man is to paye, wch. is now agreed shall be iij. s. a peece, as findinge by last yeare's experience, it cannott be lesse, to bear out the full charge.

"And for that, at such great feasts, venizon is esteemed to bee a most necessary complement, the Court hath thought fitt that letters be addressed in the name of the Companie unto such noblemen and gentlemen as are of this Society to request this favour at their hands, and withall their presence at the said Supper."

Dr. John Donne preached as requested on the 13th of November, and the

X

the Rev. Robert Bolton[1] for his honesty and sufficiency in learning, and he was despatched to Elizabeth City, now Hampton, made vacant by the removal of a Rev. Mr. Stockton, but subsequently preached in Accomac. The Rev. Haut Wyatt remained at Jamestown for four or five years,[2] and then returned to England, and became vicar of Bexley, in Kent, and in the days of Archbishop Laud was arraigned before the High Commission.

About the time that Wyatt and Bolton came, the Rev. Wm. Bennett arrived with the settlers for Edward Bennett's private plantation in the Nansemond country, and on the 21st of September the London Company wrote to the colonial authorities as follows:—

"The Company is by divers ways informed that there is a great want of worthy ministers, therefore they have entertained, and now send along Mr. Thomas White, a man of good sufficiency for learning, and recommended for integrity and uprightness of life, and of so good zeal to the plantation that he is content to go with that small allowance the Company's stock is able now to afford him, and to put himself upon such pre-

---

supper was held at Merchant Tailors' Hall, twenty-one does were served, and three or four hundred were present. Davenport and Donne were the only preachers of the annual sermon. On November 12, 1623, "a l're from an unknowne p'son beinge presented to the Court and read, wherein was enclosed two peeces of gold of 40s. for a sermon to be preached this year, as was the last before the Companie. It beinge taken into consideracon, it was thought fitt, and so agreed, the sermon should be respited for a time in reguard of the present troubles of the Companie."

In June 1624 the Company was dissolved.—*London Co. Trans. MSS.*

[1] Perhaps the Rev. Robert Bolton, made Bachelor of Divinity at Oxford, December 14, 1609.—*Wood.*

[2] On a monument to his memory at Bexley, it is stated that some of his children remained in Virginia. The name is still common there.

ferment there as he shall deserve, and you shall be able to accommodate him with, which, if it be of the places belonging to the Company, we have promised him here an addition to the small allowance he hath now received, and now likewise that your godly care and wisdom will provide for him in some competent manner till he may be furnished with the full number of tenants belonging to the ministry, which we hope, for him and all others, shall, in the beginning of the spring, be accomplished. If he finds entertainment from any private hundred, then we shall expect from them the restitution of our charges, that is, six pounds for his passage, and eight pounds delivered him toward the making of some provisions; we doubt not but you will be able to supply them out of the libraries of so many that have died."[1]

In October, Mr. Robert Staples, a minister much commended, offered to go as minister, "but the Company, wanting means to furnish him out, did move that some of the particular plantations would employ him. Whereupon Mr. Darnelly signified that he thought Martin's hundred wanted a minister, to whom he was recommended."

About this period, the Rev. Robert Paulet of Martin's

---

[1] Governor Wyatt and Council of Virginia, in a letter written the following January, say :—

"We must give you great thanks for sending over Mr. Thomas White, who we hope shall be accommodated to his good liking, so that it is our earnest request that you would be pleased to send us over many more learned and sincere ministers, of which there is so great want in many parts of the country, who shall be assured to find very good entertainment, for the inhabitants are very willing to lay every part of the burthen thereof upon yourselves."—*Virginia Records MSS.*

Hundred had been appointed one of the Governor's Council. The next spring Mr. Staples renewed his request to go to Virginia, and in the transactions of the Company, on April 10, 1622, is the following entry:—
"Mr. Staples, minister, recommended by Mr. Abra. Chamberlin, and by certificate under the hands of near twenty divines, continuing still his earnest request unto the Company for some allowance towards the transport and furnishing out of himself, his wife, and child to Virginia, where he hath a brother living, which moves him the rather to go; the Court, taking it into consideration, did at length agree that although their stock was spent they could strain themselves to give him £20 to pay for his said passage, and to furnish him with necessaries, and for that it was moved that they might have some testimony of his sufficiency by a sermon, he was desired to preach upon Sunday come se'nnight, in the afternoon, at St. Sythe's Church, which he promised to perform."

In the winter of 1622-3, a Rev. Mr. Leate, or Leake, was sent over by the Company, but he soon died. The General Assembly of Virginia, alluding to the state of religion in the colony in 1623, make the following statement:—"Ministers to instruct the people there were, some whose sufficiency and ability we will not tax, yet divers of them had no orders." For ten years after this there appears to be no reference to the clergy, except that in 1632 a man was placed in the stocks for calling the Rev. Mr. Cotton of Accomac a "black-coated rascal."[1]

[1] MS. Records of Accomac County.

In the days of Governor Harvey, about the year 1638, the first brick church at Jamestown, Virginia, was begun. Richard Kemp, Secretary of the Colony, having been told that the Rev. Anthony Panton, Rector of York and Chiskiack, called him a "jackanapes,"[1] and criticised his foppery, banished him from the colony in 1639 for alleged "mutinous, rebellious, and riotous acts." The clergyman was not a man to tamely submit to injustice, and his report of the matter in England excited displeasure against the Secretary.

Kemp wrote to Lord Baltimore on August 20, 1640, begging him to use his influence with the Archbishop of Canterbury in his behalf, but the letter seems to have had no weight, for on October 30, 1641, upon the petition of Anthony Panton, clerk and minister in Virginia, and agent for the church and clergy there, it was ordered by the House of Lords "that Sir W. Berkeley, Kt., Richard Kemp, and Christopher Wormsley shall be stayed their voyage, and forthwith answer the complaint in the said petition."

In 1642, the Puritan parish of Nansemond was divided into three, which obtained from Massachusetts Knowles, James, and Thompson, as ministers, and after they left, the Rev. Thomas Harrison, who had been Governor Berkeley's chaplain, preached to the Nansemond people. When Harrison was obliged to leave Virginia, he went to England and complained of the arbitrary course of the Governor; and, on October 11, 1649, the Council of State wrote to Berkeley that they had been informed by

[1] MS. Virginia Records in Library of United States of America.

petition of the congregation of Nansemond, that their minister, Mr. Harrison, an able man of unblameable conversation, had been banished the colony because he would not conform to the use of the Common Prayer Book, and they wrote,—"As the Governor cannot be ignorant that the use of it is prohibited by Parliament, he is directed to permit Mr. Harrison to return to his ministry, unless there is sufficient cause approved by Parliament."

During the Cromwellian era there were none who strictly conformed to the liturgy of the Church of England, of whom we have any record. A Rev. William Wilkinson of Maryland has been said to have been an Episcopal minister, but the records of the colony do not confirm the statement, but show that, with his spiritual work he connected the occupation of planter and storekeeper. One of his bills[1] to the administrators of the estate of a deceased person contains the following curious mingling of items and charges in tobacco weight:—

"For the use of his boat and a boy, . . lbs. 50
  „ boarding at his house 7 or 8 days and 2 men, 400
  „ funeral sermon, ... 100
  „   „ dinner, ... 300
  „ a plank for his coffin, . . . 60"

Outside of the Puritan settlements of New England, during the seventeenth century, the ordinances of religion were hardly observed. The Rev. Francis Doughty, who was the son of a Bristol alderman, and had been

---

[1] MS. Maryland Records at Annapolis.

vicar of Sodbury, Gloucester, and arraigned before the High Court of Commissions for contempt of his sacred Majesty, having spoken of him in prayer as "Charles, by common election and general consent, King of England," came to Massachusetts in 1639, but shortly after his brother-in-law, William Stone, was made Governor of Maryland, he moved to that province.[1]

The Rev. John Yeo, who was minister of the Church of England at Whorekill, now Lewes, Delaware, in a letter to the Archbishop of Canterbury, written on May 25th, 1676, from the Patuxent river, stated that there were at least twenty thousand souls, "but three Protestant ministers of us yet are conformed to the doctrine and discipline of the Church of England," and then remarks :[2]—

"Others there are, I must confess, that run before they are sent, and pretend they are ministers of the Gospel, yet never had a legal call or ordination to such an holy office; neither indeed are they qualified for it, but for the most part such as never understood any thing of learning, and yet take upon them to be dispensers of the Word, and to administer the sacraments of baptism and sow seeds of division amongst the people, and no law provided for the suppression of such in the province.[3]

"Society here is in great necessity of able and learned

---

[1] After leaving Massachusetts, he preached to the English-speaking members of the Reformed Dutch Church at Manhattan, now New York city, where his daughter Mary married Adrian Vanderdonk, a lawyer. After his death, she became the wife of Hugh O'Neal of Patuxent. Doughty was living in Saint Mary Co. in 1659.

[2] The whole letter may be found in Anderson's *Colonial Churches*.

[3] The Dutch Mennonists had a colony at Lewes, Delaware.

men to confute the gainsayers, especially having so many perfect enemies as the Popish priests, who are encouraged and provided for. And the Quaker takes care and provides for those that are speakers in their conventicles. . . . I doubt not but your Grace will take it into consideration, and do your utmost for our eternal welfare; and now is the time that your Grace may be an instrument of a universal reformation with the greatest facility. Cecilius, Lord Baron Baltimore, being dead, and Charles, Lord Baron Baltimore, and our Governor being bound for England this year, as I am informed, to receive a further confirmation of his province from His Majesty, at which time I doubt not but your Grace may so prevail with him, as that a maintenance for a Protestant ministry may be established. . . .

"Yet one thing cannot be obtained here, viz., consecration of churches and church yards, to the end that Christians might be decently buried together, whereas now they bury in the several plantations where they live," etc.

The Archbishop referred this letter to the Bishop of London, who, on July 17, 1677, wrote:—

"In Maryland there is no settled maintenance for the ministry at all, the want whereof does occasion a total want of ministers and divine worship, except among those of the Romish belief, who, 'tis conjectured, does not amount to one of a hundred of the people."

To the application of the Bishop, Charles, Lord Baltimore, replied—"The Act of 1647, confirmed in 1676, tolerates and protects every sect. Four ministers of the Church of England are in possession of plantations which afforded them a decent subsistence. That from the various religious tenets of the members of the Assembly, it would be extremely difficult, if not impossible, to induce it to consent to a law that shall oblige any sect to maintain other ministers than its own."

It is difficult to tell who the ministers of the Church of England referred to by Lord Baltimore were. Francis Doughty, Matthew Hill, Charles Nicholet, and John Coode are the only clergymen of whom we have any record. Hill was a native of Yorkshire, educated at Magdalen College, and preached at Thirsk until ejected for non-conformity, and about the year 1669, moved to Maryland and lived near Potopaco, where he may have partially conformed. Nicholet preached for a time in Maryland, and then was pastor of a Congregational church at Salem, Massachusetts, but in 1672 returned to England. Coode was a worthless man, more distinguished as a political agitator than an expounder of religious truth.

About the year 1664, an earnest young clergyman, Morgan Godwyn, the son and grandson of a distinguished divine, who had received in 1661 the degree of A.B. at Oxford, arrived in Virginia, and exerted an influence which is felt to this day. He was horrified at the degraded state of morals which allowed of the buying and selling of black men as if they were chattels, separating man and wife, and mother and children with the same unconcern as they would the dogs of the kennel, and caused men to smile at the idea of caring for the soul of a negro.[1]

Returning to England, he became the pioneer in the agitation in which Wilberforce and Clarkson, a century later, engaged, for improving the condition of Africans, and in 1680 he published a work called the *Negro and Indian Advocate*, and five years afterwards delivered a discourse in Westminster Abbey, exposing the inhumanity of the slaveholder, which was published under the title of "Trade preferred before Religion, and Christ made to give place to Mammon, represented in a Sermon relating to Plantations."

When he was in Virginia, the affairs of religion had no supervision, and each local secular vestry hired and discharged ministers as they pleased, frequently preferring a lay-reader, because he could be obtained at a cheap rate. Jamestown for more than twenty years, except for brief periods, had no preacher, and Godwyn indignantly states that "two-thirds of the preachers are made up of leaden lay-priests of the vestries' ordination."

The letter of Yeo, and the stirring appeals of Godwyn, were not without effect, and by the direction of the

[1] As slaves multiplied, slaveholders became arrogant. In 1721 the Virginia Assembly endeavoured to exclude black freemen from voting,—a privilege they had before enjoyed. A law to this effect was sent to England for approval, but, to the honour of the Government, was rejected, *on the ground that no worthy man should be deprived of his vote, on account of the colour of his skin.* The slaveholder persisted, however, until he created a white man's party, and when the constitutions of the Slave States were formed, after independence was established, changes were introduced, restricting the elective franchise to white men! As soon as the slaveholders' rebellion was subdued, all citizens, black, white, and red, were declared *politically* equal, in the new constitutions of the late Slave States of the United States of America.

Bishop of London, a large number of bibles and prayer-books were sent to the colonies.

In 1681 also the Rev. Jonathan Sanders [1] was sent to Maryland, and his passage paid out of the secret service fund of the King, and the next spring the Rev. James Sclater went to Virginia, and Dr. John Gordon was Chaplain to New York garrison. In 1683 the Rev. William Mullett and Duel Read [2] were designated for Maryland, and the Rev. Thomas Fenny sailed the next year for Virginia.

The ministers designated for Maryland either died or took charge of Virginia parishes, and in 1685 there was not an edifice in the province for the worship of God in accordance with the rites of the Church of England.

This condition of affairs distressed a Christian mother, the wife of Michael Taney, the Sheriff of Calvert County, and the ancestor of the late Chief-Justice of the Supreme Court of the United States of America, and on July 14, 1685, she wrote the following pleading letter to the Archbishop of Canterbury, accompanied with a petition :—

"MAY IT PLEASE YOUR GRACE,—I am now to repeat my request to your Grace for a church in the place of Maryland where I live ; but first I humbly thank your Grace that you were pleased to hear so favourably, and own my desires very reasonable, and to encourage the inhabitants to make a petition to the King.[3]

"Our want of a minister, and the many blessings our

---

[1] He settled in Virginia.
[2] Read took a parish in Virginia.
[3] The petition and letter appear in Strickland's *Seven Bishops*.

Saviour designed us by them, is a misery which I and a numerous family, and many others in Maryland, have groaned under. We are seized with extreme horror when we think that for want of the Gospel our children and posterity are in danger to be condemned to infidelity or to apostasy. We do not question God's care of us, but think your Grace, and the Right Reverend your Bishops, the proper instruments of so great a blessing to us. We are not, I hope, so foreign to your jurisdiction, but we may be owned your stray flock; however, the commission to go and baptize and teach all nations is large enough. But I am sure we are, by a late custom upon tobacco, sufficiently acknowledged subjects of the King of England, and therefore by his protection not only our persons and estates, but of what is more dear to us, our religion. I question not but that your Grace is sensible that without a temple it will be impracticable, neither can we expect a minister to hold out, to ride ten miles in a morning, and before he can dine ten more, and from house to house in hot weather, will dishearten a minister, if not kill him.

"Your Grace is so sensible of our sad condition, and for your place and piety's sake have so great an influence on our most religious and gracious King, that if I had not your Grace's promise to depend upon, I could not question your Grace's intercession and prevailing. £500 or £600 for a church, with some small encouragement for a minister, will be extremely less charge than honour to his Majesty. One church settled according to the Church of England, which is the sum of our request, will prove a nursery of religion and loyalty through the whole province. But your Grace needs no arguments from me, but only this,—it is in your power to give us many happy opportunities to praise God for this and other innumerable mercies, and to importune His goodness to bless his Majesty with a long and prosperous reign over us, and long continue to your Grace the great blessing of being an instrument of good to His Church. And now that I may be no more troublesome, I humbly entreat your pardon to the well-meant zeal of—Your Grace's most obedient servant,   MARY TANEY."

PETITION.

"To the Most Reverend the Archbishops, and the rest of the Right Reverend the Bishops, the humble Petition of Mary Taney, on the behalf of herself and others his Majesty's subjects, inhabitants of the province of Maryland,

"*Sheweth*,—That your petitioner, in her petition to the King's Majesty, setting forth 'That the said province being without a church or any settled ministry, to the great grief of all his Majesty's loyal subjects there, his late Majesty King Charles the Second, of blessed memory, was graciously pleased to send over thither a minister and a parcel of Bibles, and other church books of considerable value, in order to the settlement of a church and ministry there.

"That the said minister dying, and the inhabitants, who have no other trade but in tobacco, being so very poor that they are not able to maintain a minister, chiefly by reason of his Majesty's customs here upon tobacco, which causes the inhabitants to sell it there to the merchants at their own rates. By means whereof so good a work as was intended by his said late Majesty is like to miscarry, to the utter ruin of many poor souls, unless supplied by his Majesty.

"Praying his Majesty that a certain parcel of tobacco (of one hundred hogsheads or thereabouts), of the growth or product of the said province may be custom free, for and towards the maintenance of an orthodox divine at Colvert Town, in the said province, or otherwise allow maintenance for a minister there.

"Your petitioner therefore most humbly prays, that your Lordships will be pleased not only to mediate with his Majesty, and in your petitioner's behalf request him to grant her desire in said petition, but likewise that your Lordships will vouchsafe to contribute towards the building of a church at Colvert Town, as your Lordships in charity and goodness shall think meet.

"And your petitioner, as in duty bound, shall ever pray."

A few months after this appeal had been made to Sancroft, there were sent the Rev. Paul Bertrand to labour in Maryland,[1] and the Rev. James Blair, a graduate of Edinburgh, and the Rev. Benjamin Boucher, with John Miller, gentleman, a schoolmaster, to serve in the

---

[1] In the accounts of the Secret Service Fund of Charles the Second and James the Second, published by the Camden Society, there is this entry allowed July 19, 1684 :—

"To Josias Clark, clerk, bounty on the charge of his transportation to New York, whither he is going chaplain, £20."

parishes of Virginia, and within two years they were strengthened, by the arrival at Jamestown of the following clergymen, Robert Scamler, John Gordon, Stephen Fouace, and James Boré.

Blair was in a few years made by the Bishop of London his commissary for Virginia,[1] and amid much opposition from cold-hearted associates, he laid the foundations of religion, and succeeded in establishing the College of William and Mary.[2]

The accession of William and Mary led to renewed effort to establish the Church of England in Maryland. Lord Baltimore, while allowed to enjoy the rental of the lands of the province, was deprived of the political administration, and the King in 1691 appointed Lionel Copley governor of Maryland. After his arrival, the Assembly in 1692 passed an Act for the establishment of the Protestant religion, and divided the ten counties into twenty-five parishes. The opposition of the Quakers and Roman Catholics to an establishment was so great, that the law was a dead letter.

After the death of Copley, Francis Nicholson in 1694 became Governor of Maryland, and with him, in the month of August, there arrived six clergymen sent out

---

[1] In 1696 the following clergymen were in Virginia:—

James Sclater.	Jonathan Sanders.
Cope D'Oyly.	Charles Anderson.
William Williams.	Francis Fordyce.
Henry Pretty.	Andrew Cant.
Joseph Holt.	John Alexander.
George Robinson.	James Wallace.
John Ball.	George Monroe.
Andrew Monroe.	

[2] See page 174, where Blair is said, by a typographical error, to have been sent in 1683, instead of 1685, to Virginia.

by the Bishop of London, making the whole number of clergy in the province, nine. Nicholson was a zealous but not discreet churchman, and he immediately sought for additional legislation by the Assembly, in behalf of the Church of England, and public worship was soon disallowed to the adherents of the Church of Rome.

The Assembly of 1695, under the complaints of Quakers and Papists, repealed the invidious legislation in behalf of the Church of England, but the next year it was enacted that the Church of England in the province should enjoy all the rights established by law in the kingdom of England, and the friends of Episcopacy about the same time, petitioned the Bishop of London to send over a suitable divine, to preside at the meetings of the clergy, and act as his commissary.

Under the auspices of Nicholson, an Episcopal church was commenced at Annapolis,[1] and there were four or five plain edifices begun in other parts of the colony.

As long as Lord Baltimore appointed the governors of Maryland, no steps were taken for the establishment of schools, and planters who had the means sent their sons to Scottish[2] or English universities, while the children of the masses grew up ignorant of the rudiments of learning. But Nicholson, in order that a perpetual succes-

---

[1] This church was a very plain building. A rhymer, a few years afterwards, called it the "meanest building in the town."

[2] It is worthy of note, that the first legacy of an American colonist to a British university, was by Colonel David Browne, a Presbyterian, of Somerset county, Maryland. In his will, made in 1697, is the following : "I give and bequeath unto the Colledge of Glasgow, as a memoriall, and support of any of my relatives to be educated therein, to be paid in cash, or secured by good exchange to the visitours, the full soume of one hundred pound sterling current money of England, with all convenient speed after my decease."

sion of Protestant divines of the Church of England might be provided, caused a law to be passed, in 1696, for erecting a school in each county; and one was commenced at Annapolis, to the building of which the Governor gave £50 sterling, the Secretary 5000 pounds of tobacco, the Council 15,000, and the House of Burgesses 45,000 pounds of the same staple. It was called King William's School, the design of which, says Sir Thomas Lawrence, the Secretary of the colony, was for " instructing the youth of the said province in arithmetic, navigation, and all useful learning, but chiefly for the fitting such as are disposed to study divinity, to be further educated at his Majesty's College Royal in Virginia, in order, upon their return, to be ordained by the Lord Bishop of London's suffragan[1] residing in the province, both for that purpose and to supervise the lives of the clergy thereof, for whose support also, at the request and recommendation of the Assembly, his Excellency hath settled a fair and competent maintenance."

Dr. Thomas Bray, after being appointed Commissary for Maryland, remained in England two years, and employed his talents and energies in collecting parochial libraries of choice and useful books for the perpetual use of the clergy of the American colonies.[2]

[1] It had been proposed by Governor Nicholson and the Episcopalians of Maryland that a bishop should be appointed, who should, as a representative of the clergy, have a seat in the Upper House of the Provincial Assembly.— *Bray MSS. in Sion College, London.*

[2] The following parochial libraries were sent to America early in the eighteenth century:—

Maryland.	Books.
Annapolis,	1095
St. Mary's,	314

He also induced several clergymen to offer their services for America, one of whom, Mr. Clayton, cast his lot in the city founded by Penn, and by a prudent course persuaded many who had belonged to the Society of Friends to unite with Christ Church, the first Episcopal organization in Philadelphia.

In March 1700 Dr. Bray arrived in Maryland, and was received with respect by the Legislative Assembly of the province before whom he preached, and received their thanks. During the sessions of the Assembly the friends of Episcopacy, with his advice, prepared a bill, which became a law, and enacted that the Church of England should be the Established Church of the Province.

Maryland—continued.	Books.
Herring Creek,	150
South River,	109
North Sassafras,	42
King and Queen's Parish,	196
Christ Church, Calvert County,	42
All Saints,	49
St. Paul's, Calvert County,	106
Great Choptank, Dorchester County,	76
St. Paul's, Baltimore ,,	42
Stepney, Somerset ,,	60
Porto Batto, Charles ,,	30
St. Peter's, Talbot ,,	15
St. Michael's ,,	13
All Faith's, Calvert ,,	11
Nanjemoy, Charles ,,	10
Piscatoway, ,, ,,	10
Broad Neck, Ann Arundel ,,	10
St. John's, Baltimore ,,	10
St. George's, ,, ,,	10
Kent Island,	10
Dorchester,	10
Snow Hill, Somerset ,,	10
South Sassafras,	10

The Quakers, as on previous occasions, determined to use their influence to prevent the approval of the King, and Dr. Bray was appointed to go back to England to resist their opposition.

His biographer says, "Though the law, with much solicitation and struggling, was preserved from being totally disannulled, yet many of the exceptions which the Quakers made against it sticking with the Lords of Trade, all that could be obtained was that Dr. Bray might, with advice of council, draw up another bill according to the instructions of that board, and sending that bill to Maryland to be passed into a law, had the promise that his Majesty, upon its return, would confirm it here."[1]

	Maryland—continued.		Books.
St. Paul's, Kent County,			30
William and Mary, Charles County,			26
Somerset, Somerset	,,		20
Coventry, ,,	,,		25
St. Paul's, Talbot	,,		25
	Virginia.		
The College books to the value of £50.			
Manicanton on James River,			33
	South Carolina.		
Charles Town,			225
	Pennsylvania.		
Philadelphia,			327
	New Jersey.		
Amboy,			30
	New York.		
Albany,			10
New York,			211
	Massachusetts.		
Boston,			221

[1] At a meeting of the governors and visitors of Annapolis Free School, on May 7, 1700, he was present.—*Sion College MSS.*

After the bill, which he prepared in accordance with these suggestions, had been thrice amended, it was at last approved by the Plantation Board.

Early in the year 1701 Dr. Bray presented a petition to the King for the spread of the Gospel in America, which led to the incorporation of the Society for the propagation of the Gospel in foreign parts.[1]

In the first report of this Society, published in 1704, there is an account of the state of religion at that time in the English colonies on the Atlantic coast of North America. In the whole of New England there was no Church of England congregation except at Boston, whose ministers were the Rev. Mr. Miles and the Rev. Mr. Bridge, and at Braintree, which parish was then expecting a minister to be sent to them by the Bishop of London, also at Newport, Rhode Island, the rector of which was the Rev. Mr. Lockyer. In New York provision had been made for one minister in the city and vicinity, at £100 per annum, for two in Queen's County, on Nassau Island, for two in West Chester, for one in Richmond,

---

[1] Although absent in body, the interests of the Episcopal Church in Maryland were not forgotten, and a Rev. Mr. Hewetson, of Ireland, was recommended as a Superintendent of the clergy. In a letter, written at Chelsea, August 27, 1703, and addressed to Mr. Smithson, Speaker of the Maryland Assembly, Bray alludes to the rude treatment by the Governor of himself, and the clergyman whom he had suggested for suffragan or commissary, and proposes that the Maryland legislature shall set apart one of the best parishes as the cure, of a suffragan to be appointed by the Bishop of London, and build a house for his residence. He further suggested that the glebe[1] should be stocked with ten negroes, twenty cattle, and twenty hogs. It had been proposed that the suffragan should have a seat at the Council Board of the province, but this did not receive his approval, and he thought that this officer should not reside on the same side of the Bay as the Governor of the province.

[1] *Bray MSS.*

and an allowance of her Majesty for the chaplain of the forces. The grants by the Society for the province of New York had been £50 per annum, and a benevolence of £30 to Mr. John Bartow, at West Chester, £50 to Elias Neau, a French Huguenot and catechist in New York city, £50 per annum, and £35 for books to Mr. Alexander Stuart, at Bedford, and £50 per annum to Patrick Gordon, Rector of Queen's County, who had died before the report was published. On Long Island the Rev. William Urquhart was maintained by the subscriptions of the Yorkshire clergy. In New Jersey there was no Church of England clergyman, but in Shrewsbury Colonel Morris was building a church, and at Amboy, Hopewell, and Burlington, church edifices were either contemplated or being built.

In Pennsylvania the Church erected in 1695 had secured a large congregation,[1] and the services were conducted by the Rev. Mr. Evans and his associate Mr. Thomas, and the Society had granted £50 to Mr. Nichols, Rector of St. Paul's, Upland, and £50 per annum, and £15 for books, to Mr. Thomas Crawford, at Dover, in Delaware.

In Maryland there were sixteen ministers with a competent maintenance, their glebes settled and libraries fixed, and the only grant was one of £6 in money and £4 in books to George Macqueen. Virginia had about thirty chapels; and the Society granted £20 to a Mr. Tyliard, and £15 for books to a Mr. Prichard. In Caro-

[1] There were the following places of worship at that time in Philadelphia: —One Quaker, one Presbyterian, one Independent, one Anabaptist, and one Swedish, at Wicaco, in the suburbs.

lina there was the Rev. Mr. Marston at Charleston, and Samuel Thomas at Goose Creek.

The Rev. George Keith and John Talbot, his assistant, were also maintained by the Society as itinerant missionaries.

While at the beginning of the eighteenth century, the Church of England was firmly established in Maryland and Virginia, under the auspices of the devoted Bray and Blair, yet it could not progress in the southern colonies.

Educated men were fewer in these colonies than in the northern, and were generally lovers of pleasure and scoffers at religion. Anderson, the accurate historian of the Colonial Church, remarks :—

"Wealthy planters became notorious for their indulgence of dissolute and idle habits, and passed most of their time in drinking and card-playing, at horse-races, and cock-fights. Their slaves, and servants, and other classes of the population, were not slow to copy." The slave colonies were only saved from materialism and licentiousness by the advent of enthusiastic Methodists, who, with little education, but undoubted piety, with no possessions but a Bible, horse, and saddle bags, rode through the sparsely settled districts, and stopping in front of country stores, or upon the green lawn of the court-house, declared, with a terrible earnestness, that men were living on the brink of hell, and that they must all appear before the judgment-seat of Christ.

The imaginative and emotional African shook with fear, as these glowing men grossly portrayed the horrible future of a lost soul. The roué and debauchee were first enraged and scurrilous, but became silent and thoughtful, and the old planters forbade these noisy fanatics, as they deemed them, to enter their gateways. In spite of difficulties, Wesleyanism made rapid advances, and drew away the people from the parish churches, and became the controlling religion of the late Slave States[1] of North America.

But while the Church of England was declining in the southern, it gained ground in the middle and northern colonies, from the fact, that in these was a class of educated and thoughtful persons, who found Quakerism and Presbyterianism either too cold or intellectual, and the liturgy of the Church of England a devotional form of public worship, and the Thirty-Nine Articles a more satisfactory expression of the doctrines of the sacred Scriptures, than the elaborate chapters of ponderous confessions of faith.

[1] The following statistics, taken from the census of 1860, show the relative influence of religious denominations in the late Slave States:—

Number of Church edifices in	*Maryland.*	*Virginia.*
Episcopal,	158	188
Presbyterian,	58	300
Baptist,	34	787
Methodist,	541	1403
Roman Catholic,	82	33

Number of Church edifices in all the late Slave States—

Episcopal,	752
Presbyterian,	1805
Baptist,	7225
Methodist,	9416
Roman Catholic,	553

INDEX.

	PAGE
ABBOTT, Archbishop,	106
—— opinion of Calvert,	200
Accomac Plantation,	224, 243
Albion Nova,	261
Alexander, Sir William,	177, 205
Altham, Jesuit Father,	266, 268, 272
Ambrose, Alice, whipped,	299
America, first legislature in,	113
—— educational statistics,	175, 176
—— religious statistics,	343
Anacostan Indians,	226
Annapolis, battle near,	255
—— Puritans at,	92
—— Church,	336
—— School,	337
Anthony, Dr. Francis,	114
Archer, Captain Gabriel,	21, 22
—— Letter of,	32
Argall, Captain Samuel,	57
—— goes with Delaware to Virginia,	60
—— names Delaware Bay,	60
—— explores with Sir T. Dale,	60, 219
—— ascends Potomac,	61
—— captures Pocahontas,	70
—— dishonourable conduct,	62-65
—— ill-treatment of Brewster,	66
—— absconds,	66
—— sends out a piratical ship,	66
—— knighted,	67
—— nominated Governor of Virginia,	67
Arthur, Prince, in America,	162
Apsley on short route to China,	104
Augustine's, St., "City of God,"	123, 320
BALTIMORE, LORD. *See* Calvert.	
Baltimore, an Irish hamlet,	204
—— song about,	204
Baptism of East India boy,	207
Bargrave, Rev. Thomas, gives library to Virginia College,	319
Basse, N., Virginia Councillor,	260, 279

	PAGE
Beaver skins,	229, 230
Bennett, Edward, plantation,	279
—— Philip, visits Boston,	281
—— Richard, Parliament Commissioner,	253
—— ——, in old age,	257, 258
—— Rev. William,	280, 322
Berkeley, Sir William, surrenders to Parliament	253
—— re-elected Governor,	257
—— ill-tempered,	286
Bermudas, Gates and Somers at,	34
—— petition for toleration,	180
Berry, William, Maryland Quaker,	295, 305
Bertrand, Rev. Paul,	334
Bible for Virginia College,	139
Bishop of London on State of religion in Maryland,	328
Blackwell, Elder Francis,	98
Blair, Rev. James,	174, 175, 334, 335
Bluett, Captain, and Virginia Ironworks,	136, 137
Bolton, Rev. Robert,	322
Boré, Rev. James,	335
Boston, Church of England in,	340
Bosworth, Captain,	296
Boucher, Rev. Benjamin,	334
Bowles, Sir G., Mayor of London,	109
Boyle, Robert, on Massachusetts intolerance,	304
Bray, Dr. Thomas,	337-340
Brawnde, Captain Edward, voyage to New England,	91
—— letter to Captain Smith,	92
Brent, Margaret, a strong-minded woman,	252
Brewster, Captain Edward, accompanies Lord Delaware to Virginia,	45
—— unjust arrest,	65
—— conforms to Church,	100
—— William, the Puritan,	64
—— early life,	95

	PAGE
Brewster removes from Leyden,	101
—— William, a Virginia colonist,	96
Brinsley's, John, school-book,	130-132
Brock, Father, Maryland Jesuit,	272
Brown, David, legacy to Glasgow University,	336
Brownists denounced,	40
Buck, Benoni, an idiot,	315
—— Rev. Richard, chaplain of Gates,	34, 113, 315
—— sermon before Lord Delaware,	46
—— prayer at first legislature,	134
Buckingham writes to King James about Calvert,	196
CALVERT, GEORGE, *first Lord Baltimore*, early life,	182
—— letter to Sir Thos. Edmondes,	183
—— Clerk of Privy Council,	185
—— assists King James in writing,	186
—— knighted,	186
—— made Secretary,	187
—— M.P. for York,	191
—— opposed to people's party,	192
—— pleads for the King,	193
—— his wife and children,	194
—— favours Spanish match,	195
—— his festival dress,	196
—— cold-shouldered by Buckingham,	196
—— at his country retreat,	197
—— sells the secretaryship,	199
—— described by Archbishop Abbot,	200
—— described by Bp. Goodman,	200
—— connection with Virginia Company,	201
—— his New Foundland colony,	204
—— proposes to emigrate,	206
—— not a religious exile,	206
—— influence on Wentworth,	207
—— goes to New Foundland,	207
—— second visit to New Foundland,	208
—— letter to Buckingham,	208
—— captures French ships,	209
—— goes to Virginia,	210
—— refuses the oath,	211
—— called a liar,	213
—— his Maryland charter,	214-218
—— death of,	215

	PAGE
Calvert, Cecilius, *second Lord Baltimore*, marries Arundel's daughter,	195
—— obtains Maryland charter,	239
—— sends ships,	239
—— letter to Earl of Strafford,	239
—— controversy with Clayborne,	241
—— wishes to be Governor of Virginia,	245
—— a political trimmer,	254
—— compromise with Cromwellian commissioners,	256
—— death of,	258
—— coldness toward Jesuits,	274
Calvert, Charles, *third Lord Baltimore*, at Quaker meeting,	308
—— reply to Bishop of London,	328
—— his wife described by Quaker preacher,	308
Calvert, Leonard, factor of the St. Claude,	209
—— Governor of Maryland,	240
—— confers with Fleet, a trader,	240
—— disputes with Maryland Assembly,	246
—— death of,	251
—— appoints Margaret Brent his attorney,	252
Calvert, Philip, illegitimate son of first Lord Baltimore	259
—— Secretary of Maryland,	295
Cape Cod fisheries,	93
Carolana, charter of,	216
—— settlement of,	213
Caroloff, Mr., and East India school,	171
Cecil, Robert, Earl of Salisbury,	182
Charles the First grants letters of marque to Baltimore,	248
Charles City, free school at,	127
Chapman, Thomas, Virginia Quaker,	215
Chesapeake Bay explored,	260
Chew, Samuel, a Quaker,	311
Child, Sir Josiah, describes Virginians,	173
Children of London transported,	158, 160
Christ Church of Philadelphia,	338
Christopherson, Wenlock, Quaker preacher,	304
Church, Bow, London,	143, 144
Church of England in New York,	340
—— in Massachusetts,	340

INDEX. 347

	PAGE
Church of England in New Jersey,	341
—— Pennsylvania,	341
—— Maryland,	341
—— Virginia,	341
—— Carolina,	342
—— St. Dennis, London,	107
—— St. Michael's,	143
Clarke, Rev. Josias,	334
Clarkson, Robert, Quaker, letter of,	293
Clayborne, William, ancestry of,	219
—— surveyor of Virginia,	220
—— Accomac planter,	224, 243
—— defeats Pamunky tribe,	224, 240
—— difficulties with Calvert,	243
—— Parliament commissioner,	253
—— notice of,	257
—— has copy of Perkins' works,	320
Clayton, Rev. Mr.,	338
Coale, Josiah, Quaker preacher,	294
Cockaine, Sir William, Mayor of London,	158
Coins of Maryland,	257
Cole, William, Quaker preacher,	300, 303
College for Virginia,	112, 113, 116
—— books for,	123, 319
—— Harvard,	172
—— Henrico,	112, 113, 116, 172
—— William and Mary,	175-177, 335
Common-Prayer Book presented,	139
Communion furniture presented,	115, 116
Convicts sent to Virginia,	201, 202
Coode, Rev. John, an agitator,	329
Copeland, John, loses an ear,	298
Copland, Rev. Patrick,	106
—— returns from East Indies,	106
—— preaches before officers of East India fleet,	108
—— letter to Hulsebus,	108
—— sails for Japan,	109
—— collections for Virginia,	124
—— proposes a Virginia school,	125
—— grant of land to,	129
—— to peruse Brinsley's book,	130
—— sermon at Bow Church,	144
—— chosen Rector of College,	168
—— at Bermudas,	179
—— at Eleuthera,	180
Copley, Lionel, Governor of Maryland,	335
—— Thomas, Jesuit missionary of Maryland,	268

	PAGE
Cotton, Rev. Mr., of Accomac,	325
Crakanthorp's sermon,	26
Crashaw, Rev. William, sermon of,	36
—— rebukes players,	37
—— urges strict laws,	40
—— prayer of,	50
Cutts, John, New England, captain,	255
DALE, Sir Thomas, goes to Virginia,	51
—— a disciplinarian,	52
—— seeks to obtain sister of Pocahontas,	78
—— his wives,	78
—— brings Pocahontas to England,	81
—— goes to East Indies,	107
—— death of,	108
Davenport, Rev. John, 280, 293, 320, 322	
Davis, Captain James,	43
Davison, Sir William,	149
—— Christopher,	149
Delaware, Lord, Captain-General of Virginia,	26
—— sermon before,	37
—— ancestry of,	38
—— at Jamestown,	45
—— his strict code,	49
—— returns home sick,	51
—— second voyage,	57
—— ordered to arrest Argall,	65
—— dies at sea,	57
Delaware Bay explorations,	259
Dennis, Captain Robert,	253
De Vries, Captain,	262
Donne, Dr. John,	177, 321
Donations for Virginia,	116, 117, 139
Doughty, Rev. Francis,	327, 329
Drayton's Ode on Virginia voyage,	15
—— lines on George Sandys,	149
Dublin, cathedral at,	288
Dunton, John, Master of Warwick,	222
Durand, William,	254, 280, 293, 294
Dust and Ashes, letters of,	117, 133
Dyer, Mary, hung at Boston,	299
EAST INDIA COMPANY,	104, 105
"Eastward Ho," play of,	3-5
Edmondson, William, Quaker preacher,	257, 312

348   INDEX.

	PAGE		PAGE
Educated men desired as settlers,	48	Gold, Box of, presented to Virginia Company,	121
Elderton, William,	231	Gondomar, Spanish Ambassador,	187, 193, 195
Eleuthera Isle,	181	Goodman, Bishop, his opinion of Calvert,	200
Elfred, Captain, brings negroes to Virginia,	66	Gookin, Daniel, early planter,	148, 255, 280, 282
English girl for Prince of Sumatra,	105	Gordon, Rev. John,	331, 335
Episcopal Church in Maryland,	331-334	Gorges, Sir Ferdinand,	94
Evans, Owen, girl stealer,	160	Gosnold, Bartholomew, 2, 5, 7, 8, 11, 17, 22	
		—— death of,	19
		—— Anthony,	19
FAIRFAX family in America,	188	Gould, Daniel, Quaker,	301
—— Thomas, first Lord,	188	Gouge, Rev. Wm., of Blackfriars,	80, 278
Featly, Daniel, D.D.,	122	Grave, John, Quaker,	301
Fendall, Governor of Maryland,	295	Gravener, a Maryland Jesuit,	261, 268, 272
Fenny, Rev. Thomas,	331	Gulston, Dr. Theodore,	115
Ferrar's House in London,	115, 122, 139		
Ferrar, Nicholas, senior,	122		
—— junior,	122, 177, 179		
—— John, Deputy of Virginia Company,	116, 117, 122	HAKLUYT, REV. RICHARD,	2, 3, 5, 16
—— Virginia,	122	—— letter to Virginia Company,	27
Finch, Lady, her unruly son,	151	Hall, Rev. Henry,	309, 311
Fisher, Father Philip, S. J.,	273	Hamor's, Ralph, Narrative,	73
—— letter of,	275	Harmon, Charles, trader,	225, 226, 234
Fleet's, Henry, Journal,	219-237	Harris, Elizabeth, Quakeress,	293
Fleet, Edward,	225, 229	Harrison, Rev. Thomas, Berkeley's chaplain,	283
Fletcher, Elizabeth, enthusiast,	290	—— letter to John Winthrop,	285
Fouace, Rev. Stephen,	335	—— banished from Virginia,	286
Fox, Geo., Quaker preacher,	295, 302, 303	—— chaplain of Henry Cromwell,	287
		—— Sermon on Oliver Cromwell's death,	288
GARY, ALICE, whipped at Boston,	299	—— arrest at Chester,	289
—— John,	303	Harvard University,	172
Gates, Sir Thomas, Lieutenant-General of Virginia,	31, 34	Harvey, Governor,	235, 236, 237, 241, 242, 243, 244, 325
—— arrives at Jamestown,	34	Hawley, Gabriel,	239, 263
—— abandons Jamestown,	45	—— Jerome,	244-246, 263
—— visits England,	51	—— letter of,	263
—— second voyage to Virginia,	51	Hayman's lines on Rev. Mr. Sturton,	208
—— wife dies,	51	Henrico College,	113, 114, 116
—— daughter's return,	52	Herbert, George, poet,	178
—— employed by East India Company,	108	Hereckines tribe,	231, 233
—— death of,	108	Higgins, Rev. Theophilus,	184
Gervase, Thomas, Jesuit,	266	Hill, Rev. Matthew,	329
Gibbons, Captain Edward,	284	Hodgson, Robert, Quaker preacher,	297
Gilbert, Captain Raleigh,	90	Holder, Christopher, Quaker preacher,	297
Glasgow University, donation by Maryland Planter,	336	Holt, Rev. Joseph,	335
Godwyn, Rev. Morgan, early opponent of American slavery,	329	Hopkins, Stephen, Brownist,	314
		House of Commons on religious toleration,	180, 284

Howgill, Rev. Francis, becomes a Quaker,	293
—— visits Ireland,	294
—— on Maryland intolerance,	296
Hudson, Leonard, carpenter for Virginia School,	167
Hughes, Rev. Lewis,	318
Hulsebus, Adrian, Dutch chaplain,	108
Hunt, Rev. Robert,	19, 314
INDIAN CHILDREN, Education of,	117, 118, 121, 122, 133
—— girl sick,	86
—— girls sent to Bermudas,	87
—— intermarriages,	70
Ingle, Captain Richard,	248, 249, 250, 275
Ireland, cattle and men from,	148
—— Coleraine and Derry plantations,	56
Irish people,	130-132
Ironworks in Virginia,	136, 137
Isle of Kent,	241, 260
JACOB, REV. HENRY,	280
James the First writes against Vorstius,	185
—— caricatured,	192
—— arrogance of,	193
—— death of,	201
James, Rev. Thomas,	281
Johns, Richard, Quaker,	305, 309
Jones, Captain Thomas,	103, 259
Jonson, Ben, on Pocahontas,	84
KEITH, REV. GEORGE,	342
Kirk, Captain, of Canada,	231
Knowles, Father, S. J.,	266
—— Rev. John,	281, 282, 325
LABOURING men described by Crashaw,	29
—— women described by Crashaw,	30
Laud, Archbishop,	244
Lawrence, Sir Thomas,	311
Lawne, Christopher, plantation of,	279
Laws of Virginia strict,	49
Leate, or Leake, Rev. Mr., death of,	324
Lee, Mary, hung for a witch,	296

Lee, Colonel Richard, Cromwellian,	253
Lewger, Rev. John,	269
—— Secretary of Maryland,	270
—— death of,	277
Leyden Nonconformists,	96, 171, 278
—— Articles of Faith,	96
—— people emigrate,	101, 102
Lincoln, Countess of, her daughters,	172
London children transported,	158-166
Longfellow's New England Tragedies,	298
Lorkin, Rev. Thomas,	112
Lottery for Virginia,	52
Lowe, Captain Richard,	239
MACOCK, SAMUEL, a scholar,	62
Maids sent for wives,	155
Manhattan fur trade,	259
Martin, the Armenian,	154
Martin, Captain John,	17, 20, 33
—— master of ironworks,	46
—— Richard, Attorney for Virginia Company,	53
—— plea for Virginia,	54
—— censured by House of Commons,	55, 56
Maryland Charter,	214, 218
—— Assembly oppose proprietor,	246
—— Act of Religion,	92, 286, 287, 293
—— Quaker meetings,	303
—— Quakers' petition,	305
Massachusetts intolerance,	304
Massacre, Indian, in 1622,	169
—— Indian, in 1644,	283
Massomack Indians,	226
Masts of pine sent to England,	51
Mather, Cotton, alleged letter of,	307
Matthew, Tobias, Archbishop of York,	28
Matthews, Captain Samuel,	244, 245
Mease, Rev. William,	318
Miller, John, schoolmaster,	334
Molasco, a Polonian,	155
Mostikums, an Indian tribe,	231
Mowhaks, an Indian tribe,	221
Mullett, Rev. William,	331
NACOSTINES, Indian tribe,	226, 229
Nanamack, an Indian lad,	81
Nansemond parish,	280, 285, 325

INDEX.

	PAGE
Naval fight in James River,	283
—— at Wiggomoco,	243
Nayler, James, Quaker fanatic,	290
Negroes first in Virginia,	66, 67
—— vote of,	330
Newce, Sir William, of Ireland,	148
—— goes to Virginia,	148
New England tragedies,	298
New Foundland, Calvert's colony,	205
—— Religious dispute,	209
—— sickness at,	210
Newport, Captain Christopher,	7, 8, 10 15, 22
—— his relation,	14, 23
—— explores James River,	18
—— second voyage to Virginia,	21
—— third voyage to Virginia,	23
—— sails with Gates and Somers,	32
—— retires from Virginia,	34, 52
—— in East India service,	57
Nicholet, Rev. Charles,	329
Nicholson, Governor of Maryland,	331
—— erects church in Annapolis,	336
Norfolk, Duke of,	335
—— county of,	336
North Virginia colony,	90
Norwood, Richard, surveyor of Bermudas, and teacher,	179
Nova Albion of Plowden,	261, 265
OGILBY, father of the author, draws a Virginia lottery prize,	53
PALMER, EDWARD, noticed,	220, 260
Palmer's Isle,	220, 260
Panton, Rev. Anthony, agent of Virginia clergy,	325
Parliament, debate in Virginia,	53
Parochial libraries in Maryland,	337-339
—— schools in Maryland,	337
Patobanos, Indian village,	235
Paulet, Rev. Robert,	323
Peabody, George, legacy and death,	162
Peirce, John, and Leyden people,	101, 119, 120
Penn, William, his conversion,	306
—— called a scamp,	307
—— his tart letter,	311
Percy, George,	19, 33, 46
—— elected President of Virginia,	33

	PAGE
Perkins, Dr. Wm., books of,	123, 319, 320
Perrot, Quaker enthusiast,	301
Peyton on false Virginia pedigrees,	173
Piscataway in Massachusetts,	221, 223
Piscataways of Maryland,	227, 229, 232
Play of "Eastward Ho,"	3-5
—— "Tu Quoque,"	50
Plowden, Sir Edmund, his patent,	261
—— notice of,	264, 265
Pocahontas in girlhood,	68
—— Strachey describes,	69
—— her capture,	70, 71, 73
—— Dale wants her sister,	78
—— attends a play,	82
—— portrait of,	82
—— death of,	83
—— child of,	83
—— descendants of,	88
Poets allude to Virginia,	3, 15, 149, 177, 178
Pope Peter, a Bengala boy,	107, 109
Popham colonists in Maine,	32
—— build the pinnace called "Virginia,"	32, 43
Popham, George,	90
—— Judge,	90
Pory, J., Secretary of Virginia,	213, 219
—— notice of,	153
Potomac River, exploration of,	221
—— Falls of,	228
Potopaco, or Port Tobacco,	235
Pott, Dr., Governor of Virginia,	210
Prescott, Captain, accused by John Washington,	297
Preston, Richard, Quaker,	255, 295
Pring, Captain Martin,	109, 168
Purchas, Rev. Samuel,	23, 59
QUAKERS of America,	290
—— of Maryland,	305
—— of Maryland oppose establishment of Church of England,	337-339
—— Yearly meeting of,	312
RABNET, FRANCIS, of Maryland,	244
Raleigh, Sir Walter,	123, 187
Randolph family,	89
Ratcliffe, Capt. John,	7, 8, 17, 20, 22, 32
Read, Rev. Duel,	331
Richardson, Elizabeth, hung,	297

INDEX. 351

Robertson, Quaker preacher, hung, 297, 299
Rofe, George, Quaker preacher, . 299
Rolfe, John, infant of, dies in 1610, 34
—— white wife of, . . . 71
—— union with Pocahontas, . 76
—— early tobacco planter, . 79
—— Lady Delaware complains of, 84
—— his death, ... 85
—— his white widow and children, 85
—— Henry, brother of John, . 85
—— Thomas, son by Pocahontas, 89

SANDERS, REV. JONATHAN, . . 331
Sandys, Archbishop, on ritualism, 319
—— Sir Edwin, President of Virginia Company, 100, 112, 121, 122, 161, 319
—— on Indian education, . 135
—— George, Treasurer of Virginia Colony, . . . 149, 153, 170
Sayle, Governor of Eleuthera, . 284
Seal of Virginia described, . 161, 162
Settlers, respectable, needed, . 47
School at Annapolis, . . . 337
—— Charles City, . . . 127
—— in Maryland, . . . 337
Sclater, Rev. James, . . . 331
Shakespeare's "Tempest," . . 107
Sharpless, a London tailor, draws a prize in Virginia lottery, . 53
Shaunetowa Indians, . . . 227
Ships' safe arrival in Virginia, 142, 143
Slavery, influence of, . 330, 342
Slaveholders oppose black freemen, 330
Slave colonies not prosperous, . 342
—— States, Churches in, . . 343
Smith, Captain John, . . 17, 18, 24
—— charge against President Wingfield, ... 20, 22
—— described by Fuller, . . 21
—— sent to England for misdemeanour, ... 33
—— Admiral of New England, . 91
—— supposed letter of, . . 91
—— letter from Captain Brawnde, 92
—— Henry, D.D., Puritan divine, sermons of, ... 272
—— Sir Thomas, first head of Virginia Company, . . 59
—— patron of Purchas, . . 59

Smith, Sir Thomas, unscrupulous, 60
—— Island, . . . 60, 219
Snow, Marmaduke, first merchant at Saint Mary, . . . 271
Southampton, Earl of, 112, 123, 320, 321
Somers, Sir George, Admiral, . 31
—— M.P., ... 32
—— at Jamestown, . . . 34
—— dies at Bermudas, . . 50
—— Captain Matthew, false claim of, ... 50
Spanish ambassador on the marriage of whites with Virginia Indians, 70
—— Match, ... 199
Stage players, . . . 3, 5, 24
—— censured by Crashaw, . 36
—— prayer about, . . . 50
Stagg, Captain, of Westover, . 253
Staples, Rev. Robert, . . 323, 324
Stevenson, Quaker preacher, hung, 299
Stockton, Rev. Mr., . . . 322
Stone, Gover. of Maryland, 253, 254, 256
Story, Thomas, Quaker preacher, 309
Strachey, William, Secretary of Virginia, . . . 49, 51, 60
Sturton, Rev. Mr., verses on, . 208
Supper of Virginia Company, . 321
Sumatra, Prince of, asks for a white wife, ... 105
Sweden, colonists from, . . 263

TAMOCOMO, brother-in-law of Pocahontas, ... 81
Taney, Mary, letter of, . . 331
—— Michael, ancestor of late Chief Justice of United States, 331
Thanksgiving sermon by Copland, 143
Thorpe, George, killed, 123, 151, 170
Throckmorton, Sir William, kindness to sick Indian girl, . 86, 87
Thurston, Quaker preacher, . 295
"Tiger" ship captured by Turks, 156
Tilghman, Captain, . . . 254
Tillieres, French ambassador, . 193
Tindall, Robert, ... 43
Toleration Act of England, . 285
Tohoga Indians, . . 228, 233
Tompson, Rev. William, goes to Virginia, . . . 281, 282
Transportation of London poor, 158-160
Tucker, Daniel, . . . 23, 46

	PAGE
USSERAHAK Indians,	230, 233
Uty, John, Virginia Councillor,	234, 235, 243, 245
VIRGINIA pinnace built at Sagadahoc,	32, 43
—— early Code of,	49
—— convicts sent to,	201, 202
—— Company sermons,	321
—— supper,	321
—— dissolved,	203
—— first Charter,	6
—— second Charter,	18
—— third Charter,	52
—— instructions to first expedition,	7
—— lottery,	52
—— debate in House of Commons,	53
—— interest in education,	111
—— tablet for donors,	117
—— apply for poor children,	158
—— clergymen,	335
"Virginia's God be Thanked,"	163
Virginians illiterate,	172, 175
—— spurious pedigrees of,	180
Vorstius, Professor,	185, 186
WASHINGTON, GEORGE, ancestry of,	188
—— John, letter of,	297
Wentworth family in America,	188
Wentworth, Sir Thomas, letters to Calvert,	197 199
Wesleyanism in late Slave States,	343
West, Francis, Governor of Virginia,	23, 32
—— John, Governor of Virginia,	243, 248
—— Thomas. See *Delaware*.	
Whincop, John, notice of,	100
Whitaker, Rev. Alexander,	56, 62, 79, 278, 315, 316
White, Father Andrew, S. J.,	266-268, 270, 274, 275
—— Rev. Thomas,	322
Wickham, Rev. William,	62, 279
Wilkinson, Rev. William,	326
Wingfield, Edward Maria,	1, 5
—— ancestry of,	17
—— arrest of,	20
—— his defence,	22
YEO, REV. JOHN, letter of,	327
Young, Captain Thomas, explorer of Delaware River,	261, 263

www.ingramcontent.com/pod-product-compliance
Lightning Source LLC
Chambersburg PA
CBHW032046220426
43664CB00008B/883